FUNDAMENTAL PASTORAL COUNSELING

FUNDAMENTAL PASTORAL COUNSELING

FUNDAMENTALS OF PASTORAL COUNSELING

Fundamental
PASTORAL COUNSELING

Technic and Psychology

JOHN R. CAVANAGH, M.D., F.A.C.P., F.A.P.A., K.S.G.

Special Lecturer, School of Sacred Theology
The Catholic University of America

AUTHOR OF

Fundamental Marriage Counseling

Fundamental Psychiatry
    (with Rev. James P. McGoldrick, S.J.)

THE BRUCE PUBLISHING COMPANY
MILWAUKEE

NIHIL OBSTAT:

FRANCIS J. CONNELL, C.Ss.R.
Censor Deputatus

IMPRIMATUR:

✠ PATRICK A. O'BOYLE
Archbishop of Washington
February 1, 1962

Library of Congress Catalog Card Number: 62–10437

© 1962 THE BRUCE PUBLISHING COMPANY

MADE IN THE UNITED STATES OF AMERICA

TO MY PARENTS

PREFACE

This world, at its best, is not a secure place. Today, it is permeated with fear to such an extent that history may well record our time as the "Era of Anxiety." In addition to this state of fear, there are colossal tasks facing us. Half of the world is in a state of bondage which in many areas amounts to slavery; a third of the people of the world have an annual income of less than fifty American dollars or their equivalent. Another third of the people of the world are sick and have a life expectancy of less than thirty years. All the people of the world crave for love, security, and freedom from suffering.

Worry is a universal problem. Everywhere we find "free-floating anxiety." This may not always manifest itself somatically, but rather as a vague discomfort, a feeling of impending doom, a feeling of disquiet, vague physical symptoms, and muscle tension. Man has always been subject to fears. When life was more primitive, these fears dealt with nature, with famine or drought, with storms and floods, with lightning, thunder, darkness, with witches, wizards and demons. As civilization has advanced, these fears have been allayed, but as he has conquered these, man has invented more terrifying ones. Of these, perhaps the most awesome is the A bomb, and its possible sequelae due to radioactivity. Add to this the threat of communism, the fear of a new world war, the persecution of religion behind the Iron Curtain as evidenced by the imprisonment of Cardinal Mindszenty, the brutal, treacherous slaying of Imre Nagy, a crime which revealed the real face of Moscow. Add to this many other threats too numerous to mention, and we must seek escape and comfort in the statement of President Roosevelt in his first inaugural address: "The only thing we have to fear is fear itself."

The clergyman is accustomed to dealing with fear. Each of his parishioners has been afraid. Illness even in this modern age is accompanied by the fear of death or invalidism. Those who are afraid have become accustomed to seeking help from their local pastor in the presence of fear and its attendant anxiety. He has always been there when he was needed.

Members of the clergy have important contributions to make to the mental health of their parishioners.

In the sick confusion of thought in the modern world, sunk so deep in its own despairs, the question of religion's place in life is an indescribably important one and the claims of religion on the citizens of the world are vital, insistent, and pressing. The relationship of the average layman to religion is of particular significance in our own time and for many reasons. The alarming increase of mental illness in recent years associated with an increase in materialism and agnosticism is a source of grave concern. The educated Christian, because he realizes the importance of religion to his fellow citizen, cannot plead that he has no interest in these matters. However, we need not consider this plea for a return to God in purely pietistic terms. It is logical and rational for the Christian to do so. The materialistic liberals in this country would be a subject for laughter if they were not so influential in politics and education. In the political field, they have, during recent years, naïvely accepted the communist party line; they have been blind to the motives of communists in our midst; they have ingenuously accepted communist deceit in China. These and other fallacies may be laid on their doorstep. Such materialistic acceptance of false philosophies must be vigorously combated.

Serious as are their errors in the political field, they have become almost catastrophic in the field of education and philosophy. Dealing with the susceptibility of the young, they teach an atheistic, materialistic, and mechanistic philosophy which denies the supernatural and denies the axiom of St. Paul that the invisible things of God are understood by the visible things of His creations. This philosophy has led us straight to the brink of world conflict and atomic war. If there is no God, can we condemn the Russians for promoting militant atheism? Materialism has led us to moral and intellectual chaos: to moral chaos, because it denies God, the source of all good; to intellectual chaos, because it leaves the mind of man unsatisfied. It does not explain the complicated and mysterious universe in which we live. Christians, both lay and clerical, must aggressively combat this false philosophy. To the contrary, they must proclaim that there is a God, that man has a soul and an intellect and a will which are free. They must insist that there is a natural as well as a positive law which governs man's actions. This natural law is the eternal law revealed by the light of reason as directive of man's activity. Right and wrong, good and bad, and their general applications are thus made manifest to man. Acceptance of a natural law is part of man's nature. Man's nature completely grasped in itself and its reactions becomes the proximate norm of morality.

The pastor should work in harmony with the natural law as it is evident in man's nature. He should help his parishioners to understand the nature of morality and to regulate their advice to others in terms of objective right and wrong. Man is rational and should, by the power of his mind and will, regulate and subject his lower powers.

The pastor must not only be on guard against those outside of religion who teach a false philosophy, he must also be on guard against erroneous beliefs in his fellow Christians. Some of these are due to ignorance and misunderstanding; others are due to an unconscious wish to escape from the responsibilities of life. Many Christians believe that it is impossible to practice conformity to God's will and still be possessed of any dynamic force, or have definite goals of their own, or work with unremitting zeal for success in life. They do not understand that conformity to God's will in no sense whatsoever implies personal inertia or passivity or a laissez-faire approach to life. God gave men mind and will, and He wishes men to judge, to reason, and to seek goals and to make choices. Frequently, however, when we have done our utmost, the end result is not up to our expectation and we must accept what seems to be relative failure. For the moment, this relative failure must be considered God's will for us and we should not, therefore, become fearful, depressed, or anxious. We may, however, renew our efforts and see if we cannot, by new and added efforts, attain the goal we first ambitioned. One can, therefore, be intensely active and enthusiastic and still be totally conformed to the will of God.

The incidence of mental illness demands our attention. The pastor has an important role in mental illness, perhaps more in its prevention than in its cure. He has a special responsibility in the recognition of emotional and mental disturbances. Failure to do so can have serious consequences. A careful reading of the following chapters and a gradual adoption of the ideas therein will enable the pastor to approach the problems presented to him daily by his parishioners with greater confidence.

May I take this opportunity to thank those who helped me in the preparation of this volume. For their very valuable and always frank comments in regard to content, I wish to thank Dr. Alphonse Clemens, Dr. Paul Nolan, Father Luke Caimi, and Father Ramon DiNardo. My special thanks to Mr. Charles Crotty for his help and collaboration in the preparation of the chapter on Client-Centered Therapy. Valuable editorial assistance, without which the book would not have been possible, was rendered by my sister, by Miss Lorraine Bennett, Miss Jean Donohoe, and Miss Virginia Creamer. I also wish to thank all those publishers and authors who so generously allowed me to quote from their publications.

JOHN R. CAVANAGH, M.D.

Washington, D. C.

FOREWORD

For the past several decades, the art and science of counseling has been in the throes of radical and revolutionary changes. New psychological and sociological factors have induced innovations in the counseling process which should impel the attention and study of all engaged in this art. With the advent of psychoanalysis a new emphasis has been placed upon nonconscious factors in motivation. Various other emerging schools of thought have given the emotions a larger role in the behavioral sciences. The older methods and techniques, which too largely ignored or de-emphasized nonconscious and emotional factors have, as a result, been forced to give way to improved and more adequate counseling methods. In addition, the rapid decline of respect for authority coupled with an equally rapid growth of equalitarianism, has rendered the former methods based upon advice, directive, and precept, largely (though not entirely) ineffective.

Seminarians, clergy, and religious superiors need to be alert to these new trends and familiar with the new approaches to the counseling process if they are to discharge their roles with competency and effectiveness. The average good Christian always has and, according to surveys, still does resort in the first instance to his pastor for counsel in problematic matters. This is as it should be especially when such problems, as is often the case, pose obstacles to his religious and moral welfare. The obvious need of the moment is not the retreat of the clergy from the counseling role; in too many instances such counseling is an indispensable tool of their apostolate. Rather does the contemporary situation indicate the need for enhanced training and competency in the art of counseling.

The recognition of this need is rapidly growing within clerical and religious circles. Seminaries and religious orders are more and more employing the counseling process as a screening technique for applicants. Increasingly are rectors of seminaries engaging special lecturers and introducing courses designed to better prepare the future pastor for his counseling role. Many clergy are taking advantage of special courses and institutes devised for their purposes while some dioceses have themselves conducted seminars and institutes on counseling for the parochial clergy under episcopal auspices.

Facilities of this sort, despite their undeniable large advantages, remain inadequate to the full task at hand. Counseling is an intricate, complex science and art which cannot be completely mastered in a short course of one type or another. Those attending such courses can hope to have new avenues of thought opened to them, but little more. In most instances, their inability to pursue the longer sequence of training in counseling deemed imperative, makes it necessary for them to explore the new approaches further through the careful study of the available literature on this topic. To that vast majority not in the favored position enabling them to attend even a limited course of study in counseling, such literature remains their chief, if not sole, source of attaining that competency which is requisite to their priestly role.

Because of the paucity of counseling literature written from a religious point of view, the present book is an imperative addition. Its treatment of those problem areas most likely to fall under the purview of the pastor makes this work one of added worth. We have here not just another book on counseling written by a Catholic but a book on counseling written in accord with Catholic theological and philosophical principles. The author is to be congratulated for not having been caught off guard with addiction to any faddish school of thought and for not having overreacted against the more direct methods of yesterday. On the contrary, he has maintained his intellectual poise by a ready recourse and reference of his thinking to the tested principles of theological and philosophic lore. In so doing, we are presented with a book in which both the sacred and the profane sciences are integrated into a meaningful whole. Without endorsing every position maintained by the author in this work, I must single it out as the most thorough, comprehensive, and balanced treatment of the counseling process yet to emerge from our Catholic ranks.

ALPHONSE H. CLEMENS, PH.D.
Director, Marriage Counseling Center
Catholic University of America

CONTENTS

PART IV   THE PASTOR AND MENTAL ILLNESS

PART V   THE PASTOR AND RESPONSIBILITY

PART I

TECHNICS OF COUNSELING

CHAPTER I

PASTORAL COUNSELING

[handwritten: Help people help themselves as they see their problems and inner conflicts clearer.]

[handwritten: Aims At:→ Self-Knowledge. ← | " Awareness. " Organization.]

Counseling in General

Counseling has many facets. Basically, it is true, as Father Bier has pointed out,[1] that the generic aim of counseling of whatever kind is to help people to help themselves by gaining understanding of their problems and more especially of their inner conflicts. To a teacher, however, it may mean guidance; to the pastor it may mean spiritual direction; to a psychologist it may mean therapy. To clarify these many meanings the following classification of counseling is offered.

CLASSIFICATION OF COUNSELING

1. **Education** (of individuals or groups): "Long-term acquisition of knowledge."
2. **Guidance** (of individuals): "Specific, immediate, and necessary help."
   a) **Professional Guidance**

1. Legal	6. Vocational
2. Medical	7. Educational
3. Moral/*ethical*	8. Psychological
4. Spiritual Direction	9. Sociological
5. Marriage	10. Etc./*financial*.

   b) **Group Discussion Guidance**
   1. Led by a professional expert.
   2. Led by an experienced nonprofessional person.
3. **Counseling** (of individuals): "Increase of self-knowledge and self-organization."

---

[1] William C. Bier, S.J., "Goals in Pastoral Counseling," *Pastoral Psychology*, Feb., 1959, p. 10.

Types of Counseling

a) <u>Directive</u> or counselor-centered: "What the counselor feels the client needs."
   1. Active participation of counselor.
   2. Rational approach to the discussion of conflicts.
b) <u>Nondirective</u> or client-centered: "What the client feels he needs."
   1. Passive attitude on part of the counselor.
   2. Aim at emotional release.[2]
c) <u>Pastoral</u> or God-centered: "What the pastor of souls feels the client needs."
   1. Eclectic in its approach.
   2. Religious in its orientation.

Definition of Terms

Education. Education is the act or process of imparting or acquiring knowledge or skill. Education thus gives an individual the basic principles by which he forms his philosophical, theological, moral, and intellectual beliefs. Education helps him to earn a living, to live with others, to adjust to the requirements of his culture, to lead a moral life, and through this acquired knowledge to engage in research which will improve his own state as well as that of others. It is usually "the long-term acquisition of knowledge."

Guidance. Guidance is individual instruction about a conscious, specific problem, usually sought from a wiser, more mature individual. This would include moral, vocational, educational, social, personal guidance, and so forth. Guidance deals with "an immediate, specific, and necessary problem for which help is needed now." It deals with a special type of situation concerning which the individual needs instruction or clarification in the immediate future. This is the type of situation with which we are familiar as legal counseling, marriage counseling, and so forth. Some might

---

[2] James H. VanderVeldt, O.F.M., and Robert P. Odenwald, M.D., *Psychiatry and Catholicism* (New York: McGraw-Hill Book Co., Inc., 1957), p. 277: "Shostrom expresses the difference between the two trends as follows: 'In the directive approach, the most important role is played by the counselor; in the non-directive, by the client. In the first, the direction of the interview is determined by the counselor; of most importance is the problem, the determination of its cause, and treatment. In contrast, non-directive counseling focuses its attention on the client, and counseling is aimed at helping him to develop satisfactory adjustment by himself. In directive counseling, intellectual interpretation is the central technique. In non-directive counseling, the central technique is the release of feelings and achievement of insight by the client.'"

question whether spiritual direction belongs in this category, but since the aim of spiritual direction is the immediate guidance of an individual to a better spiritual life it seems more desirable to include it under guidance than counseling.[3] Guidance on an individual basis as it is understood here is given by a professional person, that is, one who has special training in one or more areas, and who has the necessary knowledge to help the individual seeking aid.

Group discussion guidance comes about when a number of people get together with a leader to deliberate upon a subject of mutual interest concerning which they desire information and clarification. The group leader must have greater knowledge than the other members. The leader may be active or passive depending on the purpose of the group. Cana Conferences are frequently conducted on this basis.

Therapy. Therapy is defined in Webster's *New International Dictionary* as: "Treatment of disease; therapeutics; now used chiefly in compounds (compound words)."

Therapeutics is defined as "that part of medical science which treats of the application of remedies for diseases; therapy." The term shall be used in this sense to distinguish it from counseling.

Psychotherapy is the application of a remedy for emotional or mental illness. Crotty makes this distinction between psychotherapy and counseling:

> Counseling should be distinguished from psychotherapy; the latter being a term referring to techniques employed by persons working with the mentally ill, those persons with deep, difficult to uncover, emotionally laden psychological problems; the former concerned with procedures employed with relatively normal people who have personal problems which they feel are beyond self-solution.[4]

Direction. Direction means the specific giving of advice or commands. Such authoritative methods come naturally to the pastor who by his training is prepared to give advice. There are many times, however,

---

[3] I am inclined to favor Fr. Charles Curran's distinction between education, guidance, and counseling. This differentiation seems useful in clarifying the parts played by various professions which deal with people. I do not fully understand why Dr. Alphonse Clemens feels so strongly that education and guidance should not be considered separately. See *Bulletin of the Guild of Catholic Psychiatrists*, Vol. VI, No. 4, Oct., 1959, p. 38.

[4] Charles Crotty, "Marriage Counseling and Psychology," *Bulletin of the Guild of Catholic Psychiatrists*, Vol. VI, No. 4, Oct., 1959, p. 12.

when a parishioner seeks consultation with the pastor when he is not seeking direction but is perhaps in need of an empathic listener, one to whom he can unburden himself. The pastor must be sensitive to this need. Because of the very nature of their vocation some clergymen carry over into their ministry the "directive" element which is so characteristic of the teaching aspect of their profession. For example, the titles of "director of souls" and "spiritual director" are commonly used. Almost by virtue of his office, then, he will continue to be "directive" in his approach to the problems presented to him by those with whom he comes into contact, be it in the pulpit, the confessional, the schoolroom, or the parlor.

Reassurance. Reassurance is the direct giving of encouragement to help restore an individual's confidence in himself. Such encouragement must be given carefully and kept within the bounds of reality. Reassurance to be realistic must deal with what is possible. To tell a patient with an incurable disease or an apparently insoluble conflict situation that it will all be straightened out — short of a miracle — is unrealistic and damaging.

Suggestion. Suggestion consists in urging the client to accept an idea or solution uncritically and only on the authority of the individual making the suggestion. Suggestion has value in some forms of therapy but is not part of counseling. Hypnosis is a form of suggestive therapy.

Rationalization. Rationalization is used in two ways: (1) as a psychic dynamism or ego defense, meaning to invent a rational, acceptable explanation for behavior which has its origin in the unconscious, or to justify unconsciously motivated behavior, or (2) as a therapeutic aid in explaining to the patient certain aspects of his behavior which he does not understand, in a way which he can understand. In this second sense, along with interpretation, rationalization has a part in therapy.

Pastor. Throughout this text the word *pastor* will be used as a synonym for clergyman. The term is intended to include assistant pastors, curates, or other clergymen who function in a parish in the care of souls. It is assumed that this clergyman is not specially trained as a professional counselor. Neither is he uninformed of standard counseling procedures and technics. He is understanding of the benefits that may accrue to his parishioner from the idea that psychology and psychiatry have some contribution to make in helping people to become better Christians.

Client. Client is used for the person who seeks assistance through personal counseling from the pastor. The term is used as a synonym for counselee, parishioner, or others seeking help.

Types of Counseling

With these definitions in mind I would like to make quite clear the distinction between the three principal types of counseling. Admittedly it is confusing to call three entities by similar names. Perhaps a new name for each would be desirable, but until they are more clearly distinguished one from the other it is better to retain the titles which have gradually evolved. In the classification given above three aspects of counseling need clearer definition, i.e.,

  a) Nondirective counseling
  b) Directive counseling
  c) Pastoral counseling

NONDIRECTIVE OR CLIENT-CENTERED COUNSELING

Client-centered counseling is the best defined of the three types. An extensive literature has developed concerning not only its technics, but also its philosophy. It is a method more for the full-time, well-trained, and experienced counselor, rather than for the pastor who usually has little training as a counselor, and although he is a professional person in his own right, his skills are not in the counseling field. Many clergymen are highly skilled as counselors, as of course are many laymen, but the important point here is that the pastor who is also a client-centered counselor is not to be categorized as a pastoral counselor. Client-centered counseling in all of its aspects is not for the untrained. In the hands of the amateur it can be harmful.

As usually discussed today, the client-centered technic which is described is that of Carl R. Rogers. As it is discussed later in this text references are to Rogerian Client-Centered Therapy.

DIRECTIVE COUNSELING

Directive counseling is probably better called guidance. The term is defined here because it seems to have gained entry into literature as in some way opposed to Client-Centered Therapy. As I understand the term it would usually not be considered counseling in our present use of that word, although the American College Dictionary (1953) gives as its first meaning for counsel: "(1) Advice; opinion or instruction given in directing the judgment or conduct of another."

As the term *counseling* is now generally used when it is unmodified, it excludes the direct giving of advice or instruction.

In its pure state, therefore, directive counseling will find little use. Under certain circumstances it undoubtedly has a place in eclectic forms of counseling.

PASTORAL COUNSELING

Pastoral counseling is a term sufficiently a part of common usage to warrant its retention in the literature on the subject of counseling. It partakes of some of the elements of all forms of counseling. It is essentially eclectic in its methods and its practitioner is not bound to any one school. It is pragmatic and expedient in its approach, elastic and adaptable in its method. It might be called "guidance" by some, but depending on circumstances it may at times use a counseling approach. It differs from other methods of counseling in that instead of the counselor-counselee approach of the directive-nondirective counselor, it specifically includes God in the counseling relationship. It is clear that the counselor-God-counselee relationship would differ in many respects from the one-to-one secular counseling relationship. The term *secular counselor* will be used in this text to distinguish the counselor with specialized training, whether he be clerical or lay, from the pastor without such specialized training.

As will be made clear later, the pastor, although he may not aim at being a specialist in counseling, does need knowledge and insight beyond his theological training before he can consider himself more than an amateur in the field. How he may obtain such knowledge and what knowledge he needs will be discussed in later pages.

Plan of the Book

How best can one introduce the pastor to counseling practice? There is a wealth of material, all of which would seem desirable to digest for him. Such a digest would, however, be of little value if he does not already have a background in counseling. I would like this book to be of value to the average clergyman and would, therefore, prefer a more direct and authoritative approach. Since I will be writing in a field where most things are still exploratory and little is settled and most students of the subject have an individualistic approach, I have no guidelines. No approach will be universally satisfactory, but after much thought it seems best, since I am addressing myself primarily to the untrained pastoral counselor, to discuss the subject under the following headings:

Part I. Technics of Counseling

This section will discuss counseling and its technical aspects, starting with a description of the general aspects of counseling and giving a close look at pastoral counseling as such. An attempt will then be made to point out wherein client-centered therapy is not a technic either useful or practical for the pastor. This will then be followed by a discussion of the specific technics of pastoral counseling.

Part II. The Pastor and Mental Health

The pastor must have some base line for his judgment concerning the mental health or ill health of his parishioners. Part II, therefore, deals with the concept of mental health and the pastor's relationship to it.

Part III. The Pastor and Personality Development

In Part III the psychological development of the individual is further discussed, again attempting to give the pastor a base line for his concept of what is abnormal. In these chapters will be discussed the personality development of the child, the teen-ager, and the adult, with particular emphasis on those aspects of the personality which are of importance in pastoral practice.

Part IV. The Pastor and Mental Health

In Part IV some of the relationships of the pastor to mental illness are discussed. Included in this is a discussion of the clergyman's relation to both the psychiatrist and the psychologist with whom he will have to deal in his daily practice. This section includes a discussion of the more important contemporary schools of psychology, so that the pastor may gain orientation by a study of past concepts of current psychological thinking.

Part V. The Pastor and Responsibility

Part V deals with a concept of responsibility which is of importance to the pastor who is concerned with moral problems. In these chapters the influence of habits, the unconscious, and the emotions on responsibility are discussed. Because of their importance in the development of mental illness, the value of ego defenses is discussed in detail.

The pastor seeing this description is quite likely to say that it does not deal with those abnormal states with which he is daily faced. There is no discussion of scrupulosity, alcoholism, sexual disturbances, or marriage problems. These, of course, are all very important, but the pastor is ill equipped to handle these unless he understands the basic facts which are contained in this book. Clinical problems will be discussed in a book soon to follow, which will be titled, Clinical Problems in Pastoral Counseling.

CHAPTER II

SECULAR COUNSELING

Relation to Pastoral Counseling

Secular counseling differs from education (the acquisition of knowledge) and from guidance (the solution of an immediate, specific problem) in that the aim of counseling is an increase of self-knowledge and the improvement of self-organization. As the term will be used in this text it refers to a relationship between a client and a professional counselor, i.e., one who has received special training and devotes a large percentage of his time to counseling practice. It is obvious, of course, that a clergyman can be a practitioner of secular counseling if he has had the requisite training and experience. He would not then be considered a pastoral counselor who by definition is not a specialist in counseling or its technics.[1]

Although counseling is divided into *directive* and *nondirective* it should be clear from the beginning that no counseling, at least considered subliminally, is entirely free of direction. One should think of directive counseling as being *largely* directive, and nondirective as being *largely* nondirective or *primarily* client-centered.

The pastoral counselor may in practice utilize either of these technics, but when he is functioning "as pastor," his counseling must be theocentric. It may be eclectic and aim to bring about "what the pastor of souls feels the client needs" by whatever technics fit the pastor best. He cannot, however, aim at what he, as an individual, "feels that the client needs," nor may he always aim to give "the client what the client feels he needs." He must in his pastoral role have a three-way relationship, with God, himself, and the client, so that his aim is to give the client "what is for the client's spiritual benefit." Maxson uses the designation

---

[1] See Chapter I, p. 3.

11

of "religious counseling" for the technic which is here called "pastoral counseling."

> The term "religious counseling" . . . is used mainly to designate the effort on the part of a religiously oriented person to aid one who is emotionally disturbed. It is generally but not necessarily thought of in connection with the professional clergy and, in more recent years, with the clergyman who has taken special clinical training. Nevertheless, it is equally applicable to anyone who endeavors to help another and does so drawing upon the spiritual resources within his orientation.

He then adds:

> The term religious counseling is in some ways unfortunate. It implies that all other counseling is nonreligious or nonspiritual in method, effect, and implications. This dichotomy is agreeable to the therapist who insists that religion is a "part" that is departmentalized and isolated from the rest of life. To the wholistically oriented counselor, however, this dichotomy does not exist. All counseling has some degree of positive or negative results or value manifested in the spiritual dimension of the counselee. All counseling draws from the resources of the counselor and his psychologic environment.[2]

With this statement I am in complete accord. The term *religious counseling* might easily lead to the belief that this type of counseling consisted strictly of using religion for the solution of the problems presented to the pastor. As I have indicated before, this is not what the term *pastoral counseling* means.

St. Thomas Aquinas on Counseling

St. Thomas Aquinas has described the basic notions underlying counseling. His emphasis on persuasion, as distinct from authoritative direction, is of primary importance:

> Counsel has two meanings: Sometimes counsel is nothing other than the action of reason inquiring about things to be done. In this sense, the relation of counsel to election is the same as that of a syllogism or question to a conclusion, as is clear from the Philosopher. Taken in this sense, counsel is not opposed to precept, for we take counsel in this way about matters of precept. Hence, obligation can arise from such counsel. It is in this sense that counsel is found in conscience in so far as it is applied to one function of conscience, when, namely, it makes an investigation into some action.
> In the other sense, counsel is called persuasion or inducement to do

---

[2] Howard F. Maxson, "Dimensions of Counseling," *Medical Arts and Sciences*, Vol. XIV, First Quarter, 1960, No. 1, p. 16.

something when it does not have compelling force. In this sense, counsel is opposed to precept. Friendly exhortations are of this sort, and sometimes conscience proceeds from that type of counsel. For the knowledge of this counsel is sometimes applied to a particular act. But, since conscience does not bind except in virtue of that which is in conscience, conscience which follows from counsel cannot bind in any other way than the counsel itself. Consequently, one is bound not to despise it, but he is not obliged to follow it.[3]

St. Thomas adheres at this point to a consistent theory. Were matters of counsel in any way prescriptive, in the sense of being strictly obligatory in some degree or other, the very foundation for religious vows, as one example, would begin to weaken. The vows are a friendly invitation, a counsel, on the part of God. Were a person bound to accept a counsel, the friendly persuasion would be missing and counsel would become mandatory.

With characteristic insight St. Thomas has outlined the structure of counseling quite adequately. As Fathers Hagmaier and Gleason state:

> Counseling, implies St. Thomas, is primarily concerned with those methods and skills which facilitate self-directed choices through personal reorganization, furthering thereby the development of the virtue of counsel and ultimately of prudence.[4]

Following St. Thomas we can come to a working definition of what we mean by secular counseling. With due regard for the fact that persuasion will involve first and foremost the intellect of man, the following definition in Thomistic terms seems quite satisfactory:

> Counseling comes about when one individual seeks out another to assist him in his "research of reason" in an attempt to find the means to the solution of a problem.[5]

Recent Authors on Counseling

In recent literature there is some difference of opinion about counseling. Modern authors find it difficult to define in a completely satisfactory way. This may be seen by reviewing some of the definitions of counseling published in the past few years. A variety of definitions is found

---

[3] Thomas Aquinas, De Veritate, q. 17, a. 3, ad 2.
[4] George Hagmaier, C.S.P., and Robert Gleason, S.J., Counseling the Catholic (New York: Sheed & Ward, 1959), p. 32.
[5] John R. Cavanagh, M.D., Fundamental Marriage Counseling (Milwaukee: The Bruce Publishing Co., 1958), p. 4.

depending on the function assigned to counseling. Its function, in turn, depends on the definer's philosophy of man.

Wrenn, for example, defines counseling as:

> A personal and dynamic relationship between two people who approach a mutually defined problem with mutual consideration for each other, to the end that the younger or less mature or more troubled of the two is aided to a self-determined resolution of his problem.[6]

Father Curran, a leading Catholic proponent of client-centered therapy, gives this definition:

> A definite relationship where, through the counselor's sensitive understanding and skillful responses, a person objectively surveys the past and present factors which enter into his personal confusions and conflicts, and at the same time reorganizes his emotional reactions so that he not only chooses better ways to reach his reasonable goals, but also has sufficient confidence, courage, and moderation to act on these choices.

In explanation Father Curran adds these comments:

> Consequently, behind all counseling relationships is a deepening communication which gradually becomes an intense sense of sharing, of understanding and of being understood. The counselor's striving is to understand, to give his whole trained sensitivity over to the other person, to become an auxiliary reasoning power, to become another self — objective, warm, clarifying, and secure. In turn, the person is struggling to be understood and to understand himself as the counselor understands and communicates that understanding back to him. The person himself is the best observer of himself in action and the constant companion and witness of himself. Looking at himself from this expert observation post, he tries to put what he sees and feels into words.[7]

Rev. Maurice O'Leary, chairman of the Catholic Marriage Advisory Council of England and Wales, in a memorandum to his organization accepted Father Curran's definition and then spoke of the counselor in these words:

> The counselor's function . . . is to enable the person who comes to develop his own prudence — first of all by developing his own counsel — to see for himself the reasons for the present confusion and difficulties — to clarify his own feelings. This objective self-clarification, as the psychologists would call it, is a most important part of counseling.[8]

[6] C. Gilbert Wrenn, *Guidance in Education Institutions*, 37th Yearbook of the National Society for Study of Education, 1938, p. 121.

[7] Rev. Charles A. Curran, *Counseling in Catholic Life and Education* (New York: Macmillan, 1952), p. 452.

[8] Rev. Maurice O'Leary, personal communication.

The organizer and most prominent practitioner of client-centered counseling, Carl R. Rogers, describes the counseling process in these words:

> . . . the attitudinal orientation which appears to be optimal for the client-centered counselor, we may say that the counselor chooses to act consistently upon the hypothesis that the individual has a sufficient capacity to deal constructively with all those aspects of his life which can potentially come into conscious awareness. This means the creation of an inter-personal situation in which the material may come into the client's awareness, and a meaningful demonstration of the counselor's acceptance of the client as a person who is competent to direct himself.[9]

Mudd offers this definition:

> Counseling (before and after marriage) consists of confidential interviews which provide an opportunity to talk over questions or problems with a well-trained and understanding person. Primarily, people gain perspective on whatever situations they are facing and counseling aims to help people deal with these situations in the manner best fitting their particular needs.[10]

Although this definition applies to marriage counseling, it is equally applicable to counseling in general.

William C. Cottle defines counseling as:

> Helping individual persons within the normal range of behavior to gain a better psychological understanding of themselves and their environment and to modify their behavior accordingly.[11]

Rev. John F. Harvey defines counseling in this way:

> . . . counseling is the art whereby one person helps another to be more completely human, to think clearly about himself, the world and God, and to use his will to the highest sort of freedom to attain his supernatural goal.

He continues:

> It is the relationship of complex growth in which the counselee grows in the knowledge of himself and in the ability to make use of all the faculties which God has given him, through the help of the counselor.[12]

[9] Carl R. Rogers, *Client-Centered Therapy* (New York: Houghton Mifflin Co., 1951), pp. 23–24.

[10] Emily H. Mudd, *The Practice of Marriage Counseling* (New York: Association Press, 1951), p. 178.

[11] William C. Cottle, "Which Catholics Should Counsel," *Catholic Counselor*, V. 3, Winter, 1959, 3:33, No. 2, p. 33.

[12] John F. Harvey, O.S.F.S., "Counseling is a Complex Art," *Catholic Educator*, 27:367–70–513–16 f, Apr., 1957.

Father Harvey goes on to say that since counseling involves not merely a technic but a philosophy of life on the part of both parties concerned in the relationship, it is necessary for any counselor to possess a correct concept of man and to know how to communicate this viewpoint to his client (see p. 27).

The following definition by Carroll A. Wise, a clergyman, seems to refer to depth therapy rather than to counseling. The counselor should not deal with unconscious material.

> "Counseling" is a word which some of us feel should be reserved for the process of dealing with ideas and behavior of persons which are rooted in emotional conditions that are beyond the conscious control of the person. These emotional conditions grow out of faulty interpersonal relationships. They are of a nature that prevents them from being handled by consciously accepted solutions, decisions, or intellectual formulations. They root deeply in the emotional life of the person, and often are largely of an unconscious nature.[13]

Father VanderVeldt follows St. Thomas in defining counseling in this way:

> Counseling is a discussion about a problem between two people, one of whom is supposed to know something concerning that problem; whereas the other knows little about it, or is in doubt, but is sincerely willing to be enlightened.[14]

When one studies this definition, it is clear that it emphasizes two very important points. In the first place, and more important, one of the parties must know something more about the problem at hand than the one seeking help. Second, the "other" party must be willing to be helped (see p. 69).

In applying these principles to the pastor, it is of the greatest importance for him to know more about the problem than the client. Nothing can be more harmful to a disturbed client than the attempt to aid him with solutions that actually have no bearing on the problem. It would be better if the pastor, instead of pretending to know all the answers, would consult a person who can adequately give the necessary help, or he should refer the client to such a person. It serves no useful purpose today to tell Mrs. Smith who is complaining that her husband spends his paycheck on alcohol and betting, that she married him for better or

---

[13] Carroll A. Wise, Ph.D., "Client-Centered Counseling and the Pastor," *The Journal of Pastoral Care*, Vol. VII, Fall, 1953, No. 3, p. 128.

[14] S. Theol., I, q. 22, a. 1, ad 1; I, II, q. 14, a. 1, ad 2; II–II, q. 52, a. 33, quoted by James H. VanderVeldt, O.F.M., and Robert P. Odenwald, M.D., *Psychiatry and Catholicism* (New York: McGraw-Hill Book Co., Inc., 1952), p. 97.

worse, and that she must accept this as her cross. She is entitled to more and better advice and the pastor should be prepared to give it. The pastor should, therefore, not attempt to handle an emotional problem when he lacks the necessary knowledge and skill. He should not offer specific advice when he does not understand the nature of the case. In this case, the clergyman should not hesitate to direct the client to a competent counselor. Only when a pastor has had the necessary training in the field of counseling can he deal with the more complex cases.

This variety of definitions has been offered so that different viewpoints may be noted. There are, however, despite differences, many points of agreement. For example, all the authors agree that counseling is a personal relationship between two people in which mutual consideration is given either to current problems or to a survey of past conflicts with a view to a self-determined solution of the subject's conflicts and the instillation of courage or confidence to act on this solution. Only three of these definitions mention that the counselor should be "one who knows more," that he should be "older, more mature, less troubled," or "well trained and understanding." Only one author (Cottle) says that counseling should be for conditions within the "normal range" of behavior. As will be pointed out later (p. 29), the counselor should deal only with individuals within the "normal range." Only one author (Wise) speaks of the unconscious in reference to counseling. The counselor should not attempt to deal with unconscious material unless he is a fully trained therapist. It is, however, not only desirable, as St. Thomas has said, but necessary that the counselor should have "greater wisdom" than the counselee (see p. 16).

From this rather representative sample of definitions, it is clear that from the standpoint of secular counseling the nondirective technic is strongly preferred by many specialists. There is no doubt that it has many advantages but from the practical standpoint, even if only the time involved, it is a luxury which the pastor, as pastor, must frequently forego. The pastor should, however, be well informed concerning it.

Definition of Secular Counseling

With this variety of criteria in mind, the following definition of counseling is suggested:

> Counseling is a definite dynamic interpersonal relationship in which the counselor, who should be more mature, more educated, and more

experienced, applies common sense in assisting another individual who is troubled to reach a beneficial self-solution of a mutually defined problem which is within the "normal" range of behavior, thinking, or feeling.

Counseling is designed primarily to help the client help himself, to help him view his problems more realistically and to do something about them. He accomplishes this through the assistance of the counselor who offers him understanding, acceptance, and emotional support. This encourages the client to look at himself with greater confidence and to take a more objective view of himself. True self-knowledge is a basic step in counseling. Confidence increases as the counselor understands and communicates this understanding to the client. The emphasis in the counseling relationship should be on the self-solution of the problem. The counselor merely shows the way. It is as if the counselor were blind and were going on a journey with the counselee. Because the counselor is unable to see, it is necessary for the counselee to describe every step of the way so that the counselor will see the sights along the journey through the eyes of the counselee.

Characteristic of secular counseling is that it is permissive, accepting, and primarily nondirective. It promotes self-understanding and self-investigation. It is a relationship between two people designed to bring benefit to the client. Directive counseling is at the present time largely confined to guidance. In secular counseling the counselor is passive and nondirective.

CHAPTER III

PASTORAL COUNSELING

The pastor today, as always, is looked upon by his parishioners as having a ready solution for almost any problem. To most people the pastor is the one most available for the problems they hesitate to take to others because of their personal nature. The pastor is frequently, therefore, the first to come in contact with these "troublesome" cases. Dr. Robert Felix, Director of the National Institute of Health in the United States Public Health Service, estimates that perhaps forty per cent of people first take their personal problems to a clergyman.[1]

Definition

It is clear that the pastor's primary function is the salvation of souls and that his primary duties are of a religious nature. His counseling activities, therefore, will be secondary to these purposes and will be aimed primarily at making his parishioners more accessible to his pastoral ministrations. There will, therefore, be for the pastor two aspects to counseling:

a) Primary — those directly aimed at the accomplishment of his pastoral function.

b) Secondary — those which indirectly aid his parishioner and thus make him more accepting of the pastor's primary ministration.

Father Bier says that pastoral counseling must be related to the pastor's over-all aims if it is to be distinct from secular counseling.

> My solution to the problem would be to distinguish two goals in pastoral counseling, a proximate and an ultimate goal. The two elements would correspond to the two elements involved in the notion of pastoral counseling, namely, that it is counseling (the proximate goal) in the

[1] Quoted by William C. Bier, S.J., "Goals in Pastoral Counseling," *Pastoral Psychology*, Feb., 1959, p. 9.

service of pastoral aims (the ultimate goal). In the distinction suggested, the proximate goal would be psychological, the ultimate goal religious, and the effective combination of them would constitute the characteristic feature of pastoral counseling.[2]

In our description "primary" would be the equivalent of Father Bier's "ultimate," and "secondary" would be Father Bier's "proximate." Pastoral counseling would consist of an effective combination of both aspects of counseling.

Pastoral counseling differs from secular counseling in its aims, in its methods, and in its technics. It is a three-way relationship of which God is the third member. "Consequently," according to Father Curran, "pastoral counseling, as I conceive it, is a unique kind of relationship between the person and the counselor, a relationship which implies and introduces God as a third party."[3] Pastoral counseling is essentially eclectic. It accepts the best from all other methods. It may at times be directive, authoritarian, and nonpermissive, although at others it may be permissive, nondirective, and accepting. It must always have in mind the pastor's primary religious goal.

Dr. Braceland says:

> Although I am a strong believer in the use of counseling in pastoral work, I emphasize equally strongly that such counseling should always be kept subservient to over-all religious and pastoral goals.[4]

Dr. Royden C. Astley expresses the same opinion:

> The clergyman has always been taken up with the whole man, for he sees the body as the temple of the soul. When the clergyman steps away from his primary concern about the soul, however, he denigrates his own calling. There are, of course, people who for one reason or another doubt the existence of a soul or of God; but not the clergyman. If concern about the soul be his main business, he lessens his dignity and his efficacy if he removes himself from it. Although the objections I have mentioned touch frequently on this problem, the fact that the clergyman is legitimately interested by inference in the whole man leaves room for true cooperation.[5]

---

[2] *Ibid.*, pp. 10–11.

[3] Rev. Charles A. Curran, "A Catholic Psychologist Looks at Pastoral Counseling," *Pastoral Psychology*, Feb., 1959, p. 22.

[4] Francis J. Braceland, M.D., "A Psychiatrist Examines the Relationship Between Psychiatry and the Catholic Clergy," *Pastoral Psychology*, Feb., 1959, p. 13.

[5] Rabbi I. Fred Hollander, Professor Hans Hofmann, Dr. Royden C. Astley, William C. Bier, S.J., "Some Considerations of Early Attempts in Cooperation Between Religion and Psychiatry," *Group for the Advancement of Psychiatry*, Symposium No. 5, Mar., 1958, p. 331.

Characteristics of Pastoral Counseling

The pastor must listen with all available patience, he must direct with all available wisdom, he must correct and admonish with kindness, he must delve into a difficulty with all diligence and prudence. The pastoral counselor must extend his field beyond the confessional to the rectory parlor and office whenever it becomes necessary. When the pastor extends his interest from the purely religious field into the area of general living, he enters the counseling field. If in doing so, he refrains from offering solutions to the problems brought to him, "and renounces the imparting of advice in favor of an attempt to get people to understand themselves, he begins to adopt what is essentially a counseling approach."[6]

From this brief definition we can deduce that very frequently, in contrast to the secular counselor, the pastor offers guidance or direction rather than counseling as it has been described. The pastor, as pastor, frequently cannot be nondirective, completely permissive, or indiscriminately accepting. The relationship between the pastor and parishioner cannot be client-centered or counselor-centered, but must be theocentric. Only by stepping out of his priestly role can the pastor practice secular counseling. *He may wear two hats, he may be a professional (secular) counselor, and he may be a pastor. He cannot be both simultaneously.*

Ordination by the grace of office does not make the pastor a counselor. His purpose as a pastor is to look after the souls entrusted to his care. He uses the ordinary pastoral means to achieve this end, e.g., teaching revealed doctrine and doctrines connected with revelation, offering the sacrifice of the Mass, and administering the sacraments. His main duty is not helping people in emotional or mental trouble, but rather the salvation of souls. The pastor may use specific technics which he has acquired from the mental health field, but he does so only in order to reach an individual and help him through pastoral methods. Though the pastor can and should frequently be permissive, he may urge the subject to discuss any matter whatsoever, in whatever way he wishes to do so; he must also at times have an attitude of authority in pointing out the Church's laws and teachings as applied to the client's case. The pastor must bear in mind that he is primarily a clergyman and, though some knowledge of mental illness and its treatment will be helpful to him, this is not his primary concern. His conviction must be that he counsels,

---

[6] Bier, op. cit., p. 9.

not primarily mentally disturbed persons who happen to be members of his congregation, but members of his congregation who happen to be emotionally or mentally disturbed. This opinion is shared by Hofmann:

> Another questionable approach on the part of the pastors toward the growing outreach and success of psychiatry consists of a "dilettantish" imitation of psychotherapeutic skill and practice in the realm of pastoral counseling in order to dress this up and channel some of the water passing to the psychiatrists back over their dams.[7]

In his counseling the clergyman should attempt to handle only what is conscious. Only the professional counselor should deal with the unconscious. With this Father Bier is in agreement:

> The ordinary clergyman who engages in counseling should limit himself to the problems of normal people, leaving to the professional counselor or to the psychotherapist people with genuine personality disorders. Emotional problems which are realistically related to the circumstances of life, such as illness, death, or natural catastrophe, are the domain of the counselor; not those disturbances that are irrational and unrelated to reality. The latter belong to the domain of psychological disorders and are properly reserved for the psychotherapist.[8]

Many Clients Do Not Need Counseling

Many of the cases which the pastor receives in the parlor are not in need of psychotherapy or counseling; much of the work of the pastor for this reason will be directive in nature because "most of it deals with problems of a religious or moral nature and the priest, on account of his pastoral function and in view of his aim to bring the people to Christ cannot remain indifferent as to whether the counselee accepts these religious directives or not." There can be no soft-pedaling of principles nor minimizing nor compromising of dogmatic and moral truths. However, "it may take a great deal of counseling to bring about the acceptance of dogmatic truths and moral principles; in such instances the pastor has to use all his tact and skill to make the interested parties accept the principles, even though they may hurt."[9]

Throughout all counseling the clergyman must remember that he is first and foremost a representative of the supernatural order. Help has been sought from him precisely because of this fact. In the counsel

---

[7] Hans Hofmann, op. cit., p. 323.

[8] Bier, op. cit., p. 9.

[9] James H. VanderVeldt, O.F.M., and Robert P. Odenwald, M.D., *Psychiatry and Catholicism* (New York: McGraw-Hill Book Co., Inc., 1957), p. 209.

sought, the counselee does not expect the pastor to be a therapist. The pastor is looked upon as one who is interested in people in addition to being a specialist in religion; his parishioners may, therefore, seek guidance on personal problems.

Counseling and Spiritual Direction

The pastor in exercising his office may have to consider the relation between counseling and spiritual direction.

Father Byrne[10] discusses the relationship of counseling to spiritual direction and concludes that the relationship is a complementary one. They should go hand in hand though preferably given by different persons. It is most necessary for counselors to recognize when there is a need for spiritual direction and make the proper referral. Father Noel Mailloux has pointedly complained of a need for more study of this relationship:

> . . . theologians are no more exempt than others from the temptation of neglecting the facts which do not immediately fit into the sphere of their current personal thinking. Totally absorbed in building up the well-integrated structure of moral virtues, destined to become the flexible and efficient instrument of Divine Grace, we often show some reluctance at giving due consideration to serious obstacles encountered in the acquisition of fully rational functioning which supplies the normal basis for the higher achievements of supernatural life.[11]

He then pleads for an improvement of the practice of spiritual direction by giving it the "necessary empirical basis it is still awaiting."

Also worth our consideration is the great advantage it is for the pastor to master counseling procedures and to utilize them as an adjunct to the known, tried, and tested methods of spiritual direction. Spiritual direction itself is not necessarily the lost art some say it is. The need for it, and its use today, puts the pastor in a most fortunate advantage as far as basic technic in counseling goes. Many of the technics are interchangeable.

With this parallel in mind, I would like to show the closeness of the relationship between the pastoral counselor and the spiritual director. This comparison is not by any means complete, but it will serve the purpose of pointing to the close relationship between the two fields. It

---

[10] Rev. John T. Byrne, "The Counselor and the Spiritual Director," *The Homiletic and Pastoral Review*, Vol. 59, No. 6, p. 537, Mar., 1959.

[11] Noel Mailloux, S.J., *The Proceedings of the Institute for the Clergy on Problems in Pastoral Psychology* (New York: Fordham University Press, 1956), p. 62.

will also indicate how the spiritual director is equipped to serve as counselor, and how he would profit greatly, as Father Mailloux points out, by beginning to give an empirical basis to his art. I have deliberately chosen those qualities which are relevant to the subject of this chapter and which we might call qualities common to spiritual direction and to counseling.

Those who write on spiritual direction will tell us that the director must be a man of outstanding knowledge and be as well eminently virtuous and prudent. The following paragraph is illustrative of the charity which should be characteristic of the spiritual director:

> The director will cultivate kindness for and interest in all, but will never permit himself any undue familiarity. . . . Time and again he will deal with the same problems, which are often as tedious and tiresome as they are unforeseen, presenting unexpected questions and unsuspected difficulties. Under such trying circumstances consummate virtue is required; an impulsive, uncontrolled, impolite, imprudent or impatient person could in a moment destroy what he has labored long years to build up in his penitents.[12]

Father Sackett goes on further to explain the need for great tact. These are all qualities that are basic to counseling as well.

In an impressive article, Father Cesar Vaca, O.S.A., has written with keen insight on spiritual direction. He urges the director to have what he calls sociability; he pleads for sympathy, for a delicate balance in stability and flexibility, for a sensitive power of suggestion, for a balance between involvement and indifference, and for an intimate understanding of, and sympathy for, human love.[13] When one glances even cursorily over a few of the qualities of a good counselor, he is struck again by the way in which a pastor is fitted to counsel and by the number of things he can learn from the counseling process which will be of value in his ministry.

Limitations of the Pastor as a Counselor

It is obvious that the pastor represents certain values in society. Those approaching him for help in emotional problems feel that he is competent

---

[12] Frederick D. Sacket, O.M.I., "The Spiritual Director in an Ecclesiastical Seminary," *Universitas Catholica Ottaviensis. Dissertationes in facultatibus ecclesiasticis conscriptae. Series Canonica, Tomus 13* (University of Ottawa Press, 1945), pp. 104–105.

[13] Cesar Vaca, O.S.A., *Guias De Almas* (Editorial Senen, Martin, 1949), Chapter 10.

because of his religious training. His religious training does not, however, equip him for counseling, so for this reason he needs to acquire special knowledge and training. It is by no means enough to "want" to "help people." There are certain general attitudes of a clergyman which may prove detrimental to counseling. "Clergy are likely to be guilty of the attitude of 'know-all' because of their training in dogmatic sciences. For this reason priests make poor counselors in general. . . . Priests too often are allegedly on the one end of the continuum of counseling-philosophies, i.e., firm believers in the ultra-directive approach."[14]

This statement would be especially true if we were to think of the pastor in the same way in which we think of the secular counselor. Pastoral counseling differs, however, from other forms of counseling. It differs radically in that, to the relationship of counselor and counselee, God is added as a third party. This limits the permissiveness of the counselor. No counselor may condone evil, but the lay counselor need not always correct his client. The pastoral counselor must ordinarily do so, if it appears necessary, at some time before the interview is terminated. There can be exceptional cases in which the pastor can abstain from making a correction, for example, when he knows the parishioner to be in good faith about something and feels that a correction would do no good, and there will be no public harm done if the person will keep on committing merely material sin. It is imperative that the secular counselor or therapist avoid making judgments, correcting, or criticizing the counselee at least early in the process.

The secular counselor must usually avoid value judgments unless the counselee makes a direct request for information. Under certain circumstances the pastoral counselor may no longer be permissive but must be directive. These statements should not be interpreted as criticism of the secular counselor. Secular and pastoral counseling are two different processes.

The pastor is usually well disposed toward counseling, but poorly trained. Father Van Greunsven is quite correct in saying that the average pastor is not adequately trained in counseling and should not consider himself a counselor unless he has special training.[15] But should we expect each pastor to be a trained counselor? I believe not. Counseling

---

[14] Byrne, op. cit., p. 537.

[15] Norbert Van Greunsven, "A Priest Looks at Marriage Counseling," *Bulletin of the Guild of Catholic Psychiatrists*, Vol. 4, No. 4, Oct., 1959, p. 33.

is a specialty for which years of training and experience are necessary. It would be impractical and unnecessary for each pastor to receive such training because for pastoral counseling such intensive training is not necessary. The pastoral counselor should have some training in eclectic methods of counseling. It is unwise to train him in only one orientation. The pastoral counselor, for example, who is given a short course in client-centered therapy alone may experience intense feelings of guilt because he finds it impractical to apply this method to his everyday work. He may feel, therefore, that he is doing second-rate counseling. This is usually not true.

The Pastoral Counselor Needs Training

The pastor has always been looked upon as a person capable of offering assistance and guidance. Now, however, with life's problems more complex, many people seek help from professionally trained persons who are experts in their fields. Even in this changing scene the clergyman has excellent opportunities to offer counseling in the entire scope of a person's life problems from moral, vocational, educational, and social guidance to personal counseling. Technics which were formerly quite adequate to resolve problems are no longer wholly efficacious. The counselor must have some training in this field. He must learn to recognize problems which he is not competent to handle and make the necessary referrals. The pastor will deal most frequently in personal counseling, counseling concerning emotional problems which arise from the tensions and conflicts of modern life. At the least he should be prepared to do some counseling of this type. Father Van Greunsven insists that additional training beyond that offered in the seminary is necessary and that a course in pastoral counseling is a must in the training of the pastor.[16] It is not always practical for the pastor to take such a course, however.

In determining the type of counseling that will be most effectively used by the pastor we must consider him specifically in his vocation. The pastor will be dealing mostly with parishioners who approach him first. The counselees respect and trust the pastor and on many occasions come to him with problems for which they are seeking a definitive answer. Under such circumstances the question arises as to the function

---

[16] *Ibid.*, pp. 31–36.

of the pastoral counselor. What is his role in such cases? Is counseling different from guidance or in the work of the pastor do these two go together? Wherein is its uniqueness? Maxson feels that there are at least three specific contributions which the pastor can make in addition to those offered by the secular counselor:

> First, there is a spiritual enrichment of the counselor's natural ability to do psychotherapy. Second, there is the offering of a source of power above and outside oneself that is still available to the patient who feels he has reached the end of his own strength and resources. Third, there is a contribution to the meaning of life. These assets are unique to religious counseling in that mature religious orientation is especially adapted to meet these needs.[17]

To these could be added the facts that the pastoral counselor:

a) Knows that man is composed not only of a body but also has a substantial soul and is destined for a future life.

b) Knows that in this future life man is ordained for union with God.

c) Knows that grace builds on nature and that man must work with grace to achieve his ultimate goal.

d) Knows of the reality of sin and is able to distinguish between guilt and feelings of guilt.[18]

The pastor has many of the necessary prerequisites to become a counselor and could easily become a good one.

A factor in counseling is the concept one holds concerning the nature and destiny of man and the purpose of life. It is axiomatic that guidance can be satisfactory only in so far as it is in conformity with the nature of the one guided. The pastor receives an education that gives him a correct understanding of the nature and dignity of man as a being composed of body and soul, endowed with intellect and free will, responsible for his actions and destined for an eternal life.

> The basic element in the background preparation must be a formulation of a philosophy of life and education in terms of which guidance responsibilities may be related to the whole Christian education for life.[19]

The pastor is well suited, therefore, for the work of counseling because

---

[17] Howard F. Maxson, "Dimensions of Counseling," *Medical Arts and Sciences*, Vol. XIV, No. 1, First Quarter, 1960, p. 18.

[18] John W. Stafford, C.S.V., "What is a Catholic Counselor?" *The Catholic Counselor*, Vol. 4, Winter Number, 1960, No. 2, p. 41.

[19] William A. Kelly, "Training the Catholic Counselor," *The Catholic Counselor*, Vol. 1, Winter number, 1957, No. 2, p. 2.

"the theological dimension, religious factors, and values add to counseling effectiveness, and indeed to all forces of healing or personal aid."[20] The role of the counselor's religious values as a factor in counseling is a topic of concern for those proposing the diverse systems of counseling. The proponents of Rogers' school (if they follow his philosophy) tend to eliminate religion from the counseling situation.

> It would seem from the Farson study that the counselor who communicates his values in such a way that the client conforms to them rather than to his own is likely to be less competent. The counselor's religious values have no place within the counseling relationship in so far as he would want to communicate to others.[21]

In these instances the studies probably involve counseling relationships between persons of different beliefs. No doubt where there are two different religions involved the counselor cannot communicate his values without resistance if the point at issue touches upon religious convictions. However, the counselor is responsible for his system. He is responsible for the direction in which he guides a person, and this ultimately depends on the counselor's religious convictions. The pastor possesses the principles of theology and in dealing with his clients these principles necessarily come into play. He must take what is best in the findings of clinical psychology and consider these natural truths in the light of the revealed word of God. As a pastoral counselor he "tries to integrate his knowledge of theology and philosophy with his study of the individual. He is not adverse to prudent client-centered therapy, but insists that in dogmatic and moral questions he must be prudently and gently directive."[22]

Educational Needs of the Pastor Counselor

The pastor deals with the everyday problems of his parishioners which are quite likely to differ very little from the type of problems which

---

[20] Rev. Charles A. Curran, "The Counseling Relationship and Some Religious Factors," Journal of Counseling Psychology, Vol. 6, Winter, 1959, No. 4, 6:4, p. 266.

[21] Stanley J. Segal, "The Role of the Counselor's Religious Values in Counseling," Journal of Counseling Psychology, Vol. 6, Winter, 1959, No. 4, p. 270.

[22] John F. Harvey, O.S.F.S., "Counseling is a Complex Art," The Catholic Educator, Vol. XXVII, No. 1, Sept., 1956, p. 521. "No counseling, therefore, can be adequate which fails to take into account the supernatural purpose of man, and the constant and dynamic factor of divine grace, however mysterious its operation. To be a realistic counselor means to see the whole picture. But Rogers sees only the needs of the individual as the individual himself sees them and expresses them." Ibid., p. 371.

Father VanderVeldt assigns to the secular counselor. The problems are the same, although the method of handling them may be different:

> The personal problems which the professional counselor assumes to treat are more or less everyday problems such as indecision, lack of concentration, failure in school, maladjustment to family or school associates, failure to get along with teachers or superiors, hostility to authority and to regulations, lack of friends, marital, religious, and financial difficulties, difficulties with regard to sex, feelings of inadequacy and inferiority, emotional instability, maladjustment of servicemen when they enter and leave the service, and other maladjustments which, at least temporarily, are liable to make an individual unhappy or ineffective.[23]

The pastor needs to have some knowledge of psychiatry and psychological principles both for an understanding of the problems presented to him and in order to know when and how to refer the client for specialized care.

> The call then is for the psychiatrist to treat the emotionally and the mentally ill, and the priest-counselor to be prepared to advise on the fears, anxieties, and other normal, perplexing problems which arise in the everyday lives of his parishioners. The art (and a certain necessity) comes in knowing who can be helped by pastoral counseling and who needs to be referred for expert treatment.[24]

A course of training for the pastoral counselor is difficult to outline, but it seems clear that there should be certain minimal requirements which he should attempt to meet. Some of these may have been acquired during his seminary training, some through reading, some through clerical conferences. He should have some knowledge of the various schools of psychotherapy and counseling; he should have a knowledge of personality development, of neuroses, of psychoses and personality disorders. He should have some knowledge of psychodynamics, and should especially be informed concerning disorders most likely to be seen in pastoral practice, such as alcoholism, scrupulosity, homosexuality, and the like. His knowledge of specific disorders need not be great, since it is unlikely that he will be expected to do more than direct "the abnormal cases" to someone else. His handling of most illnesses will be in their recognition and proper referral. For this reason he should have some knowledge of the community resources available to him. He should be informed as to the availability and reliability of the medical, psychological, and psychi-

---

[23] VanderVeldt, op. cit., p. 275.
[24] Braceland, op. cit., p. 19.

atric services in his community. Most of this knowledge he may acquire through selected readings.

Summary:

1. The pastor is primarily a clergyman and only secondarily a counselor or therapist.
2. The pastor should have some knowledge and preferably some training in eclectic methods of counseling.
3. The pastor, as pastor, must at times be directive. This would seem to be clear because of his obligation to fraternal correction.
4. The pastor under certain circumstances cannot be as permissive and accepting as the secular counselor.

Dr. Braceland summarizes pastoral counseling very well in these words:

> Admittedly, the mission of the priest is the care of souls, but in pursuit of his spiritual mission all types of other pressing problems are brought to him for solution. He is used to considering the plight of lost souls, but the plight of a "lost generation" is new to him as it is to everyone else. There is an urgent need for enlightened pastoral counseling, a kind of counseling founded upon the understanding of the psychological reactions which underlie the complicated and bizarre problems which are presented to the priest in the course of his pastoral duties.[25]

---

[25] *Ibid.*, p. 19.

CHAPTER IV

CLIENT-CENTERED THERAPY

Before discussing more specifically the functions of the pastoral counselor, a description of the Rogerian concept of client-centered therapy is desirable. This is desirable for the sake of clarity because, although many clergymen have heard of client-centered therapy, few have studied it. During the past twenty years, Carl Ransom Rogers and his ideas have received considerable attention from persons in psychology and related fields. Among Catholics, Nuttin[1] speaks of Rogers and his "new concepts" in psychotherapy. Curran[2] endorses to a very considerable extent the ideas and practices of Dr. Rogers. VanderVeldt and Odenwald[3] have critically evaluated Rogers' nondirective point of view. Moral questions have been raised as to the application of Rogers' form of psychotherapy, and Grau,[4] among others, has spoken on this subject with considerable conviction. In a very recent publication, Hagmaier and Gleason[5] appear quite impressed with the prospect of applying Rogers' ideas in the area of pastoral counseling. Still others have been, to say the least, unfriendly to the client-centered point of view. One thing can be said, anyone making a serious study of the field of counseling and psychotherapy must reckon with the viewpoint held by Dr. Rogers or, I think, should be considered scientifically myopic.

It is not the purpose of this chapter to evaluate the contributions of

---

[1] J. Nuttin, *Psychoanalysis and Personality* (New York: Sheed & Ward, 1953).

[2] C. Curran, *Counseling in Catholic Life and Education* (New York: Macmillan, 1952).

[3] J. VanderVeldt, and R. Odenwald, *Psychiatry and Catholicism*, 2nd ed. (New York: McGraw-Hill Book Co., Inc., 1958).

[4] Albert F. Grau, "Acceptance in Non-Directive Counseling," *American Catholic Psychological Association Newsletter*, Sept., 1955.

[5] George Hagmaier and Robert W. Gleason, *Counseling the Catholic* (New York: Sheed & Ward, 1959).

Dr. Rogers. It is my purpose to attempt, as far as it is possible, an objective statement of Dr. Rogers' position in a relatively unbiased fashion, a statement which may provide the basis for later critical evaluation. Before criticizing Rogers' position, it seems one should first know what it is. I doubt that this requirement is always met satisfactorily by Rogers' critics.

Definition of Terms

One way to present Rogers' position is in terms of a statement and analysis of recurrent significant concepts and terms which are found in his writings. This I will try to do. These terms or concepts may then be combined into a definition of the client-centered approach. The order of presentation of the terms here follows no inherent hierarchy.

Client-Centered

Client-centered is most assuredly a central concept in Rogers' scheme of things. What is it that makes his approach distinctly "client-centered," and what modifying properties does this term have for Dr. Rogers? It seems that when Dr. Rogers uses the term client-centered, he does so in order to contrast it with the idea of "problem-centeredness" or a "symptom-centered" approach. It is to focus on Rogers' idea that when therapy is indicated, it is the person treated who must in some way change. It is the person, the client, who must be dealt with essentially, and only incidentally the problem which this person has. The person comes first and the problem comes after. The person must be helped directly (if not directively) and in this way the problem is "treated" indirectly. As the person is helped, he can, hopefully, solve his present and future problems. Another reason Dr. Rogers uses the term client-centered is to emphasize the concept that the client is the central point in the therapeutic relationship and not the counselor. This emphasis is related to the question, who has responsibility for the conduct of the therapeutic interview? This will be considered later in this chapter in the discussion of the term responsibility (p. 44). For the moment, I wish to emphasize that the answer to this question is crucial for Rogers in determining what therapy means, what place diagnosis has in relation to therapy, and in what does therapeutic progress consist.

Therapy

Therapy is a term used by Rogers in a very broad sense to mean help or assistance for growth or self-change. Dr. Rogers seems to make no distinction between counseling and psychotherapy. Therapy in the client-centered context means psychotherapy, but psychotherapy of a very special kind, the Rogers kind.

Client

The client is a person who is involved in a therapeutic relationship with a counselor. The client may come for therapy or may be brought for therapy. Rogers naturally prefers that the client come voluntarily. The client may seek help with a variety of expectations: he may want help; he may want an audience; he may want approval; he may want advice; a person sophisticated in his approach to client-centered therapy may want a relationship and an atmosphere conducive to self-directed growth; or he might be coming to please someone else who thinks he needs help.

Counselor

The counselor, that is, the client-centered therapist, can be identified by his distinctive markings; he holds a unique and compelling *hypothesis*. "The counselor chooses to act consistently upon the hypothesis that the individual has a sufficient capacity to deal constructively with all those aspects of his life which can potentially come into conscious awareness. This means the creation of an interpersonal situation in which material may come into the client's awareness, and a meaningful demonstration of the counselor's acceptance of the client as a person who is competent to direct himself. The counselor acts upon the hypothesis in a specific and operational fashion, being always alert to note those experiences (clinical or research) which contradict the hypothesis as well as those which support it."[6]

Not a Technic

Dr. Rogers feels that if the client-centered approach is to be successful it cannot be considered as a technic. The term *technic*, he says, places

---

[6] Carl R. Rogers, *Client-Centered Therapy* (Boston: Houghton Mifflin Co., 1951), p. 24.

emphasis on the counselor using a tool to accomplish his purposes. The client-centered approach, rightly considered, emphasizes an attitude, a deeply held conviction on the part of the counselor that the client is capable of knowing and changing himself, and the counselor allows him to do this freely, at the client's own pace. The counselor provides an atmosphere not only conducive for becoming aware of oneself, but also for this new-found awareness as one chooses. The training and growth of the counselor himself, to a great extent, is a process of developing this attitude and of learning to "implement" the central hypothesis. In the "implementation" of the hypothesis, the counselor's role is not merely to be a passive listener. To be passive, Rogers feels, is to show but minimal concern for the client and his problems. The intent of the client-centered therapist is not merely "stay out of the client's way," nor is it to actively interpret and clarify statements made by the client. Such interpretation and clarification on the part of the counselor, Dr. Rogers feels, deprive the client of the opportunity of clarifying and interpreting himself to himself. Rogers' formulation of the role of the counselor is that "it is the counselor's function to assume, in so far as he is able, the internal frame of reference of the client, to perceive the world as the client sees it, to perceive the client himself as seen by himself, to lay aside all perceptions from the external frame of reference while doing so, and to communicate something of this empathic understanding to the client."[7] The counselor *actively* strives to accomplish this internal frame of reference. Rogers feels that if the counselor can successfully adopt this internal frame of reference, he cannot at the same time view the client from without, be diagnostic, be critical, or be judgmental. He does not consider these characteristics to be in the best interests of a good therapeutic relationship. It is realized that the counselor cannot be entirely internal, in terms of perceiving as the client perceives, at all times. It is, however, an ideal to be striven for, and Rogers feels that the counselor can improve himself in this regard.

The client-centered therapist attempts to see as the client sees without feeling, hoping, or hating as the client feels, hopes, or hates; without having his vision blurred by the client's internal emotions. It is in this sense that the client-centered relationship is considered to be *empathic*.

Rogers relates the difficulties in obtaining and maintaining an internal frame of reference to certain Gestalt phenomena. "Just as, by active

---

[7] *Ibid.,* p. 29.

concentration, one can suddenly see the diagram in the psychological text as representing a descending rather than an ascending stairway or can perceive two faces instead of a candlestick, so by active efforts the counselor can put himself into the client's frame of reference. But just as in the case of the visual perception, the figure occasionally changes, so the counselor may at times find himself standing outside the client's frame of reference and looking as an external perceiver at the client."[8]

It is the counselor's role to attempt to see as the client sees and to indicate to the client the extent to which he, the counselor, is in tune with the client's attitudes and feelings.

The counselor's role is as Rogers calls it an "implementation of an hypothesis." Rogers says, "For the present, it would appear that for me, as counselor, to focus my whole attention and effort upon understanding and perceiving as the client perceives and understands, is a striking operational demonstration of the belief I have in the worth and the significance of this individual client. Clearly the most important value which I hold is, as indicated by my attitudes and my verbal behavior, the client himself. Also the fact that I permit the outcome to rest upon this deep understanding is probably the most vital operational evidence which could be given that I have confidence in the potentiality of the individual for constructive change and development in the direction of a more full and satisfying life."[9]

Relationship

Relationship is another key concept in the Rogerian scheme. Whatever takes place therapeutically between the client and counselor takes place in a relationship. Hence, the attitude that the counselor takes toward the client and the conception the counselor has of his role are significant because of the effect they have upon the client in a social relationship. That is, the behavior of the counselor is not isolated behavior but has the potential for affecting the client's behavior, attitudes, and emotionally colored perception of himself.

The emphasis which Rogers places upon the relationship derives from the influence that Freud, Horney, Sullivan, French, and Alexander, to a lesser extent, and Rank, Taft, and Allen to a greater extent have had

---

[8] *Ibid.*, p. 32.
[9] *Ibid.*, p. 35.

upon Rogers. This latter group holds that the relationship itself, if it possesses certain qualities, can be curative.

Responsibility for Self

Within the confines of the therapeutic relationship, the counselor must create an atmosphere conducive to the personality growth of the client. This atmosphere must possess, according to Rogers, certain properties in order to be therapeutic. As part of this therapeutic relationship there is communicated to the client the idea that he is responsible for himself and for working out his problems. This may or may not be communicated verbally and specifically to the client, and usually is not by client-centered therapists. The client-centered therapist does not interpret his statements or make his decisions for him. In this way, by refusing to take over for the client, the counselor communicates the notion that the client can and must learn to rely upon himself. There are other ways in which the client is allowed to direct himself and be responsible for himself. For example, the client is free to come to sessions or not, and is responsible for being on time or not. If he is late, but the session was supposed to begin at a definite time, it will end on time even though the client missed the first part of the session.

Understanding

Another quality of the therapeutic atmosphere is understanding. This has already been treated in considering the attempts made by the counselor to see through the eyes of the client and by so doing to understand the client's problems as they appear to him.

Respect

Rogers speaks of respect as a further ingredient of the therapeutic relationship. The counselor should look upon the client as an equal, as a person of worth, as one to be valued by the counselor, as a person possessing the potentialities for mature, self-directed action.

Permissiveness, Acceptance

Permissiveness is yet another quality of the relationship. The person should be allowed to be himself, to feel and say things that are a part of him but which are ordinarily not allowed to penetrate into conscious awareness. This quality of permissiveness helps the client to drop his defenses. In this atmosphere he can feel that these thoughts, these feelings are permitted here; defenses are not necessary. Permissiveness contributes to providing an atmosphere in which the client can express himself freely. Permissiveness is a precondition for material to be brought up and freely expressed.

The attitude taken by the counselor in the fact of admissions made by the client is even more important, according to Rogers. This attitude must be one of *acceptance*. To this writer, acceptance has not been definitely defined by Rogers. This is strange since it is perhaps the most important concept in Rogers' formulation of therapeutic change. The term *acceptance* appears in different forms in Rogers' writings; for example, he says, "The therapist . . . must concentrate on one purpose only; that of providing deep understanding and acceptance of the attitudes consciously held at this moment by the client as he explores step by step into the dangerous areas which he has been denying to consciousness."[10] Again, "It was only when another self looked upon her behavior without shame or emotion that she could look upon it in the same way. These attitudes were then objectified for her, and subject to control and organization. The insights which were almost achieved in her room became genuine insights when another had accepted them, and stated them."[11] In another article, Rogers says, "Let us try to restate this idea in another way. In the emotional warmth of the relationship with the therapist, the client begins to experience a feeling of safety as he finds that whatever attitude he expresses is understood in almost the same way that he perceives it, and is accepted. . . . He can experience himself as a person having hostile as well as other types of feelings, and can experience himself in this way without guilt. He has been enabled to do this (if our theory is correct) because another person has been able to adopt his frame of reference, to perceive with him, yet to perceive with acceptance and respect."[12] Rogers quotes Bown, who says, "We speak very often, for example, of the emotional impact of acceptance where rejection is expected."[13] In another place Rogers states, "The other element in the relationship is the attitude of the therapist toward the newly discovered aspects of experience. To the

---

[10] *Ibid.*, p. 30.
[11] *Ibid.*, p. 40.
[12] *Ibid.*, p. 41.
[13] *Ibid.*, p. 165.

client they seem threatening, bad, impossible, disorganizing. Yet he experiences the therapist's attitude of calm acceptance toward them. He finds that to a degree he can introject this attitude and can look upon his experience as something he can own, identify, symbolize, and accept as a part of himself."[14] Rogers reports a study by Sheerer, whom he quotes as saying, "Acceptance of self, according to the definition used, means that the client tends to perceive himself as a person of worth, worthy of respect rather than condemnation."[15]

In a more recent publication, Rogers speaks of acceptance under the heading of a factor called "unconditional positive regard." In describing this he says, "To the extent that the therapist finds himself experiencing a warm acceptance of each aspect of the client's experience as being a part of that client, he is experiencing unconditional positive regard. This concept has been developed by Standal.[16] It means that there are no conditions of acceptance, no feeling of 'I like you only if you are thus and so.' It means a 'prizing' of the person, as Dewey has used that term. It is at the opposite pole from a selective evaluating attitude — 'You are bad in these ways, good in those.' It involves as much feeling of acceptance for the client's expression of negative, 'bad,' painful, fearful, defensive, abnormal feelings, as for his expression of 'good,' positive, mature, confident, social feelings, as much acceptance of ways in which he is inconsistent as of ways in which he is consistent. It means a caring for the client, but not in a possessive way or in such a way as simply to satisfy the therapist's own needs. It means a caring for the client as a separate person, with permission to have his own feelings, his own experiences."[17]

It would seem that in these different formulations Rogers states that acceptance is a quality of not rejecting the client, of being convinced of the essential worth of every client and of communicating this conviction to the client. It would seem that acceptance has to do with the counselor holding the view that there is an essential core of the person which is highly valued, and this valued core is there and remains in spite of detracting features which may be present. (One is tempted to see

[14] Ibid., p. 194.
[15] Ibid., p. 138.
[16] Standal, S., The need for positive regard: a contribution to client-centered theory, unpublished doctor's dissertation (Univ. of Chicago, 1954).
[17] Carl R. Rogers, "The Necessary and Sufficient Conditions of Therapeutic Personality Change," Journal of Consulting Psychology, 1957, 21, p. 98.

some similarity between this view and one prizing the person as a unique individual made to God's image and likeness.) Rogers seems to relate this worth of the person to the dignity which is idealized, if not always realized, by a person in a democratic society.

Rogers' whole approach to learning about people and helping people is very *empirical* and *tentative*. It is a series of successive approximations, a constant hacking away at the numerous unknowns in the fields of personality and therapy. He and his group make their observations (largely taken from electronic recordings of therapeutic sessions), offer and test hypotheses in attempts at verification, and combine their findings into two explanatory theories, a *theory of therapy* and a *theory of personality*. These two theories are then productive of further hypotheses which can be tested, and on the basis of these results the theory is, to a degree, confirmed or modified. The average pastor is not concerned to a large extent with theories and hypotheses. For the reader who has such interest a comprehensive outline of Rogers' "Theory of Therapy" and "Theory of Personality" are included as an appendix (see p. 293 ff).

To summarize this discussion of client-centered therapy it seems appropriate to do it in Dr. Rogers' own words. This lengthy quotation graphically describes the process of client-centered therapy.

> Let us suppose that our individual, now vaguely or keenly disturbed and experiencing some internal tension, enters a relationship with a therapist who is client-centered in his orientation. Gradually he experiences a freedom from threat which is decidedly new to him. It is not merely that he is free from attack. This has been true of a number of his relationships. It is that every aspect of self which he exposes is equally accepted, equally valued. His almost belligerent statement of his virtues is accepted as much as, but no more than, his discouraged pictures of his negative qualities. His certainty about some aspect of himself is accepted and valued, but so are his uncertainties, his doubts, his vague perception of contradictions within himself. In this atmosphere of safety, protection, and acceptance, the firm boundaries of self-organization relax. There is no longer the firm, tight gestalt which is characteristic of every organization under threat, but a looser, more uncertain configuration. He begins to explore his perceptual field more and more fully. He discovers faulty generalizations, but his self-structure is now sufficiently relaxed so that he can consider the complex and contradictory experiences upon which they are based. He discovers experiences of which he has never been aware, which are deeply contradictory to the perception he has had of himself, and this is threatening indeed. He retreats temporarily to the former comfortable gestalt, but then slowly and cautiously moves out to assimilate this contradictory experience into a new and revised pattern.
> Essentially this is a process of disorganization and reorganization, and

while it is going on it may be decidedly painful. It is deeply confusing not to have a firm concept of self by which to determine behavior appropriate to the situation. It is frightening or disgusting to find self and behavior fluctuating almost from day to day, at times being largely in accord with some new, vaguely structured gestalt. As the process continues, a new or revised configuration of self is being constructed. It contains perceptions which were previously denied. It involves more accurate symbolization of a much wider range of sensory and visceral experience. It involves a reorganization of values, with the organism's own experience clearly recognized as providing the evidence for the valuations. There slowly begins to emerge a new self, which to the client seems to be much more his "real" self, because it is based to a much greater extent upon all of his experiences, perceived without distortion.

This painful dis- and re-organization is made possible by two elements in the therapeutic relationship. The first is the one already mentioned, that the new, the tentative, the contradictory, or the previously denied perceptions of self are as much valued by the therapist as the rigidly structured aspects. Thus the shift from the latter to the former becomes possible without too disastrous a loss of self worth, nor with too frightening a leap from the old to the new. The other element in the relationship is the attitude of the therapist toward the newly discovered aspects of experience. To the client they seem threatening, bad, impossible, disorganizing. Yet he experiences the therapist's attitude of calm acceptance toward them. He finds that to a degree he can introject this attitude and can look upon his experience as something he can own, identify, symbolize, and accept as a part of himself. . . . Where the client does face more of the totality of his experience, and where he adequately differentiates and symbolizes this experience, then as the new self-structure is organized it becomes firmer, more clearly defined, a steadier, more stable guide to behavior. As in the state in which the person felt no need of therapy, or in the defensive reorganization of self, positive self feelings return, and positive attitudes predominate over negative. Many of the outward manifestations are the same. From an external point of view the important difference is that the new self is much more nearly congruent with the totality of experience — that it is a pattern drawn from or perceived in experience, rather than a pattern imposed upon experience. From the client's internal point of view, the new self is a more comfortable one. Fewer experiences are perceived as vaguely threatening. There is consequently much less anxiety. There is more assurance in living by the new self, because it involves fewer shaky high-level generalizations, and more of direct experience. Because the values are perceived as originating in self, the value system becomes more realistic and comfortable and more nearly in harmony with the perceived self. Valued goals appear more achievable.

The changes in behavior keep pace with the changes in organization of self, and this behavior change is, surprisingly enough, neither as painful nor as difficult as the changes in self-structure. Behavior continues to be consistent with the concept of self, and alters as it alters. Any behavior which formerly seemed out of control is now experienced as part of self, and within the boundaries of conscious control. In general, the behavior is more adjustive and socially more sound, because the hypotheses upon which it is based are more realistic. . . . Underlying this entire process of functioning and of change are the forward-moving forces of life itself. It is this basic tendency toward the maintenance and enhancement of the organism and of the self which provides the motive force for all that we have been describing. In the service of this basic tendency the pre-therapy self operates to meet needs. And because of this deeper force the individual in therapy tends to move toward reorganization, rather than toward disintegration. It is a characteristic of the reformulated self which is achieved in therapy that it permits a fuller realization of the organism's potentialities, and that it is a more effective basis for further growth. Thus the therapeutic process is, in its totality, the achievement by the individual, in a favorable psychological climate, of further steps in a direction which has already been set by his growth and maturational development from the time of conception onward.[18]

Conditions Necessary for Therapeutic Personality Change

In a recent presentation, Rogers enumerates six conditions hypothesized to be necessary and sufficient for therapeutic personality change. These six conditions were arrived at by Dr. Rogers on the basis of his experience as a therapist. They are hypotheses subject to test but at present unverified.

The first condition is that "the two persons are in psychological contact." Rogers feels that a minimal relationship between the therapist and the client must exist and that no "significant positive personality change" occurs except in a relationship.

The second condition is that "the first, whom we shall term the client, is in a state of incongruence, being vulnerable or anxious."

The third condition is that "the second person, whom we shall term the therapist, is congruent or integrated in the relationship." In explaining what is meant by this condition, Rogers states "that the therapist should be, within the confines of this relationship, a congruent, genuine integrated person. It means that within the relationship he is freely and deeply himself, with his actual experience accurately represented by his awareness of himself. It is the opposite of presenting a façade, either knowingly or unknowingly. It is not necessary (nor is it possible) that the therapist be a paragon who exhibits this degree of integration, of wholeness, in every aspect of his life. It is sufficient that he is accurately himself in

[18] *Client-Centered Therapy*, pp. 192–196.

this hour of this relationship, that in this basic sense he is what he actually is, in this moment of time. It should be clear that this includes being himself even in ways which are not regarded as ideal for psychotherapy. His experience may be 'I am afraid of this client' or 'My attention is so focused on my own problems that I can scarcely listen to him.' If the therapist is not denying these feelings to awareness, but is able freely to be them (as well as being his other feelings), then the condition we have stated is met."

The fourth condition is that "the therapist experiences unconditional positive regard for the client." This has already been discussed (see p. 38).

The fifth condition is that "the therapist experiences an empathic understanding of the client's internal frame of reference and endeavors to communicate this experience to the client."

Roger's final condition is that "the communication to the client of the therapist's empathic understanding and unconditional positive regard is to a minimal degree achieved."[19]

Later in this same article, Rogers discusses the implications which might follow from these six conditions. He does this by considering what these six conditions do not imply. He says that they do not imply that one kind of client can be helped when these six conditions are met but that other conditions must be met to deal with other types of clients. He feels that these conditions apply to all kinds of clients.

He does not say that these conditions apply to client-centered therapy and not to other therapeutic approaches.

He does not say that the therapeutic relationship is a special kind of relationship different in kind from other interpersonal relationships.

He does not say that special knowledge — "psychological, psychiatric, medical, or religious" — is required of the therapist.[20] For further discussion see page 16 f.

Finally, Rogers does not say that an accurate diagnosis is necessary for the success of psychotherapy. He does feel that some therapists feel more secure in their procedures when they have a diagnosis to lean on; but this does not make diagnosis an essential prerequisite for therapy (see p. 53 f.).

In another place, Rogers states the client-centered viewpoint regarding diagnosis when he says, "Behavior is caused, and the psychological cause

---

[19] *Ibid.*, pp. 95–103.
[20] *Ibid.*, p. 101.

of behavior is a certain perception or a way of perceiving. The client is the only one who has the potentiality of knowing fully the dynamics of his perceptions and his behavior. . . . The final diagnostician . . . is the client or patient. In order for behavior to change, a change in perception must be experienced. Intellectual knowledge cannot substitute for this. . . . The constructive forces which bring about altered perception, reorganization of self, and relearning, reside primarily in the client, and probably cannot come from outside. . . . Therapy is basically the experiencing of the inadequacies in old ways of perceiving, the experiencing of new and more accurate and adequate perceptions, and the recognition of significant relationships between perceptions. In a very meaningful and accurate sense, therapy is diagnosis, and this diagnosis is a process which goes on in the experience of the client, rather than in the intellect of the clinician."[21] See page 53.

Transference

One final subject deserves attention. This is the client-centered attitude toward transference. Dr. Rogers feels that transference attitudes do occur in client-centered therapy to an extent. They are handled by the therapist in the same way as other attitudes are handled. The therapist accepts these attitudes, tries to understand empathically what the client is perceiving, and attempts to communicate his acceptance and understanding to the client. The transference relationship, so called, does not develop in client-centered therapy and is in no way focal to it as it is in analytic therapy. In Rogers' own words, "If transference attitudes are defined as emotionalized attitudes which are inappropriately directed to the therapist, then transference attitudes are evident in a considerable proportion of cases handled by client-centered therapists. Both the analyst and the nondirective therapist deal with such attitudes in the same fashion in which they deal with any other affect. For the analyst, this means that he interprets such attitudes, and perhaps through these evaluations establishes the characteristic transference relationship. For the client-centered therapist, this means that he attempts to understand and accept such attitudes, which then tend to become accepted by the client as being his own perception of the situation, inappropriately held. Thus, the emotionalized, dependent relationship between client and

---

[21] Carl R. Rogers, Client-Centered Therapy (Boston: Houghton Mifflin Co., 1951), pp. 221–223.

therapist almost always becomes the heart and focus of successful analytic therapy, whereas this does not seem to be true of client-centered therapy. In the latter therapy, the client's awareness of his attitudes and perceptions may be said to be the focus of therapy. Put in another way, the awareness of self as perceiver and evaluator appears to be central to the process of reorganization of self which takes place."[22]

The Client-Centered Interview

The question is often asked, "How does a client-centered counselor conduct a counseling interview; what technic does he use?" I think that Dr. Rogers might answer the question by saying that a client-centered counselor does not concentrate on technic in the sense that if one uses this or that approach or tool he will get the best results of counseling. The client-centered counselor does implement certain hypotheses and attitudes. Each interview, each counselor statement, is in a sense an experiment, testing the hypotheses which, taken together, form a theory of therapy (see p. 304).

The fundamental hypothesis being tested by the client-centered therapist is that which states that the client has within himself the capacity for self-realization, that the client can find himself in a sense. It is hoped that this self-realization will occur in a relationship with the counselor. To this end the counselor provides acceptance or unconditional positive regard and empathic understanding which are communicated to the client. The counselor does not set up requirements for the client to meet; the relationship between counselor and client is not conditional; the counselor does not communicate to the client that he will like the client if he meets such and such requirements which the counselor has set up for the client. Acceptance is instead unconditional.

The counselor attempts to attain an empathic understanding of the client's internal frame of reference, to see, as far as possible, as the client sees, and to communicate this understanding to the client.

One might ask what part reflection plays in the relationship between counselor and client; that is, does the client-centered counselor reflect statements by the client? I think he does, but only if the reflection is to convey acceptance or empathic understanding, not merely to parrot the statements of the client. The counselor is not merely a looking glass, though he may serve as a mirror for the client at times. The counselor

[22] Ibid., p. 218.

is another person, more than a mirror; the counselor may reflect, but he does more, he accepts and he understands. Ultimately, it must be said that he loves. The counselor must love the client to accomplish the ends of counseling. This, apparently, is why Rogers holds that counseling cannot consist of a set of technics. Technics are put on as a coat is put on, under certain circumstances. The chemist "puts on" certain technics when he works with chemicals. He does not have a special regard for the chemicals; he does not see in them a certain dignity; he does not love his chemicals; he does not allow them to be free; he manipulates them. The counselor must respect the client as a person; he must appreciate the dignity of the person who is his client. The client is an equal and not something to be manipulated. This is a person who can be free, can choose, and is not to be determined by the counselor. The counselor cannot "put on" technics; he must be genuine; he must be himself, and in addition to his ability to love, he must be patient, to accept and understand. All of the qualities which flow from his ability to love will enhance or detract from his counseling.

The client who feels loved can drop his defenses. He does not need to distort and deny his feelings. He is accepted for what he is and in this climate of acceptance he can come to know himself. There is no need for diagnosis, according to Dr. Rogers. After all, he asks, of what value is it that the counselor be able to diagnose the client's problems? It is the client who must change; it is the client who must view himself in new ways; it is the client who must be able to diagnose himself if he is to remedy his problems. The client can do this if he can accept things about himself, if he does not need to deny and distort perceptions of himself (see p. 53). It is hypothesized that the client can do this, can accept himself, because he is accepted, understood, and loved by another person, the counselor.

It must be mentioned that the presence of the qualities of acceptance, understanding, and love in the counseling relationship is not a question of all or none but a matter of degree. That is, no counselor is completely accepting or empathic at all times. The counselor may say things which are taken by the client as rejecting or as evidence that the counselor does not understand.

Certainly there is an ideal in counseling, and no counselor completely reaches the ideal. However, it can be said that in the Rogerian scheme the extent to which acceptance and empathic understanding are present can be taken as a measure (not the only measure) of the success of counseling from the counselor's point of view. These qualities are the counselor's contribution. They are factors which facilitate the client's self-realization, the client's finding or perhaps becoming a self, an independent, integrated, free entity.

Summary

Taking into consideration all the elements treated here, it can be said that client-centered therapy is designed as a therapeutic approach, based upon empirical and tentative theories of personality and therapy; an approach designed to help individuals grow as selves and to become more realistically oriented to life through the efforts of a therapist to create a relationship characterized by acceptance, respect, permissiveness, and empathic understanding.

CHAPTER V

CRITICISM OF CLIENT-CENTERED THERAPY

There is much of value for the counselor in any orientation in the methods of client-centered therapy described in Chapter IV. We should recognize, however, that many of the attitudes and technics of the client-centered therapist are not peculiar to this method of counseling. There is actually very little that is new in client-centered therapy in regard to its practical application and in the relationship between the client and the counselor. Dr. Rogers and his associates have done much valuable research into the theory and practice of counseling, but the basic Rogerian technic has been used by counselors for many years. As a technic, it lends itself well to certain types of cases. What is new about it is its presentation as a complete method of therapy applicable to *all types of cases*. Lest there be any doubt that this is a factual statement, I will quote Dr. Rogers:

> The element which will be most surprising to conventional therapists is that the same conditions are sufficient for therapy, regardless of the particular characteristics of the client. It has been our experience to date that although the therapeutic relationship is used differently by different clients, *it is not necessary nor helpful to manipulate the relationship in specific ways for specific kinds of clients*. To do this damages, it seems to us, the most helpful and significant aspect of the experience, that it is a genuine relationship between two people, each of whom is endeavoring, to the best of his ability, to be himself in the interaction.[1] (Italics added.)

To a medical therapist this is akin to saying we will use the same treatment for all disorders. It seems more likely that what is meant is that in a particular type of case suitable for counseling by the client-centered counselor one type of technic is desirable. The same technic, however,

---

[1] Carl R. Rogers, and Sigmund Koch, *Psychology: A Study of a Science* (New York: McGraw-Hill Book Co., Inc., 1959), pp. 213–214.

is not suitable to all cases. One who has attended a psychiatric clinic could not feel otherwise. The sociopath, the mental defective, the depressed, and the psychotic would not be handled in the same way as one would treat the neurotic or the homosexual. Although Dr. Rogers states that his method applies to all types of cases, there must be some type of selection employed by the client-centered therapist, because the enthusiasm of even the most ardent client-centered therapist would be dulled by attempts to counsel the sociopath and the pseudo-neurotic schizophrenic, to mention only two types of patients.

The reader, I hope, will realize that the criticism of client-centered therapy contained in this chapter is not a condemnation of the method, but only a judgment concerning certain aspects of it. Although client-centered therapy has real value in selected cases, it can be harmful if it is used indiscriminately and by those who do not recognize its limitations. For the relatively untrained pastoral counselor, a special alertness to these limitations is necessary. To a "conventional therapist" such as myself, this method presents many features which are not acceptable, for example, the attitude its practitioner takes toward suicide (see p. 59 ff.).[2]

The criticisms in this chapter are based entirely on statements made in published works on the subject. Some of these are listed in the bibliography. Comments made by students of the subject lead one to believe that there are constant changes in both the theory and practice of client-centered counseling. Although this is undoubtedly correct, I would expect that the substantial body of opinion on the subject would be in published articles and would be reflected in the developing literature on the subject.

There are several aspects of client-centered therapy which require discussion:

1. Is the client-centered method a form of "counseling" or of therapy?
2. The training of the client-centered counselor.
3. Obtaining historical data in client-centered counseling.
4. The need for diagnosis in client-centered counseling.
5. The applicability of client-centered counseling to all types of cases.
6. Attitude toward suicide in client-centered counseling.
7. Is the client-centered approach consistent with the role of the pastor as pastor?

---

[2] Carl R. Rogers, *Client-Centered Therapy* (Boston: Houghton Mifflin, Co., 1951), pp. 47–48.

1. Is Client-Centered Counseling a Method of "Counseling" or "Therapy"?

Father Charles A. Curran distinguishes among education, guidance, and counseling (see p. 5). He states that in many instances people who have received an adequate education and the necessary individual guidance are still unable to make this information and direction active in their daily living. In this event, a third approach becomes necessary or desirable; this is counseling. *Counseling* Father Curran defines as a definite relationship where, "through the counselor's understanding and skillful responses, a person objectively surveys the past and present factors which enter into his personal confusions and conflicts and, at the same time, reorganizes his emotional goals but has sufficient confidence, courage, and moderation to act on these choices."[3]

According to Father Bier, psychotherapy is basically a derivative of psychology, not of education. "Psychiatry," he states, "deals with mental disorder (psychopathology), its diagnosis, treatment, and as far as possible, its cure. Psychotherapy is, in general, the (nonphysiological) method of treatment and cure attempted by psychiatry. Psychotherapy, therefore, is the domain of psychiatrists and to a lesser extent of the clinical psychologist, but by no means that of the pastoral counselor."[4] With this conclusion of Father Bier, I am in complete agreement.

Therapy is a term used for the treatment of disease. No one should treat disease unless he is qualified by training to diagnose as well as treat such disorders. Even the clinical psychologist should treat mental illness only under the supervision of a psychiatrist. The counselor should certainly not attempt to do so. Dr. Rogers' client-centered therapy is not a method of therapy, but of counseling, and as the method is used by Dr. Rogers and his adherents, it should be limited to "normal" or "near normal" cases.

2. The Training of the Client-Centered Therapist

The counselor should have greater knowledge of the subject than the counselee. This is an opinion also of St. Thomas Aquinas who stated:

> Hence, in the research of counsel, man requires to be directed by God, who comprehends all things: and this is done through the gift of

---

[3] Rev. Charles Curran, personal communication, April 9, 1956.
[4] William Bier, S.J., "Goals in Pastoral Counseling," *Pastoral Psychology*, Feb., 1959, p. 9.

counsel whereby man is directed as though counseled by God, just as in human affairs, those who are unable to take counsel for themselves seek counsel from those who are wiser.[5]

Dr. Rogers does not agree with this opinion. He states that experience, not intellectual information, is necessary in the training of the counselor:

It is not stated that special intellectual professional knowledge — psychological, psychiatric, medical, or religious — is required of the therapist. Conditions 3, 4, and 5,* which apply especially to the therapist, are qualities of experience, not intellectual information. If they are to be acquired, they must, in my opinion, be acquired through an experiential training — which may be, but usually is not, a part of professional training. It troubles me to hold such a radical point of view, but I can draw no other conclusion from my experience. Intellectual training and the acquiring of information has, I believe, many valuable results — but becoming a therapist is not one of those results.[6]

To me this statement means that special training in the four areas mentioned is not required in the education of a therapist. He needs only "experiential training." This would mean that training in psychodynamics, clinical psychology, various special areas of knowledge peculiar to specialized fields of counseling and similar subjects are not necessary for the counselor. It troubles me, to paraphrase Dr. Rogers, to see such a statement written by so influential a person. I have been told by several individuals that this is not what the statement means. It does say this, even though it may not mean this. Taken literally, it seems to me that it does say that experience, supervised it is true, is all that is necessary in training the counselor.

Experience is certainly necessary in the training of counselors. Unfortunately, in most cases experience is not intense enough or lengthy enough. In addition to training, it is absolutely essential, however, for the counselor to have greater intellectual attainments in his area of counseling than does the client. No period of experience will make a good

---

[5] *Summa of St. Thomas Aquinas* (New York: Benziger Bros., 1947), II–IIae, q. 52, reply to Objection I, p. 1412.
* These conditions are:
  3. The second person, whom we shall term the client, is in a state of incongruence, being vulnerable or anxious.
  4. The therapist experiences unconditional positive regard for the client.
  5. The therapist experiences an empathic understanding of the client's internal frame of reference and endeavors to communicate this experience to the client.
[6] Carl R. Rogers, "The Necessary and Sufficient Conditions of Therapeutic Personality Change," *Journal of Consulting Psychology*, Vol. 21, No. 2, Apr., 1957, p. 101.

counselor of the unskilled, uneducated, or inadequate. It is equally true that intellectual training will not make a good counselor. Needed in addition is aptitude, a personality adapted to the work, clinical training, and experience.

Contrast the above statement of Dr. Rogers with the requirements for marriage counseling given by Father Stafford, who is himself an avowed client-centered therapist. In the opinion of Father Stafford, it is clear that he considers more than experience necessary to do marriage counseling. Experience is certainly necessary, but so is intellectual knowledge, especially of the field in which the individual is counseling.[7]

The counselor, no matter what his orientation or area of interest, needs training at least in psychodynamics. One who is counseling in the area of marriage should certainly have greater intellectual knowledge in this field than the counselee. This would apply also to other fields of counseling, such as job counseling. This would in a very special way apply to the pastoral counselor who must be at times authoritative and directive.

It is not stated by Dr. Rogers in the article quoted above whether any of this experience is to be gained under supervision, although this is implied in the use of the words "experiential training." It is stated that such experience is not usually part of professional training which is too frequently true. Unguided experience would be of little value. More than self-help is needed. Supervised clinical training is necessary before one can consider himself a competent counselor. The pastoral counselor may not be able to enjoy the luxury of such supervision, but he should seek every opportunity to discuss such subjects and his cases with those more experienced than himself.

Pastoral counseling such as we have been describing does not require the extensive training of the secular counselor because it is more practical, more common-sense, and more direct. Without some formal training, however, the counselor will not understand what is happening during the interview. Without such knowledge, the interview becomes little more than catharsis for the client. Without such knowledge, the plan of treatment by the counselor becomes haphazard. It is not sufficient that the counselor be able to fit himself into the client's frame of reference. This makes him merely a mirror to reflect the attitude of the

---

[7] John W. Stafford, C.S.V., "The Equipment of the Marriage Counselor," *Marriage Counseling* (Washington, D. C.: Family Life Bureau, N.C.W.C.), pp. 39–43.

client. The counselor must do more than this if he is to help the client. To be a good listener is not enough.

3. The Obtaining of Historical Data in Client-Centered Therapy

It would seem important to have some sort of historical information as a background against which to get the proper perspective on the patient's problem. Some Rogerian counselors speak of "intake interviews," but are divided as to whether such intake interviews are done by the individual who is to counsel or by a social worker or clerk.

> The position of the non-directive school is clear. One never, neither at the beginning nor later, introduces new topics. One does not even ask questions which directly flow from material the patient has introduced. One must restrict oneself to reflecting back to the patient the feelings one discerns in the remarks he introduces.[8]

Direct questioning would seem contrary to the method, but without historical data the counseling will be handicapped. Is the client single or married? What is his age? Are his parents happily married or divorced, or dead or dying? What about his siblings? Is he an only child? What is his educational background? Is he employed? Does he know where his next meal is coming from? There are innumerable other questions, the answers to which would seem to be necessary as a frame of reference to evaluate his productions. Can we depend on the client to be truthful? Without some questioning and background information, how are we to know that the client's story is not delusional? How are we to evaluate the boy who comes in and confesses to having committed a crime? Are we to say only: "So you committed a crime"? — or are we to ask a few questions to see if he really did so, or is this an hysterical confession to gain attention? To obtain such information, a direct approach may be necessary. Without background information, no real plan of treatment can be outlined. Without a plan, treatment loses much of its effectiveness. It would be as if the counselor had stepped from a raft of his own to that of the client, and they start bouncing around on a chartless emotional sea without understanding of their mutual helplessness. It would be like coming into the middle of a motion picture. A few direct questions will frequently save much useless floundering.

---

[8] Merton Gill, M.D., Richard Newman, M.D., Fredrick C. Redlich, M.D., *The Initial Interview in Psychiatric Practice* (New York: International Universities Press, 1954), p. 80.

4. The Need for Diagnosis in Counseling

In client-centered counseling, diagnosis is regarded not only as un-necessary but undesirable.[9] This is a *sine qua non* of other methods of treatment.

One must remember, of course, that the need for a diagnostic evalua-tion will not be so acutely experienced if the therapist has only one method of treatment available to him. The nondirective school has only one technic; therefore, the Rogerian counselor deals only with problems in which such counseling is not contraindicated and with very few dis-turbances, if any, in which some other kind of therapy is clearly indicated. Consequently, he has no real diagnostic problem such as there would be in most psychotherapeutic clinics. Despite the fact that different types of patients have been counseled by "nondirective" methods, diagnostic pressure is diminished because undoubtedly some form of preselection operates in those who seek help in a non-directive clinic. This pre-selection eliminates for the nondirective therapist the decisions which have to be made when a therapist is presented with the psychotic, the agitated, the suicidal, the feeble-minded, and the organic, among others. In the usual psychiatric clinic many more treatment facilities are available, and there is need of diagnostic classification so that the proper therapeutic method may be employed. Correctly or not, certain disorders are con-sidered best treated by particular therapies, and for some disorders certain therapies are considered contraindicated.

Since there are so many clients and so few counselors, some sort of selection of cases must be made. A selection by diagnostic categories would be a good method to accomplish this. Although Dr. Rogers feels that his method is applicable to all types of cases regardless of diagnosis,[10] most counselors feel that counseling methods should be used only with the "more or less" normal cases. The selection of such cases requires some sort of diagnostic classification.

---

[9] Carl R. Rogers, *Client-Centered Therapy*, p. 197. Occasionally a tendency to diagnose will even creep into their theoretical statements. For example, on page 31 of the work just cited, Rogers says: "It is natural to expect that with increasing security in clinical experience there will be an increasing variety of attempts to communicate the fact that the therapist is endeavoring to achieve the internal frame of reference of the client, and is trying to see with him as deeply as the client sees, or *even more deeply* than the latter is able at the moment to perceive." (Italics added.) Cf. Merton Gill, M.D., Richard Newman, M.D., Fredrick C. Redlich, M.D., *op. cit.*, pp. 83–84.

[10] Carl R. Rogers, *Client-Centered Therapy*, p. 231.

Diagnostic categorization in counseling aims — according to Bordin — at two things: first, to find out what kind of problem the client has, and, second, to discover, if possible, the source of it. The first question is usually not too difficult to answer because the first interview will soon make clear whether the client's difficulties concern educational, vocational, financial, pastoral, or personality problems.

The more basic question about the source of the difficulties is obviously less easy to solve. The cause may be immaturity, indecisiveness, anxiety, over-dependence, self-conflict, etc. It would be evidently impossible to diagnose the source from the start, but the diagnosis may well develop during the counseling procedure with the help of the diagnostic tools just mentioned. The "comprehensive" picture which the counselor thus acquires, so far from being inimical to the therapeutic effort, will often prove beneficial to the solution of the client's problem.[11]

Father VanderVeldt quite definitely limits the area of counseling and, therefore, indicates the need for diagnosis:

The more personal problems which the professional counselor assumes to treat are more or less everyday problems such as indecision, lack of concentration, failure in school, maladjustment to family or school associates, failure to get along with teachers or superiors, hostility to authority and to regulations, lack of friends, marital, religious and financial difficulties, difficulties with regard to sex, feelings of inadequacy and inferiority, emotional instability, maladjustments of servicemen when they enter and leave the service, and other maladjustments which, at least temporarily, are liable to make an individual unhappy or ineffective.[12]

Dr. Rogers does not seem to understand the statement so frequently heard that "therapy begins with the first contact and proceeds hand in hand with diagnosis," as a psychiatrist would interpret it:

Many analysts and psychiatrists — particularly those influenced by Rankian thinking — prefer to start therapy without a diagnostic study. The trend is most sharply shown by the fact that nearly all therapists, even in making a diagnostic study, would subscribe to the statement so popular in all orientations that "therapy begins with the first contact and proceeds hand in hand with diagnosis." It has not been sufficiently pointed out that approval of this statement means that in the mind of the psycho-therapist, therapy is not built upon diagnosis. Some aspects of it, at least, can begin before there is any knowledge of the difficulty or its causation.[13]

---

[11] James H. VanderVeldt, O.F.M., and Robert P. Odenwald, M.D., *Psychiatry and Catholicism,* 2nd ed. (New York: McGraw-Hill Book Co., Inc., 1957), p. 279.
[12] VanderVeldt, op. cit., p. 275.
[13] Carl R. Rogers, *Client-Centered Therapy,* p. 219.

Rogers quotes Fenichel with approval for his statement that the final criterion of the correctness of an analytic interpretation is the patient's reaction over a period of time. Rogers continues:

> If in the long run an interpretation is not experienced by the patient as meaningful and true, then it is not correct. The final diagnostician then, in psychoanalysis, as well as in client-centered therapy, is the client or patient.[14]

Gill, et al., comment:

> There is some truth in this statement, but to say that the patient is in this sense the "final diagnostician" is not to say that the therapist must give up his diagnostic attitude.[15]

To a psychiatrist this statement merely means that every contact with the patient is therapeutically important. It does not even hint at the fact that diagnosis is not desirable. It means only that diagnosis and therapy go hand in hand and that in psychiatry diagnosis and therapy cannot be separated. Therapy depends on diagnosis, although the diagnosis may not be established in the first visit.[16]

We might express this whole concept of the need for diagnosis in psychological terms of efficient and final causality.

The final cause is that on account of which something is done. The efficient cause is that by which something is done. Now, the final cause will determine what kind of actions the efficient cause will perform, otherwise, there is no intelligibility to the action of the efficient cause. Let us take as an example, a house to be constructed. One of the final causes of building a house will be the house itself that will actually exist after the process of building is completed. One of the efficient causes will be the carpenter who saws the wood, measures the planks, etc. It is because a house is intended to exist in the actual order that the carpenter performs the actions of sawing wood, measuring planks, etc., rather than

---

[14] Ibid., p. 221.

[15] Gill, et al., op. cit., p. 83.

[16] Ibid., pp. 81–82: "It is true that non-directive therapists strive mightily to avoid such an attitude, and in their literature designate evidences of such an attitude as unfortunate lapses (formation of diagnostic impressions). But we believe that the continued struggle against such an attitude is significant. It seems to us that though their theory rejects the diagnostic attitude, it is impossible for the interviewer to operate without this attitude. We believe that they do in fact operate with it, and that they are impelled to struggle against it because of a system of value judgments which underlies the non-directive theory, with which they are trying to make their practice consistent."

calling up a friend on the telephone or watching a baseball game on television.

We may say, therefore, that the restoration of a patient to health is the goal of the physician's activity. What actions the physician performs will be guided by this final cause. The physician ought to know what deviations from the norm are present in this patient in order to intelligently direct his actions toward the final cause, which will be a removal of symptoms and restoration of the patient to a state of health. If the physician performs no diagnosis, then he will find himself without one of his most necessary final causes. He will be like a ship at sea without a rudder.

The question of diagnosis versus therapy is not so crucial in purely psychogenic disorders, but the suggestion made by Dr. Rogers that psychotherapy should be started in psychosomatic disorders, and "if the symptoms did not improve after a reasonable length of time, the chance that they might be organic in origin could then be investigated,"[17] represents an unwarranted risk.

If a medically trained physician, after intensive and extensive training, is unable without examination to distinguish between organic and psychosomatic symptoms, should a counselor without any medical training at all take the risk of a malignancy becoming inoperable, or allowing an ulcer to rupture while he gives psychotherapy? Instances of organic disease which progressed to an incurable degree before diagnosis are very numerous. For this reason alone I would disagree with this concept of Rogerian counseling. When somatic symptoms appear, there is no place in the therapeutic picture for nonmedically trained individuals until a complete medical clearance has been obtained. This would apply no matter how mild the somatic symptoms are. A negative physical examination should precede any type of psychotherapy.

The eagerness with which a patient seeks to obtain a clean bill of health is such that it seems most unlikely that a physical or mental checkup would be an affront to the "dignity" of such an individual. Rather, the attitude of the counselor who says, "I think we should treat you for mental illness until you show clear evidence of organic disease," offends his intelligence.

Without a diagnostic formulation, how shall we distinguish the normal from the abnormal, the sociopathic personality from the schizophrenic

---

[17] Rogers, *Client-Centered Therapy*, p. 227.

individual? Is the client-centered therapist to treat indiscriminately, without regard to prognosis or to the potential danger of the individual in the community? Frequently we see patients who do not reveal themselves or who project their beliefs to others. How are we to recognize projection if we are to limit ourselves only to the voluntary verbal productions of the patient?

It is a rare patient whose confidence in therapy is not increased by a proper and complete examination. Most individuals cling to the wish that their illness be physical and not psychogenic; consequently, they are eager to seek an organic diagnosis and cannot enter wholeheartedly into therapy until this is done.

5. The Applicability of Client-Centered Therapy in all Types of Cases

Rogerian counseling is applicable to all people and to all conditions, according to its founder. For example, Dr. Rogers says that "a consideration of these elements leads to the conclusion that client-centered therapy is very widely applicable — that indeed in one sense it is applicable to all people."[18] He says earlier:

> An atmosphere of acceptance and respect, of deep understanding, is a good climate for personal growth, and as such applies to our children, our colleagues, our students, as well as to our clients, whether these be "normal," neurotic, or psychotic. This does not mean that it will cure every psychological condition, and indeed the concept of cure is quite foreign to the approach we have been considering. With some types of individuals hospital care may be necessary, or with others some type of drug therapy may be necessary, and a variety of medical aids may be utilized in psychosomatic conditions. Yet a psychological climate which the individual can use for deeper self-understanding, for a reorganization of self in the direction of more realistic integration, for the development of more comfortable and mature ways of behaving — this is not an opportunity which is of use for some groups and not for others. It would appear rather to be a point of view which might in basic ways be applicable to all individuals, even though it might not resolve all the problems or provide all the help which a particular individual needs.[19]

This statement includes at least four elements: (1) client-centered therapy is applicable to all people; (2) it does not cure every condition; (3) in fact, it does not aim to cure; (4) people need and can use deeper

---

[18] *Ibid.*, p. 231.
[19] *Ibid.*, p. 230.

self-understanding. With the last statement, I am sure that no one would disagree. But on the other hand, most workers in the field of counseling would also agree that client-centered counseling has no monopoly on "tender loving care." In his book, *Client-Centered Therapy*, Dr. Rogers seems to indicate that there is very little respect, acceptance, and deep understanding in other disciplines:

> He may, due to unfortunate previous experience with psychiatric or psychological counselors, look upon this new experience as one where he will be labeled, looked upon as abnormal, hurt, treated with little respect, and thus may deeply dread the relationship.[20]

If there is any doubt that client-centered therapy is intended to apply to serious mental illness, the idea would be dispelled by the following statement:

> The "hallucinations" are very uncommon, although not unique in experience in client-centered therapy. In general, in clients undergoing drastic self-reorganization, behaviors which would be labeled as "psychotic" from a diagnostic frame of reference are encountered with some frequency. When one sees these behaviors from the internal frame of reference, their functional meaning appears so clear that it becomes incomprehensible that they should be regarded as symptoms of a "disease." To regard all behavior as the meaningful attempt of the organism to adjust to itself and to its environment — this appears more fruitful for understanding personality processes than to try to categorize some behaviors as abnormal, or as constituting disease entities.[21]

This statement seems to indicate that the client-centered therapist is to accept his clients indiscriminately and (apparently) without regard for the dangers involved not only to the patient but also to the therapist. There is no doubt that certain types of psychotic individuals are a danger to themselves and to others, and that their behavior is abnormal, and that they are suffering from a disease. More conservative counselors feel that client-centered therapy is applicable to only a limited group of conditions. According to these authors the word *counseling* is more appropriate than *therapy* because the latter term implies the treatment of an illness — an illness which the counselor (unless he is a physician) is prepared neither to diagnose nor to treat.

Before any therapy is attempted, a diagnosis must be established (see above). If this formulation is limited only to the distinction between minor and major disturbances or "normal" from "abnormal," "adjustment

---

[20] *Ibid.*, p. 66.
[21] *Ibid.*, p. 119.

problems" from "personality problems," "neurosis" from "psychosis," it would be extremely helpful and serve as a guide for the selection of cases. Most authors are more conservative than Dr. Rogers in limiting the area of counseling. For example, Father VanderVeldt quotes Dr. Thorne favorably as saying:

> Counseling is usually reserved for the relatively superficial treatment of mild personality problems in normal people, while depth psychotherapy utilizes more intensive psychiatric or psychoanalytic methods directed at modifying deep personality organization. Counseling will usually be limited to the attempt to improve adaptive behavior in specific areas without altering basic personality structure.[22]

VanderVeldt and Odenwald are themselves quite conservative in regard to the area of application of counseling methods:

> The list of personality problems which the counselor is dealing with shows that some of these problems constitute borderline cases which might require psychotherapy. Although there is some disagreement about the difference between psychotherapy as practiced by psychiatrists and clinical psychologists, and clinical counseling, many authors are agreed that this difference concerns mainly the degree of "normality" of the cases that are treated. Counseling as well as clinical psychology and psychiatry use psychological methods, but the latter uses these methods in treating disorders of a neurotic or psychotic nature, whereas counseling limits itself to the treatment of mild personality problems of more or less normal individuals. Presupposed is the idea, advanced by Carl Rogers, that the methods of psychotherapy could be applied to normal people. Naturally, since the term "normal" allows for various shades, a certain amount of overlapping is inevitable.[23]

Benjamin Patrick briefly states in agreement:

> The counselors deal with persons who have typical problems of adjustment, and no attempt is made to handle cases of mental illness.[24]

All forms of counseling should be limited to the "normal range."

6. Attitude Toward Suicide in Client-Centered Counseling

For a form of therapy which is "applicable to all types of cases," client-centered therapy apparently has no answer to the serious question of the potentially suicidal individual. The client-centered therapist seems not

---

[22] VanderVeldt, op. cit., p. 276.
[23] Ibid.
[24] Benjamin S. Patrick, "Outpatient Pastoral Counseling in a Medical Center," Journal of the American Medical Association, Vol. 168, No. 1, Sept. 6, 1958, pp. 24–26.

to accept the experience of others in regard to the dangers of suicide in depressed individuals. And if we are to take literally the following statements, he seems to set himself up as one who gambles with life and death; for example, "all that one person can do is to describe his own experience and the evidence which grows out of that experience."[25] "To me it appears that only as the therapist is completely willing that any outcome, any direction, may be chosen — only then does he realize the vital strength of the capacity and potentiality of the individual for constructive action."[26] Such statements seem to indicate a lack of concern with the serious threat of suicide in depressed individuals. One is unable to reach many depressed patients. The severely depressed patient is illogical and unreasonable. He is frequently uncommunicative and is potentially, if not actively, suicidal. This type of patient is not a candidate for a nonmedical counselor. These patients need psychiatric care. Dr. Rogers asks the questions:

> Does the counselor have the right, professionally or morally, to permit a client seriously to consider psychosis or suicide as a way out, without making a positive effort to prevent these choices? Is it a part of our general social responsibility that we may not tolerate such thinking or such action on the part of another?[27]

He does not answer these questions, but to a medically trained individual it would seem that when a patient has lost his rational control, he needs active assistance. Although Dr. Rogers speaks freely of therapy, his method is one suitable only to counseling and is not suitable to the treatment of those who are seriously depressed or psychotic.

7. Is the Client-Centered Approach Consistent With the Role of the Pastor as a Pastor?

As long as the pastor is functioning as a clergyman, he cannot practice client-centered therapy. He cannot do so because as long as he stays in his role of clergyman, his counseling must always be theocentric. It cannot be the one-to-one relationship needed for secular counseling. The pastor is the representative of the supernatural order — of the moral order — and he should remain so. To practice as a client-centered counselor, he must, for the time being at least, renounce his priestly role. As a pastor

---

25 Rogers, op. cit., p. 47.
26 Ibid., p. 48.
27 Ibid.

he can be permissive within limits, but he cannot and should not be neutral in religious and moral matters. He need not necessarily denounce, but he cannot overlook immoral or unworthy conduct. If he does so, he loses "face" with his client, because to the client the pastor represents the religious and moral order and he respects him for it and expects him to proclaim it.

For the clergyman, especially, there are serious flaws in the philosophy of client-centered counseling. To this writer there is no doubt that, at least in his written material, Dr. Rogers is a proponent of "situational" ethics so strongly condemned by Pope Pius XII.

Writing in 1959, Dr. Rogers spoke concerning his own religious feelings in this way:

> Having rejected the family views of religion, I became interested in a more modern religious viewpoint and spent two profitable years in the Union Theological Seminary which at that time was deeply committed to a freedom of philosophical thought which respected any honest attempt to resolve significant problems, whether this led into or away from the church. My own thinking led me in the latter direction, and I moved "across the street" to Teachers College, Columbia University.[28]

Whatever the significance of this change may be, it lends a framework for the development of his philosophy of counseling. He states, for example:

> This study permits the conclusion that there is a change in the valuing process during therapy, and that one characteristic of this change is that the individual moves away from a state where his thinking, feeling, and behavior are governed by the judgments and expectations of others, and toward a state in which he relies upon his own experience for his values and standards.[29]

Rogers states further:

> There is one other attitude which I hold, which I believe has relevance for the proper evaluation of any theory I might present. It is my belief in the fundamental predominance of the subjective. Man lives essentially in his own personal and subjective world, and even his most objective functioning, in science, mathematics, and the like, is the result of subjective purpose and subjective choice. In relation to research and theory, for example, it is my subjective perception that the machinery of science as we know it — operational definitions, experimental method, mathematical proof — is the best way of avoiding self-deception. But I cannot escape the fact that this is the way it appears to me, and that had I lived two

---

28 Carl R. Rogers, in Sigmund Koch, op. cit., p. 186.
29 Rogers, Client-Centered Therapy, p. 157.

centuries ago, or if I were to live two centuries in the future, some other pathway to truth might seem equally or more valid. To put it more briefly, *it appears to me that though there may be such a thing as objective truth, I can never know it;* all I can know is that some statements appear to me subjectively to have the qualifications of objective truth. Thus there is no such thing as Scientific Knowledge; there are only individual perceptions of what appears to each person to be such knowledge. (Italics added.)[30]

Again he states:

He (the client) perceives the laws of evaluation and the laws of choice as residing in himself.[31]

Contrast the above statements of Dr. Rogers concerning the subjective nature of moral standards with this comment of Pope Pius XII in his address to the psychotherapists. His Holiness warns them against a morality which fastens its attention almost exclusively on "existential" man, *homo ut hic,* to the disparagement of those universal, objective standards which are based on "essential" man, *homo ut sic.* The Holy Father denies that between these two conceptions there lies a chasm which cannot be crossed except at the expense of traditional psychology and ethics. "Consequently," he says, "it would be erroneous to establish for real life standards which would move away from natural and Christian morality and which for want of a better word, could be called 'personalist ethics.' "[32]

Ethical Existentialism (Situation Ethics, Personalist Ethics)

Wondrous as it may seem, after almost two thousand years of *non nova sed noviter,* some individuals, and even a certain element in the Catholic Church itself, have discovered and begun to circulate a new code of morality. The term *code,* however, is not the best suited designation for this collection of teachings, since its most fundamental tenet seems to be that there is no code, for a code implies some objective body of immutable principles, and of these the new morality will have no part.

The new morality has several aliases, and, according to the Holy Father's allocution on the new concept of moral life, among them are: "ethical existentialism," "ethical actualism," "ethical individualism," and

---

[30] Rogers, in Sigmund Koch, *op. cit.,* pp. 192–193.
[31] *Ibid.,* p. 218.
[32] Pius XII, "On Psychotherapy and Religion" (N.C.W.C., Washington, D. C., 1953), par. 17, p. 6.

"morality according to the present situation." The Holy Father's first mention of the new morality was in an address broadcast at the close of a national "Family Day" sponsored by various Catholic Action groups in Italy. Then, less than a month later, on April 18, 1952, in an allocution to the International Congress of the World Federation of Catholic Young Women, the Holy Father said, "The distinctive mark of this new morality is that it is not based in effect on universal moral laws, such as, for example, the Ten Commandments"; and he warned his hearers that ". . . few, if any, of the extraordinarily numerous dangers besetting the faith, are as great or so heavy in foreboding as those which are created by the 'new morality.' "

To attain to a notion of what situation ethics really is, we need only look at some of its objectives and at some of the complaints which its proponents lodge against traditional Christian morality. First of all, they cast aside everything which is abstract and universal as an obstacle to the development of personality, so their primary aim is to "free" man from enslavement to universal principles of moral conduct. This, they say, is to be done by giving complete primacy to the present situation with all its concrete, actual, existing circumstances, for it is only the individual, not the abstract universal, which exists, and only individual acts are posited. The goal is then a personal and eminently individual morality. The chief complaint of the situationist against the traditional morality is that its moral imperatives and complicated laws stifle the spiritual life of the faithful. Therefore, another avowed purpose of the new theory of morality is to make man's moral burden a lighter one, by making it a matter between God and the individual conscience.

Thus the situationist would hold that man's moral judgment is independent of any immutable rule of action extrinsic to the individual, man being quite sufficient as his own moral guide.

Jean-Paul Sartre, perhaps the most articulate and the acknowledged high priest of the atheistic existentialists, tells us that life is desperate and absurd since there is no meaning beyond the frustrated individual aims of men. There is no totality in which man can fulfill his own destiny, for existence is temporal, contingent and uncertain. Other things exist in themselves, but man is different; he exists for himself — he is eminently free and hopelessly solitary. He is not governed by any fixed laws of nature, for there is no such thing as nature until man makes it himself. "First of all man exists, turns up, appears on the scene," says

Sartre, "and only afterwards defines himself. Thus the first principle of existentialism is that existence preceded essence."

For Sartre, existentialism is no more than a logical attempt to bring out all the possibilities latent in a consistent atheistic position. The conclusion is that there are no absolute values and no universal laws of moral obligation. Man is free and is responsible only to himself; he steps into the place of God, whose death Nietzsche had announced, and thus becomes a law to himself. But while man is his own master, he is also contingent and finite, and although he tries to overcome his instability, his efforts end only in frustration. Thus man is a useless passion. Thus it seems that Sartre offers mankind less hope than even Marxism, for at least the Marxist dialectic is supposedly working toward an earthly paradise. Some of these statements are almost indistinguishable from those which were quoted above in reference to client-centered counseling.

We can accept a technic and not the philosophy underlying it, but here the two come close together. For example, in reference to client-centered therapy, Father VanderVeldt commented:

> In the first place, client-centered therapy, as set forth by Rogers, is based on the belief that man is basically good. Catholics, too, hold that some positive, constructive elements may be found in every man, but they also hold that, as a result of original sin, man is inclined toward evil and that man, left to himself, is only too prone to follow his evil tendencies because his intellect is darkened and his will is weakened.
>
> Secondly, client-centered therapy, again as advanced by Rogers, is an anti-authoritarian system; i.e., it is based on the assumption that the source of valuing things lies exclusively in man himself. Man does not admit any authority outside himself, as he is the shaper of his own destiny. If we push this principle to its logical conclusions, it would follow that man is a law unto himself, both in moral and religious matters. In other words, client-centered therapy refuses to admit an objective norm of morality and disposes of the authority of God. In the final analysis, it makes man his own God. It should be emphasized that these principles and implications are inherent in the system itself.
>
> Obviously no Catholic can accept such implications.[33]

This statement from the first edition of *Psychiatry and Catholicism* is much stronger than the following statement taken from the second edition. There is, however, in the second edition no repudiation of the statement made above.

> There is, in the first place, the assumption that every individual has within him the capacity for self-adjustment and self-direction. The critics

---

[33] VanderVeldt, *op. cit.*, 1st ed., pp. 100–101.

agree that positive and constructive elements are found in every intelligent human being, among them the drive to personality maturation, and that counseling should stimulate the client's own resources, but they know from experience that these elements do not always become operative without outside assistance.[34]

Conclusion:

1. There is nothing new about client-centered therapy.

2. It is a method of counseling rather than a method of therapy.

3. The counselor should be better informed than the counselee.

4. Diagnosis must precede therapy.

5. The method is not universally applicable.

6. The client-centered therapist should not attempt to handle the seriously depressed or psychotic patient.

7. The method is not consistent with the role of the pastor as pastor.

8. Certain aspects of the basic philosophy of the method are unacceptable.

9. For the busy pastor this is a completely impractical technique. How many clergymen in a busy city parish can spend fifty minutes once or twice a week for an indefinite period of time in counseling? This might be ideal, but the number of people in need is too great. A less time-consuming method more generally applicable is necessary.

---

[34] *Ibid.*, 2nd ed., p. 281. John F. Harvey, O.S.F.S., "Counseling is a Complex Art," *The Catholic Educator*, Vol. XXVII, No. 6, Feb., 1957, p. 369, says: "In practice, Rogers' theory requires that the client must work out his own scale of values from things experienced and enjoyed, and not from considerations of an abstract scale of values, which is super-imposed from within. Man reflects upon the reaction of his organism to a value, and if he likes it, he chooses it. In this choice man does not admit any authority outside himself. For him reality is not what it was made to be by the Creator, but only what he perceives it to be, and no more."

CHAPTER VI

THE COUNSELING SITUATION

There are four elements in the counseling relationship:
1. The Counselor
2. The Client
3. Why the Client Seeks Help
4. The Counseling Relationship

Each of these will be discussed separately.

The Counselor

Not everyone is designed by his personality traits to be a counselor. The pastor is frequently forced into a situation where he must counsel whether he wishes to or not. Let us hope that under such circumstances he will receive special benefit from his grace of office.

To be a good counselor he must have faith in people and their ultimate ability to integrate themselves. He must be aware of the differences in people and have an interest in them. He must be aware that no matter how the individual may appear to the counselor, he may be helped to regain himself as a man made in the image and likeness of his Creator. The counselor must, therefore, be aware of spiritual values.

He must be understanding, friendly, warm, patient, empathic, prudent, tolerant, accepting, considerate, free of prejudices. He must be persistent and willing to help even when there is little hope of success. For him, discouragement is a luxury which he cannot afford. He must be kindly and have an ability to listen. He must be objective and capable of remaining uninvolved in his client's conflicts. He must be consistent so that his client will not be confused by discrepant responses. He must be emotionally controlled and sufficiently secure within himself to be able to tender help to others. His power of observation should be well developed, and he should have good self-understanding as well as a willingness to understand and accept people as they are without criticism. He should be free of disabling inhibitions and resistances. He should have a greater knowledge of the matters discussed than the counselee. He should be able to impress the client with his desire to be of help to him. He must be flexible.

Equally important are those characteristics which the counselor must not have. He must not be aloof, hurried, domineering, critical, or fault-finding. He must not blame, or shame, or act coldly. He must not humiliate the client, nor should he be indulgent, sympathetic, pitying, or argumentative.

One who could fit all of the above characteristics would indeed be a perfect counselor. Few such individuals are to be found. Conscious efforts at adjustment to meet these requirements may make up for this lack. The counselor would do well to check himself against these personality characteristics periodically and make a persistent effort to measure up to them.

There are certain characteristics which are more important than others. I would consider *understanding* and *acceptance* as those above all others which the counselor must have. Before proceeding I will define these terms as I understand them.

Understanding implies a great deal. It means knowledge, training, and awareness of the possibilities. With particular reference to the interview it means "a knowledge of what is meant by what happens" during its course. It means also that this understanding should not be too readily communicated to the subject. The fact that the client is seeking consultation means that he has *overcome certain resistances* in the process of which he has built up certain defenses. These defenses are constructed not only against the counselor but against the patient's own understanding of himself. If the counselor shows too quickly that he understands and has penetrated these defenses it may leave the client feeling helpless and naked. He may then need to escape, either literally, by terminating the interview, or into superficialities. The *primary understanding* should be of the *mental processes of the individual* rather than of *his behavior as such*. The counselor must develop the ability to communicate his feelings and understanding to the client.

Acceptance of people, a firm conviction of their basic worth, is another essential characteristic of the counselor. It implies an ability to accept people as they are, with interest and without annoyance, the ability to accept the sinner but not his sin, the ability to allow people to differ, and the ability to accept the realization that behavior is a complex pattern of thinking, willing, and feeling.

Ideally, the client must be accepted unreservedly as a person regardless of what he does or says. But suppose the client tends toward an unhealthy or immoral way of thinking or acting. Can the pastor be completely accepting under these circumstances? Here is the area in which a radical split occurs between the secular and the pastoral counselor. The question of acceptance in nondirective counseling is so important that it is worthy of a critical discussion (see pp. 36, 70 ff.).

The Client

When the client seeks help it should be an indication to the counselor that he has already overcome some resistances. For some dependent individuals seeking out the pastor may have been very easy, but for most people it is with the greatest reluctance that they will reveal themselves to the counselor. Some individuals, of course, do not come with complete voluntariness. In these days of aggressive social service the client is too frequently told "to go or else" his relief payments will be cut off. This type of client is in the minority, but the counselor should be aware that some of the attitudes shown by his counselee are the remnants of the defenses which he has put up to defend his rapidly disintegrating ego. To reveal himself to a stranger may, in his opinion, be depriving him of his last vestige of human dignity.

Even a voluntary client may need special handling so that he may be desensitized to any feeling which he may have of being threatened by the interview situation. To many persons, educated and uneducated alike, going to someone in the field of psychology, be he psychiatrist, psychologist, or counselor, means that he is "crazy." He is not clear as to what is meant by this term, but it is something which is not good. Most of the individuals seen by the pastoral counselor will probably not fall in this category.

The client also needs reassurance as to the nature of the counseling process. Too frequently the client seeks out the counselor in the hope that he will "do something to him" which "will make him better." Frequently, after the client has been speaking for a while he will ask of the counselor, "Am I helping you (to help me)?" This is one of the first discoveries that the client must make, namely, that he must take the responsibility for his own condition and recovery. The counselor does not "cure him" but is merely a guide, or perhaps a catalyst who takes no part in the reaction. It may take some time to put this message across, but it is essential to do so, at first by indirection, later more directly.

There are two needs which everyone has, but which are undoubtedly greatly exaggerated in the emotionally disturbed individual. These are the need to be understood and the need to be accepted. Both of these are discussed elsewhere (p. 109 f.). Much of the immediate relief which the client experiences in counseling, even after a single interview, results from the feeling that "here is someone who will try to understand my viewpoint and who will not reject me because I am in trouble." In this relaxing atmosphere the client may be able to lower his defenses, discover rejected attitudes which he may then be able to accept. As he investigates his personality he may be better able to accept himself as he is, or at least see the need for reorganization and means by which this may be accomplished. The counselor helps him to do this by encouragement, by acceptance, by interpretation, as each of these seems necessary or desirable.

Why the Client Seeks Help

Aside from these two basic needs on the part of the client, the reasons he seeks help are legion. Many of these may be summarized under the following headings:

1. *Somatic symptoms.* The subject has been told or is himself convinced that his physical symptoms are emotional in origin. If this is a self-diagnosis, the counselor should be very cautious because serious physical illness may be present. Insist on a complete physical examination first. If no physical illness is discovered, the counseling may be started. Somatic symptoms are frequently present in depression, as well as in the group now called the psychosomatic disorders.

2. *Tension.* This may be complained of as an "inner tension," or as trembling, usually referred to as "physical tension." It is basically an anxiety reaction which is very distressing, and the individual so affected may think at first that he is "going crazy." Tension may also affect certain groups of muscles and produce locally symptoms such as headache, backache, or jaw-ache.

3. *Feelings of guilt.* Feelings of guilt may be conscious or unconscious in their origin. The anxiety provoked by such feelings often creates a need to unburden oneself. This is not possible with everyone so the client seeks out the pastor, who is probably the most trustworthy person he knows.

4. *A feeling of being overwhelmed by responsibility.*

5. *A need for guidance in marital, social, or personal problems.*

6. *A need to talk to someone.* This may represent a need to "talk through" a problem with an understanding person, or merely a need to talk to someone due to a feeling of internal pressure.

7. *Feelings of inadequacy, insecurity, inferiority, and many others.*

The Counseling Relationship

The aim of the counselor is to establish between the counselee and himself a relationship in which the client feels comfortable and accepted and in which the counselor is empathic. In this type of relationship the client is most likely to see for himself the "why" of his present problem and confusion. Having done this much, the client may then, by using his own counsel and prudence, arrive at a decision. The role of the counselor is "to enable them to use their own counsel and prudence: to see for themselves, to decide for themselves, so that they can act for themselves."[1] This may be a counsel of perfection for the pastoral counselor. He may have to deal more directly with the problems of his client than does the secular nondirective counselor. He should be careful to avoid either spiritual or emotional harm to his client. Much more could be said on this subject, but it has already been described on page 35 in Chapter IV. There are aspects of the counseling relationship, however, which need special attention:

1. Acceptance in Nondirective Counseling
2. Sympathy Versus Empathy

Acceptance in Nondirective Counseling

How accepting may the pastoral counselor be? Certainly not as accepting as the secular counselor. Acceptance, as I am using it here, is a

---

[1] Rev. Charles A. Curran, *Personality Factors in Counseling* (New York: Macmillan, 1952), p. 274. Father Curran recognizes that complete acceptance is impossible: "It would be a mistake, therefore, to assume that freedom of non-directive counseling implies no restraints and no limitations."

synonym for permissiveness. Suppose that Father X is counseling Client A. Client A tells Father X during a counseling session that he intends that evening to have sexual relations with May B to whom he is not married. How permissive can Father X be under these circumstances? Must he point out the immorality of this action or may he be permissive? At times, even the secular counselor should condemn this proposed conduct, at least when he feels that he can avert it. But he would not be bound to condemn it to the same extent as the pastor.

> It is especially incumbent on the pastor and on confessors to deter their subjects from occasions of sin, even if those occasions are innocently entered upon. Similarly, these Superiors must admonish subjects of grave violations of Natural Law, committed, if that is possible, in good faith. The matter is more urgent in these days when false moral principles are learned in irreligious surroundings. (Italics added.)[2]

Perhaps the best way to reason about this type of "acceptance" in nondirective and/or client-centered therapy is to consider it against the background of a discussion of a client-centered therapist, Reverend Albert F. Grau, S.J.[3] My discussion of the subject is limited to the use of acceptance in pastoral counseling as it was defined on page 19. The arguments given by Father Grau favoring acceptance are not convincing. Before starting his discussion Father Grau explains the position of the counselor with reference to the client and his possible immoral choice. He states:

> Let us remind ourselves of two important facts: (a) client-centered acceptance for the purpose of therapy implies neither approval nor disapproval, and it pertains to the peculiar genius of the counselor to make this clear; (b) consequently, this "permissiveness" is related only to the client's self-expression in the client-counselor relationship.

In pastoral counseling, there is by definition an intrinsic relationship between helping the person to gain insight and improving his religious life (see p. 23). In order to achieve this goal, the pastor must limit his counseling "to people with conscious religious, moral, and spiritual problems, not rooted in deep emotional conflict."

Secular counselors may indirectly help a person to lead a better religious life, but this is only a secondary effect, since their purpose is to help him to adjust to all phases of life. In the mind of the pastor,

---

[2] Henry Davis, S.J., *Moral and Pastoral Theology*, Vol. 1 (New York: Sheed & Ward, 1936), p. 330.

[3] *American Catholic Psychological Association Newsletter*, Supplement No. 17, Sept., 1955, "Acceptance in Non-Directive Counseling."

this is his primary purpose and there is a formal connection between insight and greater religiosity.

Since this question of acceptance is one of basic importance in a method of counseling employed by a large number of clergymen, I would like to treat it at some length. For this purpose I would like to present Father Grau's arguments completely so that I can be sure they are being stated correctly. He says that he will discuss the subject of acceptance under three headings:

> The moral principles which may seem to be involved can be listed under three headings. These, expressed in the technical terminology of moral theology, are *scandal, cooperation in evil,* and *fraternal correction.* The proposition is submitted that client-centered acceptance does not conflict with the moral principles included in those three areas.
>
> It is important to emphasize that these remarks deal solely with the client-centered counseling situation in which we presuppose a completely "non-directive" orientation.
>
> (a) *Scandal.* Scandal, in the technical moral sense, we define as "unbecoming words or conduct furnishing the occasion for another's sin or spiritual ruin." Scandal in the strict sense is *direct* if the one giving the scandal intended the sin of the one scandalized; *indirect,* if the sin is not intended, but merely foreseen. If a grown-up intends that the children develop his same unfortunate habit of bad language, he gives direct scandal; if he merely foresees this, but does not intend it, he is giving indirect scandal.
>
> Applying what we have said here to the counseling situation, we maintain that no direct scandal is given, since from the supposition the client-centered counselor — who neither disapproves nor approves — does not wish the evil to be committed. Indirect scandal can be present only if the sin is foreseen, or is likely to result from the counselor's not "exerting pressure." *In our knowledge of the dynamics of counseling therapy at their present stage of development, this is not a valid prediction.*

I can agree with Father Grau that there is no direct scandal, since the pastor does not intend the sin of the client. It seems evident, however, that indirect scandal may be present.

I believe that you can make the prediction of an intended sin with moral certainty, since the client is supposedly a responsible individual. Perhaps the pastor cannot always foresee that the client will carry out the immoral action that he is determined upon, but certainly *in some cases* this *can* be foreseen. The scandal consists in the omission of any manifestation of disapproval of the intended sinful act.

The same situation is true in regard to "exerting pressure"; that is, there will undoubtedly be times when the pastor will be able to predict with moral certainty that the exertion of pressure would prevent the client from performing an immoral act.

Scandal may, therefore, be involved in the use of acceptance, since the immoral act can at times be foreseen and actually prevented by the exertion of pressure.

Father Grau then reaches his second point:

> Lending Moral Cooperation to Evil. Moral cooperation in evil, again in the technical sense, is "concurrence by counsel or silence in the evil or sinful deed of another." As is evident, moral cooperation is very similar to scandal. We call moral cooperation formal if the cooperator intends to encourage conduct which he knows to be sinful or to lead to sin: e.g., if I encourage by approbation or praise the plans of a friend to burglarize a home. The moral cooperation is material if I encourage a line of conduct, not knowing that it is sinful. We are concerned here only with formal moral cooperation. Looking at the counseling situation, we maintain that the client-centered counselor is not lending (formal) moral cooperation to sin, since he, as a client-centered counselor, cannot approve or intend the sin.

Father Grau says that in nondirective counseling there is no formal co-operation. This is true, because formal co-operation implies a desire to see the sin committed. He says that we are not concerned with material co-operation. This statement is erroneous because material co-operation is per se sinful, and would ordinarily be present if a pastor refrained from any sign of disapproval, when his client manifests the intention of committing some sin. In such a case his silence would be negative co-operation, i.e., the neglect to prevent the sin of another by one who is bound by his office to do so.

He defines material co-operation "as encouraging a line of conduct not knowing it is sinful." This is also incorrect, because a person may co-operate in an act which he knows is sinful, e.g., the nurse who is ordered to prepare a patient for an immoral operation, or the salesgirl who in order to hold a necessary job is forced to sell contraceptives. The lawfulness of material co-operation does not depend on knowledge or the lack of it, but on the person's intention and the reason for co-operating.

According to Father Francis Connell and Father Merkelbach, there is a definite obligation for the pastor to correct in such cases and only a very grave reason would destroy this obligation.[4]

Fathers Callen and McHugh state that material co-operation in evil

---

[4] *Moral Theology*, revised by Edward Farrell, O.P., Vol. 1, No. 1515, p. 620.

must be justified on the principle of the double effect. This is impossible in client-centered therapy because the act which is being performed is acceptance, and we cannot say this is good, bad, or indifferent, since it is the very thing we are trying to prove.

Father Connell says,

> Two factors must be considered in the question of cooperation in evil: (1) the gravity of the sin involved, and (2) the degree of influence of one's cooperation toward the evil act. In other words, the graver the sin the graver must be one's justifying reason; and the greater influence one's action has, the greater must be the reason.[5]

Later he mentions that a person is permitted to co-operate materially in the sin of another for a sufficiently grave and proportionate reason. It does not seem to me that there is a proportion between allowing a person to commit a seriously immoral act and the profit he will get from counseling, especially if a third party is involved. It seems that the worst that could happen is that the client would discontinue his visits to the counselor and this does not compare with serious immorality. To remain accepting would tend toward making the end (insight) justify the means (murder).

According to Father Connell, even material sins are the subject of fraternal correction:

1. When the thing involved regards something necessary by necessity of means, e.g., belief in the Trinity;
2. When it involves a material sin that induces a habit that is hard to overcome, e.g., impurity;
3. When the sin causes scandal or grave damage to another;
4. When the sin brings about grave injury to God.[6]

Merkelbach says that "even private persons are obliged to correct others in order to avert some grave evil as homicide or damage to the common good."[7] This does not flow from the obligation of fraternal correction, but from the obligation of preventing evil from happening to others.

---

[5] Very Rev. Francis J. Connell, C.Ss.R., *Outlines of Moral Theology* (Milwaukee: The Bruce Publishing Co., 1953), p. 93.

[6] Personal communication.

[7] *Summa Theologica Moralis*, Vol. I (10th ed.), 1935, Q. 438, Fraternal Correction.

Fraternal correction[8] is the third point taken up by Father Grau:

Fraternal Correction. There is finally the consideration of the obligation of fraternal correction which may apparently militate against the conclusions summarized above. Fraternal correction is defined as "admonition or advice given to our neighbor with the purpose of correcting or preventing a fault or sin." In academic discussions an appreciation of this obligation seems to be the basis of many of the objections against client-centered acceptance. It is necessary to remember that for the obligation of fraternal correction to be present, certain conditions must be *simultaneously* fulfilled. In terms of the counseling situation, these are that (a) the client's moral or spiritual danger be serious and actual; (b) that giving the admonition should not impose a great personal inconvenience upon the counselor; and (c) that there be a well-founded hope that the admonition or advice will prevent the sin.

Let us examine Father Grau's three principles in regard to fraternal correction:

1. "The client's moral or spiritual danger must be serious or actual."

This is an incomplete statement because the client is not the only person to be taken into consideration. Merkelbach also states that even material sin is the subject of fraternal correction when one (such as the pastor) is bound ex *officio* to teach others, or if because of his own ignorance grave damage will come to him, to a third party, or if scandal or irreverence to God or religion, etc., will arise.[9]

It has also been previously mentioned that even abstracting from the obligation of fraternal correction, private persons have an obligation to prevent serious evil from happening to others.

Therefore, it is erroneous to state that only the client's welfare is to be taken into consideration. Anyone who is affected must also be considered.

2. Father Grau's second principle is that the admonition should not impose a serious inconvenience on the pastor. This statement, at least, seems unobjectionable.

---

[8] According to Henry Davis, S.J., *Moral and Pastoral Theology*, Vol. 1 (New York: Sheed & Ward, 1936), p. 327: "Fraternal correction is a private admonition given to another in order to withdraw him from his sin or to prevent his sinning. It is not judicial correction, which is, as it were, public, given by legitimate Superiors, and for the common good. Fraternal correction may be given by an equal or even by an inferior, because the obligation of charity is universal. It can be given in other ways than by actual words."

[9] Merkelbach, *op. cit.*, No. 941.

3. Finally, he says there "must be a well-founded hope that the admonition or advice will prevent sin."

The phrase "well-founded hope" is somewhat misleading. Moralists usually use the term "probability." Jone, however, says, "There must be well-founded hope that the other will profit by the correction" (italics are in the original).[10]

Father Connell states that there must be some probability that the correction will be profitable. If it is equiprobable then it is to be omitted, unless the person will die in sin or grave scandal or dishonor to God will follow from its omission. A superior is bound to give it ex officio.[11]

Father Merkelbach says:

> 1. If the correction may help the person and certainly will not harm him then it must be given.
> 2. If it is equi-probable, then it is to be omitted.
> 3. Unless it is foreseen that the person will die in sin, or if a greater evil is feared of which they must be forewarned, e.g., dishonor to God, irreverence to religion, scandal or damage to many or to the state or even to one person if it is greater and more feared than the damage to the sinner; superiors must give correction ex officio even when there is small hope in order to keep discipline or prevent scandal.[12]

This comment of Merkelbach gives a quite different impression from that conveyed by "a well-founded hope." There is no doubt that at times a third party will be involved and that the success of the correction or admonition will represent at least an equiprobable opinion. Consequently, fraternal correction may be demanded because a "well-founded hope" is not necessary but only a real probability, and this requirement is lessened when someone in addition to the client is affected.

Father Grau ends his discussion with this statement:

> There is, finally, the following consideration: the entire discussion is concerned NOT with "Should we help our clients avoid sin and evil?" but, rather, "How best can we do this?" Even the obligation of fraternal correction supposes a choice of the most suitable means. In the light of the research of Carl Rogers, et al., we can validly dispute the efficacy in this regard of explicitly verbalized admonitions in the counseling situation.

It seems to me that the question which the client-centered counselor

---

[10] Herbert Jone, O.F.M.Cap., and Urban Adelman, O.F.M.Cap., *Moral Theology* (Westminster, Md.: Newman Press, 1945), p. 88.

[11] Personal communication.

[12] Merkelbach, *op. cit.*, No. 938-3.

really asks is, "How best can we do this regardless of what happens to anyone else?" Father Grau speaks of a choice of the most suitable means in fraternal correction and then concludes that according "to Carl Rogers, et al." one is not required to offer correction "in the counseling situation." What are we to think of the statements of Father Connell and Merkel-bach in this regard? Or the statement of Father Davis quoted on page 71? It would seem that their admonitions apply to the pastoral counselor regardless of "the research of Carl Rogers, et al."

For the sake of completeness, I would like to quote briefly from the answer of St. Thomas Aquinas to the question as to when fraternal correction may be omitted:

> Fraternal correction may be omitted in three ways. First, meritoriously, when out of charity one omits to correct someone. For Augustine says (De Civ. Dei, 1.9): If a man refrains from chiding and reproving wrong-doers, because he awaits a suitable time for so doing, or because he fears lest, if he does so, they may become worse, or hinder, oppress, or turn away from the faith, others who are weak and need to be instructed in a life of goodness and virtue, this does not seem to result from covetous-ness, but to be counseled by charity.
>
> Secondly, fraternal correction may be omitted in such a way that one commits a mortal sin, namely, when (as he says in the same passage) one fears what people may think, at least one may suffer grievous pain or death; provided, however, that the mind is so dominated by such things, that it gives them the preference to fraternal charity. This would seem to be the case when a man reckons that he might probably withdraw some wrongdoer from sin, and yet omits to do so, through fear or covetousness.
>
> Thirdly, such an omission is a venial sin, when through fear or covetous-ness, a man is loath to correct his brother's faults, and yet not to such a degree, that if he saw clearly that he could withdraw him from sin, he would still forbear from so doing, through fear or covetousness, because in his own mind he prefers fraternal charity to these things. It is in this way that holy men sometimes omit to correct wrongdoers.[13]

To take an extreme case, could a pastor remain permissive when he learns in a counseling review that his client is determined to seriously injure someone who might then die in mortal sin? Even a private person has the obligation in charity to prevent evil from coming to others, and needs a serious reason to overlook a serious harm which his client has determined to inflict on another.

It would seem logical to conclude that the pastoral counselor must

---

[13] Summa Theologica, Vol. 2 (New York: Benziger Bros., 1947), p. 1334, Reply Obj. 1, Reply Obj. 3.

instruct and admonish, unless he judges that greater harm than good will result from the correction. He must take into consideration not only the client but scandal to a third party, harm to religion, etc. This would be the same principle as that regarding leaving a person in good faith.

As Father Harvey says:

The counselor must be held responsible for the act of counseling itself, and for the techniques which he chooses to use during his interviews with the client. Furthermore, he is responsible for all the results that are foreseeable even in a confused way from his manner of counseling.[14]

And:

The ideal of counsel is to allow the client to discover the value for himself after he has regained insight into his problem. But the problem is how long may the counselor allow the client to wander in the labyrinth of his false reasonings, which lead to very foolish choices, choices which may cut off opportunities for a fuller life in later years. Is not the permissiveness and moral neutrality of Rogers contrary to common sense? Accordingly, therefore, the counselor may not allow the client to make a choice which will place him in a proximate danger of serious sin.[15]

Sympathy Versus Empathy

There is a very important relationship between these two reactions which must be fully understood if the counselor wishes to avoid emotional involvement with his client. For better understanding a few definitions will help to clarify the problem.

Sympathy, according to Hinsie and Shatsky's Psychiatric Dictionary,[16] means the existence of a feeling identical with or resembling that which another experiences. Aring, in a scholarly article on the relationship of sympathy and empathy in the practice of medicine, gives this definition:

If we thoughtfully examine the definition of the word sympathy, we find that it refers to an affinity, association, or relationship so that whatever affects one, similarly affects the other. The act or capacity of entering into or sharing the feelings of another is known as sympathy. Without crowding the definition we may say that this describes exactly what occurs in far too many human relationships, including the practice of medicine. I want to submit that entering into the feelings of another and

---

14 John F. Harvey, O.S.F.S., "Counseling is a Complex Art," The Catholic Educator, Vol. XXVII, No. 1, Sept., 1956, p. 513.
15 Ibid., p. 371.
16 Leland E. Hinsie, M.D., and Jacob Shatsky, M.D., Psychiatric Dictionary (New York: Oxford University Press, 1953).

becoming similarly affected may not be the constructive method that it has been supposed.[17]

Empathy, from the standpoint of psychoanalysis, is defined according to Hinsie and Shatsky, as an intellectual understanding of what is inherently foreign to our own ego, in other people. Empathy is thus a form of identification. It may be called *intellectual identification* in contrast to *affective identification* which occurs in sympathy. Again quoting from Aring, whose viewpoint on this subject is well expressed:

> The term empathy is thought to have originated with the German psychologist, Theodore Lipps, in the word *einfuhlung*. Like many foreign conglomerates, *einfuhlung* is difficult of translation. *Einfuhlung* connotes the emotional appreciation of another's feelings, as does sympathy. *Einfuhlung*, or empathy as we say, is an entrance into the feelings of another person or of a thing or concept: one may feel oneself into things contemplated or persons observed. This "infeeling," or better "feeling-into," depends a good deal on the richness of one's own experience; it has to do with the matured use of the self. It is not only an identification of sorts, but unlike the implications of sympathy it is an awareness of one's separateness from the observed. One has had one's own feelings and relationships and has worked at the understanding of them, and they will be useful in understanding those feelings and relationships of others.[18]

Identification occurs between two people when one or both share similar feelings based upon some common unconscious quality.

Rapport refers merely to an harmonious relationship which is suitable for therapy or counseling.

Transference is a phenomenon in which a patient feels and behaves toward his therapist as he did toward important figures in his childhood (usually parents, siblings, family, etc.).

Compassion is defined in *The American College Dictionary*[19] as a "feeling of sorrow or pity for the sufferings or misfortunes of another; sympathy." In Soule's *Dictionary of English Synonyms*[20] the following synonyms are given: "pity, commiseration, sympathy, rue, tenderness, kindness, kindliness, clemency, fellow-feeling, heart, tenderheartedness, mercy, etc." In this sense, compassion becomes a synonym of sympathy. With this *Webster's International Dictionary* is in agreement giving the definition: "Literally suffering with another; fellowship in feeling . . .

---

17 Charles D. Aring, M.D., "Sympathy and Empathy," *J.A.M.A.*, Vol. 167, No. 4, May 24, 1958, p. 449.
18 *Ibid.*, p. 449.
19 *The American College Dictionary* (New York: Harper and Bros., 1953).
20 *Soule's Dictionary of English Synonyms*, ed., Alfred D. Sheffield (Boston: Little, Brown and Co., 1959).

commiseration, sympathy." These words are important to the counselor. Particularly should he have clearly in mind that *sympathy and compassion are synonyms*, and that both mean an emotional identification of the counselor and the counselee. This identification is destructive of a good counseling relationship. Such an identification may cause the counselor to be drawn into activity which his intellect should warn him against. It may cause him to be tempted to overstep the limits of his competence. It is not good counseling practice to proceed blindly motivated by sympathy. There is a better way, the way of empathy.

Empathy implies action motivated by conscious awareness. Empathy encourages appreciation of another's feelings, *not by entering into them and suffering with him, but by standing off and viewing them objectively.* As noted above in the definition, empathy represents an *intellectual* identification with the counselee, whereas sympathy or compassion is an *emotional* identification. Sympathy, because of this identification, is destructive of good counseling practice. Ideally the counselor should remain unburdened by the counselee's perplexities. He should be interested but detached.

> Appreciation of another's feelings and problems is quite different from joining in them, and in so doing, complicating them beyond resolving. Empathetic understanding allows a better opportunity of defining what is transpiring and what the behavior of another signifies. It is hardly possible to overstate the importance of the uses of empathy in the practice of medicine.[21]

Sympathy occurs in the inexperienced counselors. Empathy depends largely on the depth of the counselor's own emotional experiences.

On this point of sympathy versus empathy I find myself in disagreement with Fathers Hagmaier and Gleason who in these words seem to recommend to the counselor a sympathetic or compassionate attitude:

> The priest as a listener can create an atmosphere of solicitous permissiveness in which the troubled client feels free to share the burden he is unable to carry alone. This is the true meaning of compassion. The compassionate counselor touches the emotional pulse of his client by identifying in some personal — though not in any overtly emotional — way with his anguish, his bewilderment and his interior conflict. Thereby the counselor shows that he understands.[22]

[21] Aring, *op. cit.*, p. 449.
[22] George Hagmaier, C.S.P., and Robert Gleason, S.J., *Counseling the Catholic* (New York: Sheed & Ward, 1959), pp. 34–35.

CHAPTER VII

THE COUNSELING INTERVIEW

The importance of the selection of cases for counseling which is necessarily based on some type of diagnostic screening procedure has already been discussed. It is clear, therefore, that the aim of the initial interview is primarily diagnostic. This does not imply necessarily that a disorder, if present, is to be given a name. It means essentially that an evaluation of the client's psychological status and of his suitability for counseling is made. As a secondary result, the counselor will seek to establish rapport, and as the interview draws to a close he will encourage the counselee to seek further help if his examination has led him to believe that the client will benefit by such counseling.

In regard to the appraisal expected in the initial interview, Knight quoted by Gill, *et al.*, states:

> With a great deal of intent listening and skillful questioning the examiner follows the unfolding material noting significant elements, making and testing hypotheses as he explores the psychopathology, the adaptive capacities or ego strengths, the nature and strength of the motivation toward recovery, the kind of communication of which the patient is capable, his feelings and experiences in their psychological aspects.

Gill then concludes:

> If Knight's summary statement is dissected, it will be seen that he recommends appraising, evaluating, diagnosing the patient in four main areas — the nature of the disorder, the motivation for psychotherapy, the capacity for psychotherapy, and external factors helping or hindering the undertaking of psychotherapy and carrying it through.[1]

Start Counseling With Listening

The pastoral counselor should be a listener during at least the initial interview. He should give the counselee a chance to talk. As counselors,

---

[1] Merton Gill, M.D., Richard Newman, M.D., Fredrick C. Redlich, M.D., *The Initial Interview in Psychiatric Practice* (New York: International Universities Press, 1954), p. 91.

clergymen tend to talk too much. Being in the habit of preaching and teaching, they tend to preach and teach all the time. Whatever the effects of this flow of words may be in the pulpit, school, or confessional, in counseling the results of such a practice are usually fleeting and of little value, if not actually harmful. To be effective, the counselor must develop the ability to listen, and this is especially true of the pastor. Too frequently the conscientious clergyman feels that he can by direction solve all his client's troubles. Such talking by the counselor is seldom of real value. Rather, pastoral counselors must take the attitude of learners, listening with minds not so filled with theological distinctions and conclusions as to exclude all room for empathy and patience.

The value of listening has long been recognized and practiced by wise men. It has not, however, been studied with scientific skill until recent times. Listening as a social function has always been stressed as part of the correct grooming of a gentleman. Writers today, in applying this ability to treatment situations, have had much to say about its role in the technic of counseling. The counselor by listening intently and with obvious interest quite readily establishes a working contact between the counselee and himself. Until the pastor has mastered this skill, his clients are not likely to gain the confidence in him that is so basic in the movement toward an eventual solution of his problem.

The need which some people have for patient listening is exemplified by the following note:

> In New York there used to be people who advertised as "listeners," and they charged five dollars per half hour. They were flooded with clients. They never gave any advice or said anything; they just listened.[2]

If such nonprofessional listeners can draw a steady supply of patrons, then certainly there is a place for listening as such in the legitimate counselor's technic. "Listening to a client's story is sometimes helpful in and of itself."[3]

"With this patient, silent, passive attitude, one gives these clients something they have never before received: a serious interest in their irrational fears and symptoms."[4] By showing genuine confidence and

---

[2] Ralph M. Kaufman, M.D., "The Patient-Physician Relationship," Teaching Psychotherapeutic Medicine, ed., Helen L. Witmer (New York, 1947), p. 77.

[3] Annette Garrett, Interviewing: Its Principles and Methods (New York: Family Welfare Association of America, 1942), p. 34.

[4] Trygve F. Braatey, Fundamentals of Psychoanalytic Technique (New York: Wiley, 1954), p. 153.

interest from the start, the pastor can initiate a truly helpful relationship. Thereby the often unavoidable barrier induced by the treatment situation is penetrated and progressively opened wider as the troubled counselee unburdens himself further to the receptive ears of the counselor. "Even the most rigid compulsive neurotic relaxes somewhat in this atmosphere,"[5] and as confidence grows in this permissive climate, the client will gradually open up. To begin counseling, then, one listens. In other words, the client must be received from the start with an attitude of interest in his conflicts, respect for his person, manifested specifically by a readiness to hear his story as the patient himself wishes to tell it. Start the interview with some general question or statement such as, "Tell me about yourself," or "Let us start with the beginning," or "Why did you come to see me?"

While the client is thus unburdening himself, the good listener avoids interruption while he is examining the content of what he is learning, and attempting to interpret what the client has to say.[6] By no means is the counselor passive in the sense of being merely physically present to his patient. Rather, by his interest, he is encouraging the client and responding very actively, and, although silent, he is alert in his attitude.

This should be a quiet alertness, an attitude of "tell me more," "feel free to say what is on your mind" type of attitude. This should be reflected in an intent listening posture rather than in any verbal encouragement. That others are not of this opinion can be readily seen in this statement of Dr. Karl Menninger which I mention only to say that I disagree:

> The interjection of such exclamations as "Really" (in the sense of mild astonishment), "Naturally!" (in the sense of a certain reaction being a very reasonable one), a mild groan to indicate sympathetic deploring of a tragic situation, a chuckle at an appropriate time in connection with an amusing episode, and so on, are often very useful, especially early in the analytic treatment.[7]

Although in this initial phase the interviewer makes no suggestions, gives no comfort, makes no criticism, gives no diagnostic opinion, it is not correct to say that he only listens or to imply that he is as stiff and silent

---

[5] *Ibid.*

[6] Cf. E. Boyd Barrett, "The Art of Listening," *Ave Maria*, March 6, 1954, p. 14.

[7] Karl A. Menninger, *Theory of Psychoanalytic Technique* (New York: Basic Books, 1958), p. 131.

as a statue.[8] During the entire period he is indicating his close attention through the signs noted above. While the client ventilates, the counselor directs his attention to his productions, except that he may take notes. Being an efficient listener demands a definite disposition of mind: a receptive empathy which communicates to the counselee a feeling of complete acceptance. The counselor aims at understanding.

Handling Silences

All of this is by no means an easy task. "There is more to the art of listening than appears at first glance. It is an act that calls for intelligence as well as self-control."[9] The counselor must learn to reconcile himself to periods of silence which are frequent in the "listening technic." A patient respect for silences is more helpful than a too hasty interruption if the client stops talking, since such action may leave the client with the impression of impatience or anxiety on the part of the counselor. Furthermore, "giving advice or help when the client could have thought it through himself deprives him of the satisfaction and self-esteem of having solved his own problem."[10] Just as the skill of listening itself must be developed, so the counselor must become accustomed to the long pauses that will occur and learn to estimate their value in the counseling process. Direct questioning is possible after the client's confidence has been gained securely.

Listen first and question later is a good policy. Too many questions in the beginning will confuse and block the patient's freedom to operate, if it does not obstruct him completely. The good counselor is never in a rush. Direct questions are of little value until the client has given the interviewer his complete trust. This is achieved through patient, indulgent, sincere listening with an active mind. "Generally speaking, if the interviewer talks more than one-half the time, the interview will be less productive than the one in which the client talks more than one-half the time."[11] I would prefer to see the proportion for the first interview more nearly 80 per cent for the client to 20 per cent on the part of the counselor. The "listening-to" interview, therefore, is initially a more

[8] Cf. Kaufman, op. cit., p. 44.

[9] Barrett, op. cit., p. 14.

[10] George Hagmaier, C.S.P., and Robert Gleason, S.J., Counseling the Catholic (New York: Sheed & Ward, 1959), p. 37.

[11] John G. Darley, "Conduct of the Interview," The Interview in Counseling (1940), pp. 12–19.

promising technique than the "talking-to" type of conference, and it is for the eventual recovery of the client that the counselor aims in choosing his technics.

"Towards the end of the interview, the client is assured that his talking so freely has been worth while and that he has not been acting foolishly."[12] If this is made clear tactfully, the counselor will have little trouble in persuading the client to return. It is the empathy and understanding, together with the atmosphere of hopeful recovery, born of the relationship a good listener creates that wins the confidence of the patient and draws him back for further counseling.

In summary of these comments on listening, it seems clear that the pastor will find in the "listening technic" a method with which he is less likely to make a mistake. No advice is better than the wrong advice, and with this method the pastor can feel that he is at least safeguarding the client from the harmful, inopportune, or miscalculated advice he might have given. The ability to listen well is a safe technic especially for the new, inexperienced pastor. But even listening can be dangerous; if a client anxiously demands answers to his questions they are best given.

Aids to a Productive Interview

Although counseling is comparatively new as a professional method there are many hints which can be successfully utilized by the new counselor. I will attempt to summarize some of them. During the initial session as well as in those which follow, the counselor should have in mind these general statements. There are no short cuts to good counseling but some basic principles which have been learned from experience will be of value to the beginner.

1. It is very hard for the neophyte in counseling to realize that although the consultation has been voluntarily sought *the client frequently avoids the real problem*, especially in the early sessions. This may occur for a variety of reasons, such as testing the counselor, fear, conscious resistance, etc. Under such circumstances it is best just to wait for another interview. "The truth will out," eventually. Do not expect too much from the first interview; the next, and the next will each be more productive.

---

[12] Rev. Charles A. Curran, *Personality Factors in Counseling* (New York: Macmillan, 1952), p. 58.

2. *Encourage the client to talk about himself rather than his symptoms.* Discussion of his feelings in the beginning is more important than uncovering the facts. Discourage a recitation of symptomatology. Much valuable time will be lost if too much attention is paid to symptoms or daily events. Gently lead him at first away from these subjects; later it can be done more directly.

3. *Emphasize and encourage detail* in the patient's narration. Remember that catharsis has greater value if the telling of the story is vivid. This is promoted if the client is encouraged to give examples and if he is urged to give free expression to his emotions.

4. *How the patient feels and thinks about a situation is more important,* in most cases, than the facts of the case. The facts will gradually emerge. The patient's attitude toward them as he sees them is reality for him.

5. *Reassurance should be used sparingly,* especially in the beginning of counseling. It tends to promote dependence which is usually undesirable except with very disturbed individuals in whom it may be helpful as a temporary expedient. The best reassurance comes from understanding and explanation.

6. *Objective self-evaluation may be hindered by too much interference* by the counselor. Help the client see himself as he is. The counselor's role is to enable the client to use his own counsel and prudence, to see for himself, to decide for himself, so that he may act for himself.

7. *The counseling relation is two-way.* The counselor must evaluate the client's reaction to him and evaluate the relationship between them. The counselor must remember that he, as counselor, is a participant in the interaction of the interview. At the same time the counselee is evaluating the counselor.

8. *Treat the client as a person* with dignity. Support his self-respect rather than destroy it. Be careful not to humiliate or tire the client.

9. It is not usually expedient to tell the client too quickly that he is wrong. Be slow to do so. *Be slow to blame, to moralize, or criticize.* Get all the facts first. As a pastor it may be necessary to point out the moral aspects of a situation, but hear the client through first.

10. *Reinforce the client's emotions* by letting him realize your understanding of his feelings by naming the emotion he is experiencing. The client may not understand the naturalness of his response to certain emotions. Be sure that he does understand.

11. *Be reassuring* as to the understandableness of his symptoms of fear or hostility.

12. *Do not confuse tact with timidity.* All necessary questions should be asked. They may be avoided until it is evident that the client is not going to give the necessary information. If questions are not asked the client will not usually bring up sensitive matters and a long delay or even complete failure of the counseling effort will occur.

13. *Do not let the patient push you into activity.* Premature activity before all the facts are obtained may lead to embarrassing mistakes. Delay may be an important measure of treatment.

14. *Make no promises;* merely say, "I'll try to help." When people are in distress it is sometimes difficult to avoid saying, "Yes, you will be all right." Be sure not to promise any more than you feel sure you can deliver.

15. *Answer any pertinent questions* to which you have reliable answers. Do not give a response because it seems expedient at the time.

16. *It may be necessary to structure the situation.* Some initial structuring statement is desirable to let the subject know what to expect. The counselor should guide the interview openly only if necessary.[13]

17. *Interest* and *evidence of caring* are more important than technic.

18. Be prepared to *accept the client unreservedly,* regardless of what he does or says. *Accept him as he is with warmth, interest, and without criticism.* Keep in mind that all people are to some extent lonely. Complete acceptance of the client's moral attitudes may not be possible for the pastoral counselor, but this need not be evident before he has had a chance to tell his whole story.

19. Be prepared to *ask questions* if these seem desirable or necessary.

---

[13] Structure in this sense means to explain to the client the method or procedure which is to be employed and how it may be expected to work. In client-centered therapy such structuring is no longer recommended: "It would appear that real progress or movement in therapy is greatly facilitated when both client and counselor are perceiving the relationship in similar fashion. How this may be achieved is the question which must be continually raised. Our experience is clear on one point. The perception does not come about by telling the client how he ought to experience the relationship. Meaningful perception is a matter of direct sensory experience, and it not only does not help but it may hinder a unified perception if the therapist attempts to describe, intellectually, the character of the relationship or of the process. It is for this reason that counselors operating from a client-centered point of view have tended to give up any attempts at 'structuring,' though earlier these were thought to be of value." Carl R. Rogers, *Client-Centered Therapy* (New York: Houghton Mifflin Co., 1951), p. 69.

Ask enough questions to clarify the situation both as to the past or present.

20. *Varying situations call for flexibility.* Do *not* react with a fixed pattern. Adapt your method to the situation.

21. Explain that *psychological readjustments are slow* and that rapid change is not to be expected.

22. "There is rarely, if ever, a place in . . . counseling for the counselor to be humorous or make jokes."[14]

23. *Be slow in offering advice.* Get all facts possible before doing so. If you feel that your information is still inadequate, ask for more. Ask to see other members of the family. It is surprising how frequently the one who first came to ask your advice about another — perhaps more correctly stated, to complain about someone else — is the one who is at fault, not the one who is complained about.

Special Problems of Counseling

Time for Next Interview

Most counselors see clients by appointment. It is impractical to conduct a counseling practice on the basis of, "Drop in sometime next week." This could easily involve feelings of rejection and uncertainty on the part of the client who might be afraid of coming at an inopportune time, or when the counselor was not available. Appointments should be made for the first and each subsequent appointment.

Each counseling visit should last not more than one hour. There is sometimes a temptation to continue longer, but this will rarely be of any real value. A longer interview is tiring to both client and counselor; besides, the most productive portion of any interview is in the first forty minutes. The client should be expected to be on time for his appointment and he should also expect the interview to end on schedule. This is one of the few limits placed on the patient in the counseling process.

A common practice is to make fifty-minute appointments starting on the hour. This gives ten minutes between appointments for telephone calls, discussion matters with one's secretary, and also provides a slight cushion if there is delay for any reason. It should be remembered that the counselor must also be on time and make a real effort to adhere strictly

---

[14] Emily H. Mudd, *Man and Wife* (New York: W. W. Norton & Co., 1959), p. 254.

to a schedule. Emergency cases rarely occur, but when they do, they should not be seen, if any other way is possible, at the expense of another client's time. Such clients should be seen after hours, during the lunch period, or on Saturday or Sunday.

Frequency of Interviews

The frequency of interviews should depend primarily on the client's needs, not on the convenience of the counselor. If the counselor does not have time available he should not accept the client, or at least he should explain to him that he can be seen at first for an evaluating interview but that after this his appointments will be delayed until an opening occurs. It should not be forgotten that when one makes a counseling appointment it is seldom for one visit but for several. Depending on the type of counseling, it may mean anything from ten to over a hundred visits. In general, however, if the situation does not show marked change for the better in five to ten visits the pastoral counselor should refer the client to a secular counselor for further consultation and counseling.

In most cases one visit a week is adequate, although in some acute situations more frequent visits may be advisable or necessary. In my own practice I have felt that a client who was so acutely disturbed as to need to be seen more than twice a week was not suitable for out-patient management. There will, of course, be individuals whose improvement would be speeded by more frequent visits, but this may be a luxury which neither the counselor nor the client can afford.

Frequent visits may be harmful in creating too great a dependence of the client on the therapist. This type of dependency should be carefully avoided. Interviews held too close together do not give the client time enough to digest the substance of the previous interview before he returns.

Place of Interview

The office of the counselor, whether the parlor of the rectory or one more formally located, should provide privacy and freedom from interruption and if possible freedom from telephone calls. The progress of the interview should not be interrupted except for emergencies. The office should be comfortable and, if the client's anxieties permit it, he should sit face to face with the counselor without a desk between them. It allows for greater comfort during a long counseling day if the chairs occupied by the counselor and his client are placed at an angle to each other so that they will not necessarily be looking directly at each other.

Joint Interviews

Joint interviews of the husband and wife in counseling situations are becoming more acceptable as we gain experience with the technic. The idea of a separate therapist for husband and wife is also changing, and in many instances this is no longer considered necessary. The problem of joint interviews arises most frequently in regard to marriage counseling. The pastoral counselor should approach this joint method of counseling with caution. Out of respect the couple may not give him as bad a time as they occasionally do to the secular counselor. Some of my most disturbed interviews occurred while I was trying to learn the degree of rapport it was necessary for the husband and wife to have before they should be seen together. As one gains skill in the use of this technic its value increases. The counselor must, of course, strive to be absolutely impartial. He should remain as silent as possible, except for a word here and there to encourage an interchange between the parties. If the individuals are seen alone first, care must be taken when they are seen together not to repeat to the other partner anything detrimental which has been said by his spouse.

From the initial interviews the general areas of disagreement or difficulty should be outlined so that the joint interview may start off with a general statement by the counselor delineating one of these areas. Be sure not to attempt to cover too much in any one interview. It may be necessary to introduce several topics before the couple will pick up one for discussion. An alternative plan is to start the interview by asking, "Is there anything either of you would like to bring up today?" This will frequently clear the air for more satisfactory discussion which will not get under way as long as something more acute is on the minds of the couple. Do not make the mistake of seeing one partner several times and then bringing in the other partner for a joint interview without having first seen him alone. This may lead to a bad relationship from the very beginning. In my own practice, if possible, I see the couple together on the first interview to get an over-all picture of the problem. Then each partner is seen alone once or several times and then a joint session is arranged. After this, joint sessions may continue or, if one partner seems in greater need of help, individual counseling may be instituted.

Note-Taking

Notes of interviews are absolutely essential. Memory is very undependable and records are frequently called for years later. Clients expect you to keep records. The only question, therefore, is whether these notes should be written during or after the interview. Experience indicates that only rarely will a client be disturbed by note-taking but, on the contrary, will comment on the fact if you do not take notes. The rare individual who objects to note-taking is frequently paranoid and he will be equally concerned over listening devices which may be hidden in the room. In such cases note-taking is probably best not done in the presence of the client.

It is important that if the counselor is to take notes that he do so actively. He should not merely hold a pad, or doodle, or be distracted. The client frequently will feel that the counselor writes only what is important and that if he does not make notes then what he is saying is unimportant. He will also be concerned as to "who sees the notes?" "Are they left locked up?" "Is his permission necessary before they may be released to anyone?" "Will you tell my husband, or wife, or mother, or father what I tell you?" The more satisfactorily these questions can be answered, the better the interview will be. Be sure never to leave records where they can be seen by anyone except yourself and the client.

Resistance

Resistance to revealing himself is frequently encountered even in those patients who come voluntarily. It is, of course, much more frequent in those patients who come reluctantly or against their own wish. Resistance may be unconscious or conscious.

Unconscious resistance is a psychoanalytic term meaning the instinctive opposition displayed toward any attempt to lay bare the unconscious (a manifestation of the repressing forces). This type of resistance is of only didactic interest to the counselor.

Conscious resistance is the intentional withholding of information by the client. This is frequently for reasons of which he may be fully conscious, but not infrequently it is for reasons of which he is not fully aware and for which he has a rationalization in consciousness. Some causes of resistance arise within the client such as shame, fear of rejection, fear of the consequences, distrust of the counselor, stubbornness — "You can make me come but you can't make me talk." I recall one boy of 19 years who came for 14 sessions without a word being spoken. He began to talk on the fifteenth session. Such a list of causes is not meant to be exhaustive but merely suggestive. Causes of resistance may be derived from the counselor or his attitude, e.g., a counselor who talks too much ("He tells me to talk, then doesn't give me a chance"), who interrupts, who rebukes, who is too demanding, who is late for appointments, who is impatient, who appears bored, to mention only a few possibilities.

Resistance may be manifested by refusing to talk at all or by talking only in response to questions and then in monosyllables, by talking only in generalities, by being late for appointments, by missing appointments, by insisting on making inquiries about the counselor's private life, and so forth.

Such resistances are best handled, if recognized, by explanation of their nature with an effort to explain how they have come about. This is best done by "talking through" the resistance in an effort to help the client see why it is present and how desirable it is to overcome it. If the client is merely silent the counselor should maintain an attentive attitude while he "sits out" the silence. Although he may be tempted, he should not read a book or write his sermon for the next day while he is waiting for the silence to break. As long as the client is your responsibility he deserves your whole attention.

Transference

Transference, as the term is used technically by psychotherapists, is not likely to occur in pastoral counseling. Transference in its technical sense means that as a relationship develops in the counseling situation the client begins to *invest* the counselor with qualities of some important figure from the past, and he, therefore, thinks, acts, and feels toward the counselor as if the counselor were the original object of these feelings. This was at one time mistaken for falling in love. This is far from the truth. Patients may fall in love with their counselors but this is not a transference reaction.

Transference reactions may be positive or negative. A positive reaction is one in which the client identifies the counselor with a loved or admired figure from the past. A negative transference is one in which feelings of hatred or dislike are transferred to the therapist. Both types of transference can be worked with, but it is obvious from the standpoint of both parties a positive transference is much easier to deal with. A negative transference is hard on both the client and the counselor. I recall one case in which a patient retained a strong negative transference for three years. This patient transferred to me very strong feelings of hatred that she had had toward her father. In the course of this negative reaction she told patients waiting to see me that I had taken all of her money and now refused to give her an appointment, although she had a regular appointment each week and had a slip in her hand for her next consultation. The client may, not infrequently, identify the therapist as an ideal parent.

Transference does not usually occur in counseling situations and even in therapy does not develop for several months. The counselor should be alert to its possibility and, since he is probably not prepared by experience or training to handle it, he would be wise to transfer the client to a secular counselor.

Experienced counselors know how to handle, preferably to prevent, "falling in love." At the first sign of such an event the pastoral counselor would do well to break off his relationship, either directly, or by reference of the client to a professional counselor.

PART II

THE PASTOR AND MENTAL HEALTH

CHAPTER VIII

THE CONCEPT OF MENTAL HEALTH

In a strict sense, it is incorrect to speak of the health of society; it is only the individual member of society who can be healthy. A healthy family, for example, is composed of individual healthy members. Society is healthy only as its individual members are healthy. When we speak of health, our concern is with the individual — the individual who is so frequently forgotten in today's collective societies. This loss of the identity of the individual and of his dignity as a person has made its own contribution to the decreasing mental health of the world.

To combat this tendency and for his own education, it is important for the pastoral counselor to have a firm foundation in the more normal aspects of the personality. Normal is a poor word when it is used in regard to persons. A better word would perhaps be "average," and we might then more properly speak of the "average person" or the "average range of normality." Mental health we can expect to be a characteristic of the "average person."

Mental health is more than an absence of disease. It is a positive quality. Emphasis on the positive aspects of health rather than on disease is not new. In fact, this aspect of medicine was emphasized by the first medical school worthy of the name. It was founded in A.D. 1000 at Salerno by a Greek, a Roman, a Jew, and an Arab, a truly international group, who composed its first faculty. A lack of knowledge of the causes and treatment of diseases at this time may have compelled a study of their prevention. It seems likely, however, that a knowledge of the positive aspects of health was more prevalent then than it is now.

Mental Health Difficult to Define

Mental health is an elusive concept. For instance, Eaton, writing in the *Journal* of the American Psychiatric Association, states: "Mental health as a scientific concept does not now exist."[1] Bearing in mind Eaton's comment, let us consider some of the attempts which have been made to define mental health.

It must be clear from the first that mental health is not the same as mental hygiene. Mental hygiene is concerned with the maintenance of mental health and the prevention of mental disorders. Webster's Dictionary defines mental hygiene as "the science and art of maintaining mental health and preventing the development of insanity and neuroses." Mental hygiene clinics have been established rather extensively in schools, in hospitals, and in health centers. Although they were originally most concerned with prevention, they soon, of necessity, became treatment clinics because the need for therapy was so great. The number of those demanding treatment far exceeds those who have the foresight to seek a positive development of mental health in their children. Mental health is a positive entity. It is part of our original inheritance. Mental health is God's gift at birth for those who are born with intact nervous systems. Unfortunately, influences soon begin to undermine our original healthy state and in numerous instances the seeds of neurosis and psychosis are planted in prepared soil at a very early date.[2] Most clinical studies have been directed to the maladjusted child, or to the sick child. This is commendable and necessary, but it is not these children with whom we are presently concerned. This discussion is concerned with mentally healthy adults and children. What can we do to lessen the tremendous loss to the world and the incalculable suffering caused by mental and emotional illnesses? Even a small contribution to this end would be worthwhile. The pastor must accept this challenge. A confident and determined attack on the problem will yield dividends.

Difficult as the task may be, let us attempt to understand and define mental health. Health is defined by Webster's Dictionary as "a state of being hale, sound or whole in body, mind or soul; well-being; especially a state of being free of physical disease or pain." "Healthy-minded" is defined as having a wholesome outlook on life. "Wholesome" is "that which is good for one, whether physically or morally."[3] Webster thus

---

[1] Joseph W. Eaton, "The Assessment of Mental Health," The American Journal of Psychiatry, Vol. 108, No. 2, August, 1951, pp. 81–90.

[2] John R. Cavanagh and James B. McGoldrick, S.J., Fundamental Psychiatry (Milwaukee: The Bruce Publishing Co., 1954), p. 223.

[3] Noah Webster, New International Dictionary, 2nd ed. (Springfield, Mass.: G. & C. Merriam Co., 1953).

defines mental health in terms of the obvious. Hadfield does the same thing in different words: "Mental health is the full and harmonious functioning of the whole personality."[4]

Mental health has been defined in other frames of reference. For example, Erich Fromm defines mental health in terms of social function:

> The term normal or healthy can be defined in two ways. Firstly, from the standpoint of functioning society one can call a person normal or healthy if he is able to fulfill the social role he is to take in that given society — if he is able to participate in the reproduction of society. Secondly, from the standpoint of the individual, we look upon health or normalcy as the optimum of growth and happiness of the individual.[5]

Rennie and Woodward equate mental health with individual "maturity":

> In very simple terms, a mature and mentally healthy person is one who (1) Respects and has confidence in himself, and because he knows his true worth, wastes no time proving it to himself and others; (2) Accepts, works with, and to a large extent enjoys other people; and (3) Carries on his work, play, and his family and social life with confidence and enthusiasm and with a minimum of conflict, fear and hostility.[6]

Happiness is emphasized by Karl Menninger:

> Let us define mental health as the adjustment of human beings to the world and to each other with a maximum of effectiveness and happiness. Not just efficiency, or just contentment — or the grace of obeying the rules of the game cheerfully. It is all of these together. It is the ability to maintain an even temper, an alert intelligence, socially considerate behavior, and a happy disposition. This, I think, is a healthy mind.[7]

Preston also defines mental health in terms of social adjustment.[8]

Other definitions are equally unsatisfactory. For example, the definition of the World Health Organization is a statement of obvious fact:

> Health is a state of complete physical, mental and social well-being, and not merely the absence of disease or infirmity.[9]

---

[4] J. A. Hadfield, *Mental Health and the Psychoneuroses* (London: George Allen and Unwin, 1952), pp. 1–2.

[5] Erich Fromm, *Escape from Freedom* (New York: Farrar & Rinehart, 1941), p. 138.

[6] Thomas A. D. Rennie, and Luther E. Woodward, *Mental Health in Modern Society* (New York: Commonwealth Fund, 1948), p. 334.

[7] Karl Menninger, "Are You an Associate of the World Federation of Mental Health?" (London: W. 1, 19 Manchester Street, 1950).

[8] George H. Preston, *The Substance of Mental Health* (New York: Farrar & Rinehart, 1943), p. 112.

[9] *Bulletin* of the World Federation on Mental Health, 1951, 3, 27–28. Reprinted by permission. See also L. P. Thrope, *The Psychology of Mental Health* (New York: Ronald, 1950), pp. 4–6 and Chap. IV.

The Expert Committee on Mental Health of the World Mental Health Organization produced a better but still unsatisfactory definition of mental health and mental hygiene:

> The Committee recognized the necessity for explaining as precisely as possible what is meant by the terms "mental health" and "mental hygiene." Mental health was defined as a condition, subject to fluctuations due to biological and social factors, which enables the individual to achieve a satisfactory synthesis of his own potentially conflicting, instinctive drives; to form and maintain harmonious relations with others; and to participate in constructive changes in his social and physical environment. Mental hygiene was interpreted as referring to all the activities and techniques which encourage and maintain mental health.[10]

It is interesting to note that none of these definitions makes any mention of supernatural motivation or of man's striving for his ultimate goal, although Hadfield does mention the need for completeness, which could certainly include man's need for a Supreme Being. The deficiencies of these definitions can be readily seen. A man may be very moral but still be mentally unhealthy. A good life does not protect against neuroses. Also, a man may be very socially inclined and yet not be mentally healthy. A man may be very happy, but this may be merely an indication of his disturbed mental state. On the contrary, one cannot be mentally healthy and immoral, or asocial and mentally healthy. Mental health can never be complete unless man is properly oriented toward his ultimate goal.

In any scientific attempt to achieve a satisfactory teaching program in mental health, it is necessary to know the goal for which we are striving. Steiglitz, although he does not define health, gives a conceptual framework which offers more:

> The degree of health parallels effectiveness in living; contrariwise, disease induces ineffectiveness in the somatic and psychic activities of living. The mensuration of health, which closely parallels the measurement of biological age as contrasted to chronological age, is most difficult and requires exceptional diagnostic acumen and understanding of the mechanism of homeostasis. Health measurement involves stress tests for the evaluation of functional reserves. An entirely different diagnostic philosophy is requisite; we are no longer seeking to discover specific disease

---

[10] *Ibid.*

entities or even clinical syndromes, but attempting to measure biological effectiveness in adaption.[11]

Where mental health is to be measured, it is obvious that some parallel requirement is necessary. Jahoda, for example, states:

> Yet the establishment of some criteria by which the degree of mental health of an individual can be judged is essential if one wishes to identify social conditions conducive to the attainment of mental health.[12]

I have been unable to find an adequate definition of mental health or criteria for measuring it in the literature.

Definition of Mental Health

My own definition of mental health is couched more in philosophical than in psychological terms:

> Mental health is that state of well-being in which there is a dynamic, efficient functioning of the whole man which brings about co-ordination of his powers in such a way as to develop most perfectly his psychic potentialities for the purpose of achieving his goals, both present and remote.

A brief explanation of the terms of this definition may be helpful.

1. *State of well-being* — We often speak of the "glow of health" which accompanies a state of physical well-being. A state of mental well-being would also be expected to accompany mental health. This is the condition which Bishop Sheen speaks of as "peace of soul." If we are at peace with God and the world, we certainly have a sense of well-being, but before this feeling is complete, we must also be at peace with ourselves.

2. *Dynamic* — Mental health occurs in a living body, vibrant and active. It is not static; it changes from time to time. What is mentally healthy at one time might be evidence of abnormality at another.

3. *Efficient* — The best interests of the individual must be served with the least amount of wasted motion.

4. *Whole man* — The human composite is made up of body and soul

---

[11] Edward J. Steiglitz, "The Integration of Clinical and Social Medicine," in Iago Galdston (ed.), *Social Medicine — Its Derivatives and Objectives*, The New York Academy of Medicine Institute of Social Medicine, 1947 (New York: Commonwealth Fund, 1949), pp. 76–79.

[12] Marie Jahoda, "Toward a Social Psychology of Mental Health," reprinted from *Problems of Infancy and Childhood*, Milton J. E. Senn (ed.), trans., Fourth Conference Supplement II (New York: Josiah Macy, Jr., Foundation, 1950), p. 5.

which together form the unit man. Man is neither body nor soul, but a perfect combination of both. Mental health, therefore, is of the whole man and not primarily of either body or soul.

5. *Co-ordination of his powers* — Man is an extremely complex being composed of a body and a soul. He has external cognitive powers, internal cognitive powers of the sensory order, as well as intellect. The intellect gives rise to ideas, judges, and reasons. Man possesses two appetitive inclinations: the sense inclination which follows pleasure and is not free in itself but can be controlled by reason and will; and the rational inclination called the will, which is free to choose or not to choose with respect to any good other than the infinite good perceived as such. The will depends upon intellectual appreciation of the object as upon a motive or impelling force for its own activity.

If each power of man acted without interference of other powers and under the guidance of reason, he would enjoy great peace and ease. Such was the case before the sin of Adam and Eve. Now man daily experiences difficulty in following reason because it is austere, speaks an abstract language, and recommends deferred pleasures.

6. *Psychic potentialities* — The highest psychic faculties of man are his intellect and will. Their perfection cannot help but promote mental health.

7. *His goals* — The catechism states that "man is on earth to love, honor, and serve God in this world and to be happy with Him forever in heaven." In other words, as I have stated elsewhere:

> Now God is both kindly and just and has not given man a mind and a will to frustrate him. There must, therefore, be some object that will satisfy man's rational aspirations for truth and goodness. That object is not a created one. The infinite God Himself is the object which will unendingly satisfy the thirst of the mind and will for truth and goodness. God is, therefore, man's ultimate goal. He is the infinite truth and infinite goodness sought by man's intellect and will.[13]

Characteristics of Mental Health

Although there is no generally accepted concept of what constitutes mental health, it has certain characteristics which are fundamental.

1. It is dynamic. *Mental health is not static.* It is likely to fluctuate with changes in the milieu.

---

[13] Cavanagh and McGoldrick, *op. cit.*, p. 27.

2. It *concerns the function of the whole organism* because mental and physical health form a continuum. They cannot be separated one from the other because of the perfect union of body and soul which makes man a unity. Disturbances of mental health may cause repercussions in the physical and vice versa.

3. *Mental health is more than an absence of symptoms.*

4. *Mental health is not the same for all people.* It will vary in degree.

5. *Disturbances in mental health are a quantitative rather than a qualitative disturbance in the individual.* As Eaton says: "In reality, mental health merges imperceptibly and gradually like the colors of the spectrum into mental illness."[14] This means, therefore, that mental illness is not the result of some ingredient added to the personality, such as a germ or toxic substance. It means, rather, that mental health and mental illness form a continuum. It means that the mentally ill person is one who has deviated in the matter of degree from the average normal pattern.

6. Physical heredity plays no part in mental health or illness. Social heredity is important. This follows from the fact that mental illness is an acquired trait and that acquired traits are not transmitted by physical heredity.[15]

7. In mental health, activity must be goal-directed, whether this goal be an immediate ambition or toward man's ultimate goal, the supernatural.

Genesis of Emotional Problems of the School Child

Much of the pathology which the psychiatrist must treat in the adult has its origin in the child. As Wordsworth so aptly stated many years ago, "the child is the father of the man." It is in the roots of childhood that the beginnings of the true worth of man lie. Manhood is the actualization of the potentialities of childhood. In *Paradise Regained*, Milton expressed a similar thought when he said. "The childhood shows the man, as morning shows the day." If we are to understand the thoughts and feelings of the adult man, be he normal, neurotic, or psychotic, we must first study the child. This has only recently been understood. The suffering of the adult neurotic has forced the psychopathologist to study the child at an early age where these disturbances have their origins.

---

[14] Eaton, *op. cit.*, p. 83.
[15] Cavanagh and McGoldrick, *op. cit.*, p. 27.

Until recently, the emotional disturbances of the child were considered only a passing phase which the child would either outgrow or which could be corrected by punishment. Even now, these disturbances are poorly understood, but a beginning has been made. Since we can now recognize that the origin of many adult disturbances is in childhood, we can recognize that the prevention of these disorders must also begin there. For this reason, child guidance clinics have been established. These clinics were originally intended for the guidance of well youngsters so that mental illness might be prevented. There has been, however, such an influx of children who need treatment that the original purpose of these clinics has been set aside and they are now largely devoted to treatment rather than prevention.

"How shall we define a child?" asks Father Clark. "Is he merely a small adult? Or is he a different sort of person with definite likes and dislikes, definite inclinations and tendencies, which make him live in a world of his own? I believe that all psychologists agree that he is not merely a small edition of the adult. And furthermore personalities, even among children, differ greatly, so each one is definitely an individual."[16]

Although the child has certain constitutional characteristics at birth, his development depends on his environment. He is dependent upon his parents during his early years so that they and his siblings will provide most of his environmental influence. This is especially true during his first five or six years. By this age, his basic personality pattern will have been established. *The natural tendency of the child is toward physical, psychological, religious, and social maturity.* Various factors which impede or accentuate his needs may interfere with this tendency and may produce emotional disturbances. The need for training and discipline which lead to the development of good habits and right principles is, therefore, apparent. As Alexander Pope in his *Moral Essays* said: "'Tis education forms the common mind; just as the twig is bent the tree's inclined."

Since the school child is under discussion, it is best perhaps to define him in terms of his chronological age. *Preschool age* extends "from the thirty-sixth to the seventy-second month of the child's life; that is, the child enters this period about his third birthday and passes on to the period of childhood proper about his sixth birthday. During this period

---

[16] William R. Clark, O.P., "What Parents as Educators Should Know About the Spiritual Problems of the Grade Child," unpublished manuscript, 1957.

intelligent guidance and direction of the rapid growth and development is of great importance."[17] *Childhood proper* would then extend to the teen-age, and the *teen-age* extends to the twentieth birthday.

Characteristics of Normal Social and Psychological Self in Preschool Child

Before we can discover the disturbance in the older child, it is first important to consider the normal development of the preschool child. Knowing what to expect in the average normal preschool child, it will be easier to detect what is pathological.

The average child ready for school is:

1. Individualistic and self-centered; eager to make his own decisions.

2. Beginning to develop a sense of property rights. (As a consequence, he grabs less — there is also less pushing and crying than before.)

3. Concerned over the new world he is entering, especially over his first prolonged contact with people outside the family when he is to enter school.

4. Developing an ability to enjoy co-operative play; has a preference to be "bigger than" his playmates.

5. Alternately shy and a "show-off."

6. Anxious to learn; wants to help.

7. In a constant state of activity; very energetic and restless; noisy; cross when tired.

8. Short in his attention span.

9. Becoming oriented in his relations with others, both adults and children, in his milieu. He begins to separate adults and children.

10. Reflecting the security feelings of the adults in his environment. His emotional reactions vary with his feelings of security.

11. Anxious to gain status in his group.

12. Sexually indifferent. Boys and girls mix without self-consciousness. Boys are more quarrelsome than girls.

13. Well established in his toilet habits, eating and sleeping patterns.

14. Showing rapid growth of his mental powers. Perception is remarkably active; imagination is vivid; dramatization is a favorite pastime; the

---

[17] W. A. Kelly and M. R. Kelly, *Introductory Child Psychology* (Milwaukee: The Bruce Publishing Co., 1938), p. 126.

boundary between the real and the imagined is often hazy and indistinct. *N.B.:* The ability to adjust is not the same in all children.

It must be recognized that in this brief outline we are touching only the highlights of the child's personality development. There is enough here, however, to bring out departures from the normal. Regression to levels previously achieved is usually evidence of an unresolved emotional conflict. Perhaps the most easily recognized regression is a return to enuresis (bed-wetting) after control has been achieved. Certain of these normal characteristics prove very disturbing to parents at times. *His constant activity, his constant asking of questions, and his desire to help* make the child seem to his harassed parent to be always underfoot. Parents should be thankful for this, however, because it is a sign of health.

There is one problem "which appears and re-appears at all ages, which is often thrust upon us with a suddenness which may be disconcerting, and for which we cannot specifically prepare ourselves; it is a problem common to parents, grandparents, uncles, aunts, nurses, teachers and friends, which is therefore of interest to all — the problem of a child's questions."[18] Children's questions are persistent and may indicate interest or curiosity (occasionally inquisitiveness or suspicion). The response of the parent to these questions will naturally depend on the child's motivation in asking it. Questions asked out of interest are usually asked in a leisurely, quiet frame of mind, without anxiety — "I want to know." When curiosity motivates a question, it is usually asked with urgency, impatience, and doubt — "I must know something."[19] In responding to the question, the parent should be guided by the child's emotional attitude in asking it. He should not answer too much, but, above all, not too little. The child's privacy in regard to his thoughts should be respected, and our temptation to act as amateur psychiatrists should not lead us to probe to its depths every question which arouses our curiosity. This is especially true of questions in regard to sex. In this matter, all questions should be answered truthfully but with due regard for what is appropriate to the age of the child. Curiosity in regard to sex should not be greeted with prudery or false modesty. Such curiosity should also receive a response appropriate to the age and development of the child.

---

18 John Rickman, *On Bringing Up Children* (New York: Robert Brunner, 1952), pp. 87–88.

19 *Ibid.,* p. 89.

Frustration of Needs

Threats to the individual, either from the world around him or from within himself, bring about conflicts which are frequently productive of painful emotions and destructive of mental health. These external dangers are not always susceptible to alteration. *There is, however, a large area of conflict which arises out of the frustration of certain human needs. It is in this area that the pastor can make his greatest contribution.* It is in the growing child that such frustrations are most likely to occur, although they also occur in adults.

Small frustrations are desirable and necessary for the proper upbringing of the child. Severe and repeated frustrations, however, are likely to bring about emotional disturbances. Most of the emotional disturbances of children are likely to arise out of the frustration of the child's needs. These needs may be physiological, psychological, social, or moral. We have advanced far enough in physical hygiene so that most parents will keep the child's physiological needs satisfied, except perhaps his chance to make noise. It is in regard to the psychological and social needs of the child that the parent may have a blind spot or may consciously or unconsciously bring about frustration of the child's needs.

CHAPTER IX

PSYCHOLOGICAL NEEDS AND MENTAL HEALTH

Needs

Father James E. Royce states that, strictly, "a need" is the lack of some good, and refers to an objective fact: it is the absence of something required for adequate adjustment. Good is used here in the philosophical sense, as something fitting to one's nature, either because it is suitable or because it is necessary — something which completes or perfects a person.[1]

The need may be:

1. Physiological
2. Psychological or Social
3. Supernatural

The satisfaction of physiological needs is more of an economic and political problem than it is a religious problem. Adequate food, adequate housing, adequate rest, and adequate recreation are necessities. The pastor can seldom provide these on a large scale. He can only diagnose the results of their lack and urge that they should be supplied. The satisfaction of these needs is a matter of daily concern to each of us. Failure of satisfaction of some of the physiological needs may even result in death. Gratification of such needs does not necessarily imply satiation.

The impressions received during the first years of life exert what may seem an altogether disproportionate influence on the whole course of the individual's later life. Psychologists emphasize the importance of these early years because they constitute a basic formative period of life during which the roots of mental health or ill health are deeply implanted.[2] Particularly important is the parent-child relationship, and the

---

[1] James E. Royce, S.J., *Personality and Mental Health* (Milwaukee: The Bruce Publishing Co., 1955), p. 24.

[2] John R. Cavanagh, M.D., and James B. McGoldrick, S.J., *Fundamental Psychiatry* (Milwaukee: The Bruce Publishing Co., 1958), p. 233 ff.

parents should make the most of this relationship for the welfare of the child. Proper training in every aspect of the child's life is of utmost importance, for each of the various phases is closely related to the others. Quite often the mental and moral attitudes of the child are neglected and his physical orientation given prime attention. Such an attitude is grossly in error, for the habits established in this period form the foundation of the child's future mental, moral, spiritual, and physical outlook.

It is in the field of the social and psychological needs that we can be of service. These needs may be listed as follows.

The Need

1. To be loved, to love others, to feel cared for.
2. To feel secure, to feel safe, to feel at ease.
3. To be creative, not only of material things, but of new life; to procreate.
4. To accept authority, to be free.
5. To achieve, to be praised, to be recognized, to be esteemed as a person.
6. For new experiences, for adventure, to satisfy curiosity.
7. For companionship, to be gregarious, to have consideration for others.
8. For independence, for self-control.
9. For self-understanding, to realize one's capabilities, and to be able to translate these capabilities into action.
10. For God, and for religion.

Failure of satisfaction of any of these needs will disturb mental health in the degree to which it is frustrated. At the least, it will result in frustration, inhibition, and emotional disequilibrium associated with a feeling of defeat. An exhaustive discussion of the topic is beyond the scope of this book; however, a representative sample will make the matter clear.

The Need to Be Loved

"Love is the first lesson that should be taught to every child."[3] Let the children know they are loved and because they are loved they are accepted. Parental rejection, either conscious or unconscious, is a very

---

[3] A. Auffray, Blessed John Bosco (New York: Benziger Brothers, 1930), p. 261.

potent source of emotional disorders. The children should be encouraged in a proper display of affection, and parents should not be ashamed to demonstrate their affection before the child. To be mentally healthy, a child must feel wanted because he is loved. As St. John Bosco often said, "without affection, there is no confidence, and without confidence, no education."[4]

Although it can neither be seen nor felt, love is the most powerful force the world has ever known. *Love is a powerful antidote for mental illness.* Love neutralizes hate and adds a healing force all its own.

One can safely say that from birth a child should have tender, loving care in large measure to prove to him that he is loved and wanted. In the absence of love, a great variety of symptoms may develop, the more important of which may be timidity, fear, social withdrawal, untruthfulness, stealing, and lack of a competitive spirit. In a reaction of overcompensation, the child who feels unloved may become overly aggressive, belligerent, or exhibitionistic in an effort to get attention. Much of today's delinquency arises out of the loss of love with its consequent feeling of rejection.

Imagine the effect on mental health of the unhappiness and heartache of the displaced children of World War II and of all the upheavals since that time. Not only do children suffer from lack of love, but adults as well. Life in a police state is destructive of love. Suspiciousness of one's neighbor or even of members of one's own family is strongly inhibiting under these circumstances. With love should go confidence, which would not be possible under these circumstances. No great mental effort is needed to picture a world in which love, not hate, was dominant. Suppose every man accepted the Golden Rule and each man loved his neighbor as he would like his neighbor to love him. There would then be no theft, no slander, no distrust, no suspicion, no murder, no wars. Even a small measure of any of these would loom large in a world saturated with hate.

The mother is the child's first love, and her role is important in fostering love for her child, who must first be loved before he can love his fellow men. The child must know that he is loved and that he is secure in his home, where he is given love and shown sympathy and understanding. The importance of this fact has been proved only too

---

[4] Cf. Daniel A. Lord, S.J., *Guidance of Parents* (St. Louis: The Queen's Work, 1944), p. 65.

often by the hostile or apathetic traits shown in children who have not been given the love that is their due. The frequency with which the unloved child is found among the "problem children" is a matter of record. A child who feels he is unloved by one or both parents is likely to become envious or jealous. He will tend to act out his difficulty in a way to attract attention or to assert himself. He may develop some minor illness in an attempt to secure sympathy.

It is not inconsistent to show affection to neglected and rebellious children when one firmly checks their misdeeds. The withholding of affection should never be a punishment. Such affection should be accompanied by discipline; but when the wrong has been penalized, and any loss by other children compensated for, friendly relations with the offending child should be attempted again. It is difficult in many cases to strike a happy medium between excessive sympathy or overpetting on the one hand, and neglect or hardness on the other. Nevertheless, we must seek to give the child a chance of success.

Rejection

Many parents, on realizing that they had once thought of rejecting their child, are deeply upset by feelings of guilt. To overcome these feelings, they project their feelings on the child, and place the reasons for their disapproval of the child on the child himself. The parent then demands perfection from the child who, realizing his own imperfections, faces life with a constant feeling of insecurity. Another form of rejection manifests itself as *overprotection*. This can ruin a child just as easily as neglect or rejection. The unfortunate child is not allowed any independence. He is pampered, spoiled, nagged, hovered over, and not allowed to grow up. The "silver cord" is perpetuated and "Johnny" is tied to his parents; he is not permitted to decide anything for himself. This rejection by the parents is sensed by the child and their neglect influences the child's whole life. Levy coined the term "affect hunger" to indicate "an emotional hunger for maternal love and those other feelings of protection and care implied in the mother-child relationship; this is a state of privation due primarily to a lack of parental affection, with a resulting need, as of food in a state of starvation."[5] Some parents outwardly show their dislike for a child by neglect or severity. A child

5 Levy, quoted by Leo Kanner, *Child Psychiatry* (Springfield, Ill.: Charles C. Thomas, 1948), p. 127.

naturally seeks the affection of his parents and, therefore, can sense this rejection by his parents.

Variety in forms of rejection is common. Some parents have over-solicitousness for their children, keeping them "tied to Mother's apron strings," not permitting them to take part in sports or other activities for fear of an injury. The *overtly hostile mother* might say: "I do not like him." A *perfectionistic mother* would most likely say: "I cannot like him as he is and acts; but I *might* love him if he were perfect." She demands achievements beyond the child's capabilities. The *overprotective type of mother* says: "I do not see how anyone could possibly think that I do not love my child. I am sacrificing every minute to his welfare. I deny myself many pleasures because I must devote myself to him. Doesn't this prove that I like him?"[6] Parental rejection when it occurs in severe form and in early childhood, frustrates a child's need for love and acceptance. In sensing this rejection, the child may develop an antisocial personality. He may develop negativistic behavior which is the opposite or contrary to the normal expected response to a specific situation. It is often called "contrariness."[7] In the case of rejection by the parent, the child may seek attention through this contrary behavior.

Jealousy often plays an important role in the life of the rejected child. In a family of two or more siblings where preference is usually given to a particular child, the neglected one senses this neglect. He will then, in most cases, develop a jealous attitude toward this favored sibling. The need for recognition and attention is so strong in everyone that some will go to great lengths to gain attention. In some instances, the child will seek attention by trying to be very good and obedient at home, and by working industriously at his lessons in school. More frequently, however, rejection causes the child to take the opposite course of seeking attention by being bad. He may have tantrums when he is not given what he wants or permitted to do what he would like to do. He is disobedient and shows disrespect to his parents or superiors. At school, he creates disturbances among his schoolmates and gives endless trouble to the teacher. He shows off on every occasion. Since he is usually a poor student, he cannot show off with his scholastic abilities, so he resorts to finding followers and forming a "gang" and on the play-

---

[6] *Ibid.*, pp. 129–131.

[7] W. A. Kelly and M. R. Kelly, *Introductory Child Psychology* (Milwaukee: The Bruce Publishing Co., 1938), p. 126.

ground he is known among his classmates as "the bully." Lacking encouragement from his parents, he loses interest in study. High marks have no interest for him because his parents never seem to show an interest in them. Sensing their lack of interest in his schoolwork, he soon loses interest himself and gradually develops a dislike for school.

One remote effect of rejection is having serious repercussions today. The rejected child of yesterday who is the parent of today is determined that his child will not be rejected either by himself or society. This determination leads the parent to encourage too early dating in mixed company. This too frequently leads to *going steady* at an early age. This is an enemy of successful marriage and leads frequently to a too early introduction to sex. Even though the moral conduct of such children is above reproach, the practice is very likely to be harmful psychologically. It arouses the emotions unduly and projects the children into situations for which their tender years do not prepare them. The situation is such that the parents of Charlotte, North Carolina, made an examination of the practice in eleven southern cities. They found that children were pushed socially in grammar school; that mixed parties were arranged as early as the sixth grade. This is true not only in North Carolina but in other states as well. These children are not ready for this type of activity. Most frequently they are pushed into it by parents who thus project their own need. "I want to be sure that my child doesn't lack dates the way I did." Parents must be firm and forbid the attendance of their children at these mixed parties of grade school children even though the school promotes them. They should do everything in their power to prevent the "going steady" of teen-agers and preteen-agers because it deprives growing boys and girls of much of the carefree outlook on life which they should enjoy. It puts them into a confused state regarding life which is definitely harmful to their future adult adjustments. It limits their friendships and, if continued, is likely to promote, at best, a brother-sister relationship in marriage. In addition, it may lead to a consummated sin even in the early teens.

The *need for recognition* and the *need to achieve* are similar to the need for love, but are less personal and less intimate.

The Need for Security

Next to love, our greatest need is for security: security in our material needs, security in our psychological needs, and security in our spiritual needs. An element in security is confidence in one's own ability to solve problems, to stand alone in the face of adversity. Such confidence will seldom be found in an individual who was neither secure in his childhood relations with his parents nor had a feeling of being accepted by them. It should be emphasized that the need to *feel* secure within one's self is the point at issue, not the need to be actually secure.

Mistrust of the world by children is frequently the fruit of the habitual lies of their parents. These are frequently told about quite casual things, which may not seem very significant to the parents, but which may be the steppingstones which bridge the gap betdeen imagination and reality for the child. It does not make good sense and is quite harmful to distort reality for the child during his period of growth, to have him later discover the deception which has made cause and effect seem like nonsense to him. This eventually maneuvers him into the position of not being able to trust anyone. If one cannot trust one's parents, whom can one trust?

Unfortunately, most of the world's children are frequently exposed to falsehoods or silly, illogical explanations, but it is not only the child who is exposed to falsehood and deception. Propaganda mills produce a constant stream of vilification and deceit. In a more subtle approach, entire populations are indoctrinated with a false philosophy. They are not allowed to know the truth. What security is there for such people? Another element enters into the picture under these circumstances. Men who are constantly insecure, frustrated, bewildered, persecuted, frightened, and anxious tend to regress. By regression is meant a retreat to less mature, more primitive behavior. As individuals regress, so does the culture. There is less creativity and a smoldering resentment takes its place. It is this poorly repressed resentment which so frequently breaks out in rebellious conduct of the individual and in civil war or revolution by social groups.

The Need to Be Creative

The need to create is much sinned against. It involves the whole question of the procreative aspects of sex. Deliberate frustration of this need creates many conflicts. On the other hand, involuntary sterility is also a serious source of mental distress.

In an adjusted and healthy marriage, sexual needs are satisfied with due regard for their proper place in the hierarchy of procreation. The use of sex should always be compatible with the primary purpose of marriage. Both partners should do all in their power to satisfy the needs of the other. They should each be realistically aware of the fact that psychological and personality adjustment contribute more to adjustment in marriage than does sexual compatibility. An adjusted and happy marriage implies permanence of the relationship. In some countries, divorce is becoming easier and more frequent. This is only one example of our failure to profit by experience. If we did so, we could look back to 1789. At that time, the French revolutionaries quite easily enacted a law which freed marriage from social constraints and made it as easy to get out of marriage as it was to enter it. The results of this marriage legislation amazed its enactors. Paris became a city of license. Fathers deserted by the wholesale, abandoning their wives and children; divorce was granted at the will of one party; free love, illegitimacy, and juvenile delinquency became commonplace. By 1797, one divorce occurred for each three marriages. In a similar way, the Bolsheviks, during the Russian Revolution, announced that marriage was a purely personal matter of no interest to others. By 1926, chaos over desertions and divorces forced the state to restore the civil registration of marriage. Anything which promotes security in the marriage relationship also promotes mental health.

Contraception and the deliberate destruction of new life are not only sins against the natural law; they contribute to the loss of mental health. Such deliberate frustration of the order of nature is followed by a reaction to the guilt with its inevitable psychic repercussions. The need to create new life cannot be frustrated with impunity. Demographers tell us, as they have for several centuries, that the world is getting overpopulated. They have never produced convincing proof of this, and their arguments are the same now as those of Thomas Malthus when, in 1798, he published his "Essay on the Principles of Population."

Acceptance of Authority and the Need for Freedom

The ability to accept authority is essential to mental health. This does not mean subservience but submission to properly constituted authority. Discipline and submission to authority must be learned in childhood. Children are not able to make their own decisions and to direct their own activity. They may act as if this is what they want and are apt to be resentful if parents attempt to exert control. This is usually an effort to test their parents — a test of strength, as it were. They want the parent to prove his authority. If the parent or teacher responds to the test firmly and confidently, the child will accept his authority. The child wants direction and needs it. He needs help but, perversely, may not be too willing to accept it. Those methods of modern education which encourage too much free expression are, for this reason, seriously detrimental to his mental health. Self-control is essential to mental health.

However, this statement should not be interpreted to mean that the child should not express hostility. He should be permitted to do so in the privacy of his room and not be punished for it. Later he should be given an opportunity to express his feelings.

In adults, we find this same need for the acceptance of legitimate authority. Yet we find many otherwise apparently mature people consciously and intentionally submitting to the will of totalitarian leaders who have set themselves up as dictators. By doing so, they attempt to avoid personal responsibility, by regressing to the stern father image for the security it offers.

A recently elected President of the American Medical Association found it necessary to comment on the loss of personal initiative in this country. He pointed to the increasing dependency of our citizens upon the government. The spirit of the pioneer has faded and in its place we find a weak, dependent, passive shadow of a man who is a seeker after government benefits. We may be confident, however, that there is a potentially mentally healthy individual repressed within this shadow who would leap into aggressive action if he felt that there was an actual threat to his freedom.

In other less fortunate areas, particularly those behind the Iron Curtain, this need for freedom is seriously frustrated. Many courageous souls have given their lives or their liberty to rectify this injustice. Any infringement on the four basic freedoms described by President Roosevelt should be sternly rejected in the cause of mental health. The pastor should be prepared to vigorously oppose any attack on the basic freedoms.

Freedom does not mean the ability to express every impulse. On the contrary, freedom means the acceptance of discipline.

Discipline is defined as an external system of control, the ultimate end of which is the establishment of self-control. . . . There are certain features which should designate true discipline. It should be characterized by normalcy and consistency. To attain normalcy in the training of children, we must strike the happy medium, avoiding the extremes of rigidity or laxity. These tend to reduce children to the level of animals rather than to elevate them to their true standing as creatures made to God's image and likeness.

Let us consider the overly strict parents who rule like autocrats and who make the home anything but a pleasant place in which to live. Some human beings take delight in the exercise of authority, forgetting that the source of all rightful authority is God Himself. Authority is simply the moral power to direct others and to point out just what is or is not the right thing to do. It is not an indefinite list of commands and restrictions. Certain parents get a thrill of satisfaction when their children obey with the utmost alacrity. There is a great sense of pride in knowing that their children obey promptly, but how few pause to consider that perhaps they are afraid to disobey! This attitude destroys the true purpose of discipline and, as a result, the child may develop unfavorable personality traits which will mar his character for life. Instead of cultivating a grateful, loyal spirit for his parents and home, he may degenerate into a sullen, rebellious, or even delinquent member of society. Pope Pius XII expressed himself very clearly on this matter when he addressed a group of teaching Sisters in Rome. He said: "To try to reform young people and convince them by making them submit, to persuade them by force, would be useless and not always right. You will induce them very much better to give you their confidence, if you, on your side, strive to understand them — and to make them understand themselves — save always in the case of those immutable truths and values which admit of no change in the heart and mind of man."[8]

The contrast to this exceedingly rigid attitude is the rather prevalent vice of excessive laxity. It is this lamentable trend which today is playing havoc with our modern world. Many parents are of the impression that to have a quiet, peaceful home it is necessary to give in to the desires and impulses of the child. Many educators advocate the need for self-expression, stating that the child should be free to make his own decisions. This theory is erroneous because the child certainly needs expert and intelligent guidance before he can make a reasonable choice. Worst of all, parents do go so far as to shield the child when he has done something wrong and thus prevent him from recognizing the error of his

---

[8] Pius XII, *Counsel to Teaching Sisters* (Washington, D. C.: N.C.W.C. Publications Office, 1943).

misdeed. Thus, the child fails to realize that there is a natural restraint incumbent on us as individuals in a social world. The child who has been protected during his youth will, in later life, be unable to stand on his own two feet and meet the challenges of an ever changing modern world.

The ability to accept authority is essential to mental health, but early rigid training causes confusion. The child needs firm but gentle remonstrances. He should be led along, not forced. Sarcasm, nagging, bossing do not help. We have often heard the expression that overbent twigs do not develop into sturdy trees. Florence Blake has some very apt words on this subject:

> Many adults feel discipline is a failure if it has not made the child feel miserable, afraid and repentant, but study of children has not shown this to be true. Discipline should help the child develop increased capacity for self-direction. It should increase his self-confidence and his respect for himself and his own capacities.[9]

The Need for a Sense of Achievement

All of us need recognition as individuals of worth. Too frequently, daily experience is deflating and it tends to produce feelings of inferiority. Sarcasm and unwarranted criticism on the part of those in authority promote such feelings. Severe and unjust punishments are frustrating and ego-deflating. On the contrary, encouragement and praise associated with understanding and individual treatment promote mental health. Under a totalitarian state, the loss of the value and dignity of the person is destructive to mental health and leads to regressive behavior in the individual and in the culture.

Enough has been said to demonstrate the importance of fulfilling an individual's psychological and social needs. Education will help tremendously toward an insight into the relation between failure of fulfillment of these needs and the development of mental ill-health.

The Need for Religion

Morality is important in the education of the school child and should be taught early and in accord with the child's ability to understand. Great care is necessary in handling problems relating to purity, because

---

[9] Florence Blake, quoted by Kanner, op. cit., p. 127.

severe scrupulosity in this regard is very prevalent. It frequently arises out of improper methods of instruction which create an "either-or" concept — things are either all right or all wrong. The individual with this concept does not have the ability to see varying gradations of severity. The bases of moral training during the school years are: (1) building up of habits of moderation and regularity; (2) imparting to the child knowledge of what is right and wrong; (3) guidance and direction in the performance of acts which are in accord with the child's acquired knowledge.[10]

Religious ideals should be used to reinforce moral principles. Pre-school age is not too early for moral and religious training. Such training should keep pace with mental and physical growth. The child is naturally impressed by what he sees and hears, so that stories of the life of Christ, the saints, and the presence of religious pictures and statues in the home will be vitally important as part of his environment. In the case of older children, it is often beneficial to both if the older child is allowed to explain to the younger the catechetical principles he has learned at school and how these principles are related to life.[11]

Daily training in habit formation; in the acquisition of ideas of right and wrong; in the development of attitudes of modesty, generosity, or respect for the rights and property of others; in suitable habits of personal hygiene, if effective, will lead to the development of a normal, wholesome personality. The parent should also realize that there are unlimited possibilities for the early religious training of the child, and that to wait until the child goes to school to begin his religious training is to neglect these possibilities. Religious habits, ideals, and ideas constitute much of the groundwork that will influence the guidance and direction of the physical, mental, emotional, and social development of the child.

The child, early in life, recognizes that there is a power greater than himself. He may feel very early in life that this Omnipotent Being is his parent, but as he grows older he soon recognizes this as a power of infinite proportions, and early in life recognizes the fact that he is on earth to love, honor, and serve God. This knowledge of God gives point, direction, and orientation to the child's future activity. It does not vary with the customs of the time nor with the passage of time. In spite of this intuitive knowledge, religious education is essential. Religious train-

---

[10] Kelly and Kelly, op. cit., p. 133.

[11] Cf. Laurence H. Gibney, "Suggestions to Parents," Ave Maria, Sept. 6, 1952, Vol. 76, pp. 310–312.

ing is important in the development of a proper philosophy of life. It may be stated with conviction that a belief in God and an acceptance of religion as a way of life, a belief embraced and practiced, will bring to the faithful a high degree of happiness which of itself will produce mental health. This, however, is a subject with which the pastor is more familiar than the author.

CHAPTER X

THE PASTOR AND EDUCATION TOWARD MENTAL HEALTH

The educator must have a clear idea of life's purpose, a well-developed philosophy of life, before he is prepared to plan the training of children. This is especially important if he is to contribute to the mental health of his students. His ideal may not always be realized because both he and his students are human, but if it is wholly absent, "he can but train for a life that resembles that of an ant."[1] He may even do damage. In neither case can he give his students that which makes life worth living.

This does not mean that a philosophy of life is sufficient in itself to insure successful living or successful teaching. Physical health is important; comfort is important; adequate food, clothing, and shelter are not only important but necessary. Lack of these material essentials can produce anxieties which gnaw away at a man's morale and destroy his spirit. These physical needs can seldom be provided by the pastor or teacher, but the pastor and teacher make as important a contribution to the mental health of their charges as does the home.

It is clear that education has two purposes: (1) the acquisition by the student of sufficient knowledge to earn a living; and (2) the preparation of the student to face life realistically and, even more important, to develop fully his deeper potentials, physical, mental, and moral. It is this second and more important purpose with which we are concerned.

Thus, the primary aim of education is to teach the student to face life realistically. If his training does not accomplish this, knowledge acquired will be of very little value to him. To live productively, the child must be both mentally and physically healthy. He must be happy. Mental health is dependent upon happiness. The first aim of education, then, is to bring up mentally healthy children.

---

[1] Edward Leem, *What is Education?* (New York: Sheed & Ward, 1944), p. 6.

In this task the pastor, the teacher, and the parent must co-operate. It is the duty of parents to train and discipline their children, but teachers also hold a great deal of responsibility. The encyclical of Pope Pius XII concerning the responsibilities of teachers states:

> We who are teachers and educators must be (so) ready and (so) up to the level of our office. We must be so well-informed of all with which young people are in contact, in all which influences, that they don't hesitate to say: "We can approach Sister with our problems, and she understands and helps us."[2]

Good emotional patterns begun at home will give children confidence to face school life. "Schools do want all children to be able to enter school healthy and free from anxiety or emotional disturbances."[3] This depends a great deal on the parents. Pope Pius XI made this point quite clear in speaking of the necessity of example in the home:

> The first natural and necessary element in this environment, as regards education, is the family, and this precisely because so ordained by the Creator Himself. Accordingly, that education, as a rule, will be more effective and lasting which is received in a well-ordered and well-disciplined Christian family; and more efficacious in proportion to the clear and constant good example set, first by parents, and then by other members of the households.[4]

This instruction by the parents is most important because it is in the early preschool years of life that the seeds of neurosis and personality distortion are planted.

Before parents and teachers can promote mental health, they should be as well informed as possible concerning this subject. Unfortunately, this is not easy. It is an area in which the pastor can make important contributions.

Methods of Teaching Mental Health

"St. Anselm, in his principles on how to train the young, tells us that the gentle helpfulness of others, kindness, mercy, friendly consultations, charitable support and many things of this nature are what children need most."[5] Perhaps this idea of St. Anselm is the best method of

---

[2] Pius XII, *Counsel to Teaching Sisters* (Washington, D. C.: N.C.W.C., 1951), p. 7.

[3] *Happy Journey: Preparing Your Child for School*, Foreword by Mrs. Newton P. Leonard (Washington, D. C.: National Educational Association, 1953), p. 7.

[4] Pius XI, *Christian Education of Youth* (New York: Paulist Press, n.d.), p. 27.

[5] Daniel A. Lord, S.J., *Some Notes for the Guidance of Parents* (St. Louis: The Queen's Work, 1944), p. 65.

teaching mental health, i.e., by giving a good example. This, however, is not enough. Some formal instruction is necessary. Such instruction has been seriously deficient in most schools, in religious schools, as well as in nonsectarian and public schools. Suffice it to say for the present that there are very few formal courses of instruction in any school system which I was able to study. In some schools, mention is made of mental illness in courses on social studies. This consists of a brief, inadequate discussion. In some schools, the students are taught the scholastic philosophy of the soul. This is not likely to make much of an impression on high school students and does not actually have any practical impact on mental health. Counseling service is available in some form in many schools, but is formalized in only a few. The need for counseling indicates that there is recognition on the part of the individual of a need. Counseling is not needed by the mentally healthy.

In most religious schools the only teaching on mental health is in the course on religion and in religious practices. These, although desirable and necessary, are not enough for the maintenance of mental health. Sanctity does not guarantee mental health.

Some positive means of teaching mental health should be devised. If individuals qualified in the field of education will turn their attention to such programs, they will gradually be developed. Some projects are already in progress, but have not been in action long enough to evaluate their results. The best known of these plans are:

1. Forest Hills Project[6]
2. Charlotte, North Carolina, Project[7]
3. The Bullis Plan[8]
4. The Force Plan[9]

Space and the requirements of this text do not permit a discussion of all of these plans. The plan suggested by Colonel H. Edmund Bullis of Wilmington, Delaware, seems most practical and constructive. This plan

---

[6] This project is described in *Published Reports*, 1947–1951, Vol. 1, of the Group for the Advancement of Psychiatry (Publication Office, 3617 West Sixth Avenue, Topeka, Kans.).

[7] *Marriage and Family Living: Journal of the National Council on Family Relations*, Vol. 15, No. 2 (May, 1953).

[8] H. Edmund Bullis and Emily E. O'Malley, *Human Relations in the Classroom*, Course I — 6th and 7th grades (Wilmington: Delaware State Society for Mental Hygiene, 1947).

[9] O. Spurgeon English and Stuart M. Finch, *Introduction to Psychiatry* (New York: W. W. Norton & Co., 1954), p. 582.

involves the teacher and student only; it does not require special equipment, specialized training, or great changes in the school organization and planning. Colonel Bullis and Miss Emily E. O'Malley together have written a series of lessons in mental health suitable for use in grades seven, eight, and nine. These authors select four needs of the child upon which to concentrate. These they list as adventure, security, recognition, and sex. They feel that if these needs can be satisfied, mental health will result. This information is taught in classes on human relations which are held weekly. The classes are initiated by the teacher who tells a stimulus story which is then discussed by the students with the assistance of the teacher. Some of the subjects discussed are:

Public Enemies of Good Human Relations
How Personality Traits Develop
Our Inner Human Drives
How Emotions Are Aroused
Our Unpleasant Emotions
Emotional Conflicts
Making Difficult Decisions
Assuming Responsibility
Losing Gracefully
Submitting to Authority
Our Need for Faith

The students are urged to participate actively in the discussion and to give examples from their daily lives. The teacher then ends the discussion with a summary. For example, this is the conclusion to the discussion on "Submitting to Authority":

> We cannot always suppress our emotions — it's not good to do so — for we all have to let off steam at times. However, we can try to harness our emotions constructively in the problems that face us in our daily lives. We all have to learn to submit to those in authority and not let our emotions cause us to act in such a way that we may regret it later. Keep your "team feeling" and remember that a continued effort to do your best is the most constructive reaction to over-severity, or what you believe to be an unfair decision. It is a more mature way to act than the babyish reaction of "making a scene." Prove your worth and you will be the real gainer in the long run.[10]

This plan has deficiencies, perhaps the greatest of which is that too many teachers are unfitted either by lack of training or by their own

---

[10] Bullis and O'Malley, op. cit., p. 143.

neurotic personalities to carry it out. It has not been evaluated, but it seems to be a good, practical plan, headed in the right direction. I would, therefore, recommend it for your consideration. It is better to have a plan under way than to sit waiting for the perfect plan to be developed. Thorpe[11] speaks favorably of the Bullis Plan and points out these examples of typical mental hygiene devices which are described in Colonel Bullis' book. The page numbers refer to the Bullis text:

1. Encourage children to discuss errors they have made in offending others rather than emphasizing how others have offended them. (p. 23)
2. Avoid giving direct advice. Do not be afraid to refer a problem to the class as a whole. If no pupil can suggest a solution, then you may offer your idea. (p. 43)
3. Remember to refer a question back to the children instead of answering it yourself. (p. 67)
4. Do not be afraid to tell of your own personal experiences. (p. 74)
5. Do not be afraid to deviate from the suggested plan if a child brings out a good discussion lead. (p. 134)
6. Do not forget to call on those who are not actively participating in the discussion. (p. 139)
7. By your personal interest, sympathetic understanding, and, if possible, your affection, try to give the child a feeling of personal worth, a feeling of security, a feeling of self-respect. (p. 169)

The Problem of the Maladjusted Teacher

One serious contribution to the maladjustment of children is the maladjusted teacher. Not everyone is qualified by nature to teach. Training alone cannot make a teacher. Many of the lay teachers in our schools do not have adequate training. Some teachers expect to hold the job only until they can get married; they have no real interest in teaching. I have recently seen a psychotic individual who is teaching in grade school. There should be more careful psychological screening of teachers. This in spite of the present shortage of teachers. I feel that, at least from the standpoint of mental health, no teacher at all is better than one who is mentally or emotionally ill.

Even a good teacher may be adversely affected by being overburdened with work, by having too many courses to teach, by being underpaid, or by failure of co-operation on the part of superiors or parents.

---

[11] Louis P. Thorpe, The Psychology of Mental Health (New York: Ronald Press, 1950), p. 571.

The intrapsychic conflicts of the teacher are likely to be reflected in his charges.

Basic Requisites in Mental Health

In the meantime, until more can be done, there are certain points in character discipline that should be maintained in the classroom. *First, to be on time.* The child must be taught this at a very early age. Promptness is very important throughout his entire life, especially if he is to achieve important positions.

The second point is *dependability.* The child's sense of responsibility must be well developed. It can be tested by both pastor and teacher by examining the child's work. Can he fulfill an assignment regardless of a few difficulties?

It is most important that *children learn to "take it" and take it with a smile.* Each child must learn that when he needs correction he should take it without resentment. He must expect and be prepared for disappointments. He cannot win all the time. Those who do not learn to "take it" in life are headed for a miserable future.

Point number four is *honesty.* The final blow to a reputation is to discover that a man cannot be trusted. He is kept on the outer circle and cannot hope to get a decent job. Children must be taught to be honest in even small things.

The fifth point is to be *diligent.* Instill into children the idea that they should never fear work. Hard work should be a challenge. "By laziness a man fails to realize the good that he can do."

Children *must also be taught unselfishness.* They must give themselves to others. They must start at home and then bring it into the school. They must be kind to everyone, without distinction.

Summary

Mental health is a treasure whose value cannot be estimated. As yet, there is no scientific understanding of what constitutes it. We do have some knowledge of how it may be maintained, but we are not utilizing even this knowledge in our schools. The Bullis Plan is the most practical plan available. More pastors should be familiar with this plan and encourage its use.

PART III

THE PASTOR AND PERSONALITY DEVELOPMENT

CHAPTER XI

THE PSYCHOLOGY OF CHILDHOOD

Periods of world unrest are always characterized by a marked increase in juvenile delinquency. The neurotic character of the times is reflected in growing children, and many desperate parents seek help. Those able to give such help are too few at the present time. It behooves the pastor, therefore, to make inquiries into the psychic development of the child, so that he may be able to advise these bewildered parents. Many of those who deal with people, although now willing to admit the increasing importance of a knowledge of personality development, have undoubtedly felt at least mildly frustrated because of the involved terminology found in psychiatric literature. To the nonpsychiatrist, many of the claims concerning the psychosexual development of children seem so fantastic as to be unbelievable. This is granted. It would seem, however, that for those who will in the future advise parents on the training of their children, a practical knowledge of the psychology of childhood is necessary.

Many mothers who are concerned over the development of their progeny investigate the literature on this subject and find themselves confused. They seek the help of their pastoral adviser to straighten them out. Their plea is "What shall we do?" The pastoral counselor may be prompted to remind these parents that the successful approach to the individual behavior problem comprises more undoing than doing. He should then emphasize the essential need of therapy which will undo and re-educate.

The particular appropriateness of such an approach arises from the fact that the child himself never seeks advice and that children do not outgrow asocial behavior. It is important to recognize the problem when it arises in children and adolescents; first, because of the importance of childhood experiences in determining later personality reactions, and,

129

second, because of the immediate importance of the problems of personality in childhood.

In presenting the psychology of childhood an endeavor will be made to facilitate an understanding of why children do not grow out of their asocial behavior, and why they must be treated early.

Mental growth is one long conflict between the demands of the individual, of his natural egoism (so manifest in the child and available to study), and the conditions of his environment. It need not be a painful conflict except at intervals. This would be the psychiatrist's definition. The sociologist, on the other hand, might put it this way: Growing up psychologically is a progressive socialization of the individual, more or less successful, more or less painful.

Grownups usually think of childhood as a time of carefree unconcern, the easiest part of life, not the proper subject of psychiatry, in fact relatively unimportant psychiatrically. Grownups have forgotten a great deal. Growing up is a hard job, many may never succeed, and others will have only slight success. The measure of their immaturity is the measure of the mental illness, of neurosis, of the so-called "neurotic personality of our time."

Let us remember then that it is the position of modern psychiatry that the formation of "personality" — the individual's habitual modes of reaction — occurs to a great extent during the period of infancy (birth to six years).

Very little is factually known of the early sexual development of the child. For this reason, there are many theories. One needs to be careful in evaluating the early emotional changes in infancy, because as has been emphasized by the work of Mandel Sherman, impartial observers such as students of medicine, psychology, and nursing, who could not see the type of stimulus which produced an emotional reaction in infants less than twelve days of age, could not give the correct name for the child's emotional response.[1]

Another factor that arises in the study of infantile sexuality is the difficulty in distinguishing between actions which are more or less similar to sexual acts of adults and the specific sexual experience which accompanies these acts in the adolescent and postadolescent periods. Charlotte Bühler, for example, has pointed out that although children

---

[1] Mandel Sherman, "The Differentiation of Emotional Responses in Infants," *J. Comp. Psych.*, 7: 265–335, 1927.

may handle their sexual organs in early infancy and may even seek a sexual partner for this purpose from the fifth year on, there is no evidence that these acts are accompanied by specific sexual pleasure. Bühler also points out another important distinction between the sexual play of a child and an adult, that is, that the sexual play of a child does not involve a tender, personal attachment to the play partner.[2]

It is apparent, however, that the child is capable of such attachments. This is indicated by his display of affection to adults for whom he cares. Bühler's work would seem to indicate that a tender, personal love of a nonsexual character develops in a child between the second and fourth year of life. This love has, according to her work, nothing to do with the developing sexuality of the child.

Dom Verner Moore, writing about this personal attachment, makes the following comment:

> Personal attachment should not disappear from the life of man in the adolescent period. Marital affection that is merely sexual lust is not likely to form the basis of a permanent wedlock. True friendship is possible without a sexual component. In marriage the two components, personal attachment and sexual desire, exist side by side. The true basis of marital life is a warm, tender, personal attachment that can endure on into old age, even after the sexual interest has disappeared.

Moore then adds:

> As to the presence of specific sexual experience in infancy and in early childhood, we shall never be able to solve the problem by appealing to the introspection of the infant and the child. Neither does the memory of the adult reach back to these early years so that he can tell us whether or not it is really true that in infancy and early childhood he experienced specific sexual excitement and that this was repressed and became latent, as Freud maintained.[3]

This is the nucleus of the problem. The life, sexual or otherwise, of the child is not accessible to psychological investigation. Observation can provide certain facts which may be used as the basis of a theory arrived at by inductive reasoning. This was the method influenced by Freud, who from a few cases arrived at many general conclusions. These hypothetical constructs are merely theories. Many, however, seem to overlook this fact and, in discussing the sexual life of the child, assume that these theories are postulates. The theories of childhood sexuality presented by

[2] Charlotte Bühler, *Kindheit und Jugend* (Leipzig, 1931), p. 198 ff.
[3] Rev. Thomas Verner Moore, *Nature and Treatment of Mental Disorders* (New York: Grune & Stratton, Inc., 1943), p. 48.

the Freudian psychoanalytical school are widely known and in many respects conform to observed facts. *Because they are so widely known and permeate so much of the current literature, the pastor should be familiar with these theories.* It must be understood that these concepts represent only an hypothesis which is not proven.

The Freudian Concept of Childhood Sexuality

Freud maintains that the force which holds an individual back from achieving the best of his potentialities is the result of early frustration of pleasure needs, leading to hostility, pain, and hatred. This pain of frustration and the hatred it engenders gradually form a wall within the self; a wall which inhibits, which frustrates, a wall of pessimism, of depression of spirits, of indifference and lack of generosity, and even active cruelty and oppression of others.

The human being is born into the world with certain needs which must be met by those about him (see p. 108 ff.). If he is from his infancy made physically comfortable, made happy; if he is given a chance to express himself without too much unnecessary frustration, he makes a mentally healthy beginning in life. He is the person who becomes the optimistic, hopeful individual who contributes something to the world at large and those about him. The human being whose needs are reluctantly met when he comes into the world, who is an unwelcome addition to the family, who is neglected, and who lives in an environment that is indifferent and cold toward him, receives an unhealthy and an unhappy start. It is he who tends to the development of hostility, resentment, hate, and pessimism. He will be unhappy and unable to function. Further, not having been accepted and not having satisfactorily accepted the family group, he then does not later accept, or is unable to accept, the larger social group of the community with its rules of conduct. He becomes an asocial individual.

Mental growth, the development of the personality, is a progressive modification, adaptation, and adjustment of the individual's needs and demands in his conflict with the environment. The environment of the young child consists of the family group, primarily the mother and father. We have referred several times to the needs of the individual which demand gratification, and to his inborn appetites demanding satisfaction. These natural tendencies of the individual which constantly seek gratification are called the "instincts." Instincts were originally described as those of procreation and of self-preservation. Just as we do not understand fully what constitutes life, so we do not understand the forces that strive to preserve it, or the nature of the forces tending to destroy it. It was Freud who referred to these forces as "instinctive," and who later rearranged the concept of instincts to (1) the erotic (the sex or life) instincts whose purpose is procreation and self-preservation, and the (2) aggressive instincts which are usually projected toward others as aggression.

It must be emphasized that a human being is born into the world with certain needs which must be met by those about him. The instincts continue to exert their force throughout life, following a sort of pleasure principle in seeking their own gratification, releasing the energy connected with them, trying to avoid the pain of frustration and of tension. Each one of us can recall much of this from his own experience. The appetite for food in the infant's rapidly growing body must be satisfied or the tension of hunger builds up. If it mounts too high, strong energies associated with this instinctive need of the infant are exerted to obtain relief. He cries and wiggles to make known his hunger. Ordinarily he gets his relief. If he does not, these energies build up the painful tension of hunger.

These instincts have no organization in infancy, no discipline, no control, and no fear of consequences. The child will move about, demand food, soil or wet at will, be destructive and cruel if his instincts are allowed full expression at all times. This state of undisciplined instinct gratification cannot, however, last for long. The child is soon made aware that some control of this free expression of all his desires must be brought about in order to adapt to social life. He finds that such indiscriminate relief of his tensions is not acceptable to those about him. The first social demands are now made upon him by his environment as represented by his mother. Since his need for protection and love is greater in most cases than his desire to satisfy his tension at will, the child attempts to control these tensions in order to hold the good opinion of this mother on whom he is dependent for existence. He learns to tolerate a little anxiety, a little tension so that he may feel secure in his mother's love. So a new part of the personality, a monitor, develops, which, while taking note of outside dangers, still strives to pacify the instincts. This monitor or superego has to fulfill the function of creating conditions under which the instincts can express themselves, in however distorted a way, in a manner which the environment will tolerate. It attempts to substitute a reality principle for the pleasure principle, the reality principle being the capacity of the organism to forego an immediate pleasure for a future gain, for a greater good. Its successful acceptance is the measure of adult character formation, of "growing up."

The Superego

As a result of repeated parental admonitions, the parental viewpoint is gradually taken over by the child so thoroughly that it becomes incorporated as a part of the forming personality and is called the superego. (See p. 137 for distinction between superego and conscience.) It is this superego which admonishes the ego when undesirable instincts strive for expression. It causes the ego to feel shame, fear, disgust, or embarrassment. The instincts are considered to be part of the "id" or "it" part of the personality and are essentially selfish. These three parts of the structure of the personality, i.e., the ego, superego, and "id," are not to be thought of as separate and distinct parts of the human mind. This topical division merely helps in thinking about the chaotic and difficult concept of personality.

The process of birth is the individual's first difficult experience. (One writer, Rank, contends that it is an experience from which he never recovers!) With birth, the child becomes aware of many unpleasant stimuli; the external stimuli of a dry atmosphere, noise, light, cold, and the unpleasant inner needs of hunger and thirst, all of which cause him discomfort and stimulate the instincts of self-preservation and aggression.

Oral Stage of Development

During early infancy, the increased instinctual tensions are caused mainly by internal physiological needs. These are at this time centered about the upper gastrointestinal tract: (1) hunger is felt strongly as the metabolic needs of the infant's rapid growth demand much food; (2) the oral zone has then the greatest degree of itching and this oral tension is felt as frequently as is hunger. This itching sensation in the lips is felt even at birth. Indeed, fetuses have been observed to suck their fingers in utero. At birth, before he can be hungry, merely touching the infant's lips suffices to initiate strong sucking movements. He will later suck his fingers after feeding, or even while taking a bottle. This need to suck is evidently solely for pleasure and not dependent on hunger. Other tensions and anxieties in later years often cause a reversion to this oral relief of tension, this infantile pleasure pattern. Other evidence of this reversion is the oral pleasure of the adult in overeating, drinking, and smoking. This demand for pleasurable gratification has to be reckoned with at all ages.

After the first day of life, hunger and thirst are added to the itching discomfort of the infant's lips. He responds with sucking movements of the mouth and with crying. His mother feeds him and he gets relief. As his sense organs develop, he comes to realize that his desires are a part of himself but that what satisfies them is a separate entity from himself. He comes to realize that he has discomforts and that his mother can relieve them. He learns that the presence of his mother is associated with pleasurable sensations of warmth, of touch, of taste, and of smell. Then, as his ego develops, he learns that he needs his mother to obtain the pleasure which arises from the gratification of his needs.

It is in this desire for pleasure that he comes to need his mother, to desire her constant presence, i.e., to love her. This is the beginning of love for a person outside of himself (object love), which is later to play such an important part in his life. A beginning in socialization is made with this realization. When an infant's mother does not respond immediately to his needs, allowing him to suffer hunger pains, oral tensions, or other discomforts, then the child may react with violent emotion. He kicks and pounds as though to punish his mother for her neglect.

This is the beginning of muscular aggressive activity toward the world, particularly toward objects which do not contribute to his comfort and pleasure. Such discomforts arouse strong instinctive urges; such situations stimulate self-preservative or erotic desires. These desires are very strong and are frequently felt by the child as an overwhelming need. Their overwhelming strength is unpleasant, and the child feels and expresses fear and anxiety.

Through the occasional temporary stimulation of his anxiety patterns, the child learns to tolerate small amounts of anxiety and thus becomes capable of tolerating larger amounts liberated at later critical periods of his life. He is helped through these difficult times and his fears are quieted by an early appreciation of his mother's love and protection in which he can feel secure. If not, if this affection is not offered, he becomes more fearful, doubtful, perplexed, and confused; and, as with the adult, his body may distress him as well as his mind. He may exhibit colic, vomiting, or diarrhea. It was for this reason that Dr. Holt, dean of American pediatricians, frequently used to write on the chart of a child in the pediatric ward the prescription: "This baby to be loved every three hours."

The oral period with its close association of physical needs (hunger) with pleasurable feeling (sucking) comes to an end with weaning. Now the opportunity to get the major pleasure reaction through the mouth ceases and there comes a realignment of the instinctual expressions.

If complete weaning is abrupt, there may occur the general signs of discomfort and anxiety, sleeplessness, irritability, crying, rage attacks, increased oral activity, and often illness (vomiting, diarrhea).

Each of the periods of infantile pleasure gratification should last an optimum length of time. The child should be assured of adequate nourishment and adequate pleasure in sucking.

When either his hunger or his desire to suck has been accentuated through frustration (as by too short a nursing period for any reason), the child remains constantly unsatisfied. He may develop the reaction pattern of always feeling slighted, of wanting more. If this pattern persists, he may, as an adult, meet every situation with the underlying feeling that no matter how well things turn out for him, he will not receive his deserts.

The individual who is nursed longer than the optimum, for whom the supply of milk has been overabundant, or for whom the breast has been used as a pacifier for all of his outcries, may have quite the opposite reaction. He may go through life feeling that no matter what happens, he will get what he wants and is therefore prone to extravagance and improvidence. It is to be understood, of course, that many circumstances in later development may modify this basic reaction pattern.

The Anal-Sadistic Stage

As previously mentioned, with weaning there is a realignment of instinct expression. The pleasure sensation of the excretory processes is heightened. Children (in their first and second years) may take great interest and show a good deal of preoccupation with the action of excretion. They may talk unabashedly about toilet activities, of having produced large bowel movements, and similar topics.

It is shortly after weaning that the child is faced with the next stage in development. His parents begin to institute toilet training, to insist that he relinquish oral pleasures. They demand control of his bowels and bladder from the child. The child wishes to please his mother because he needs and loves her. He chooses the path which produces the lesser anxiety, the one which seems likely to retain his mother's love. At first, he can exercise this control only with the help of his mother's constant watchfulness. Then he retains control if she is near at hand; later, even in her absence. After learning control, he may lose it on separation from his mother or when disturbed by any anxiety.

The child at first obeys the commands of his mother only when she is present. Later he assumes her attitude, makes her commands part of his personality — his superego — which stands guard over the ego and the free desires of the id — just as the mother stood guard over the child's desire for uncontrolled excretory activity.

Like the mother, the child's superego controls by the use of concepts such as must, ought, must not, ought not. In later life, this nucleus develops into an internal code of morality.

If the methods of training are severe — with punishment or extreme expressions of disgust from the mother — the child will probably feel the need to conform to her standards, to rid himself of anxiety caused by her attitude. He takes over her attitude. Henceforth, any semblances of soiling, not only of the body, but any form of mussing or disorder will be disgusting to him. He becomes the extremely overconscientious, overmeticulous, and overclean individual, the rigid personality.

If he is unable to control himself, the child may develop the feeling of failure, of having lost his mother. Consequently, he prefers not to add to his anxiety the discomfort of trying to control himself.

Often, as a result of his failure to control, his mother redoubles her efforts. The child finds that soiling himself is the one way of attracting his mother's interest and regaining the affection he is losing. This prolongs the soiling; the punishment becomes pleasurable partly because it is accompanied by his mother's attention, partly because it relieves him of the responsibility for soiling.

This type of reaction, of clinging to infantile modes of behavior through the permission given by some form of punishment, may continue throughout life. It is a mark of the juvenile delinquent or criminal whose life is an alternation of crime and punishment, who becomes a criminal because of a need for punishment.

Few children need very active training in bowel control. By the time the nerve tracts are myelinated and functioning so that such control is possible — the child is endeavoring to imitate all adult activities. Seldom is there need for more than encouragement and mild reward.

If the parent is wise enough to regulate his interest in the child in generous proportion to what he is asking of him, then the child will not be rebellious, heedless, inconsiderate, or unco-operative. Parents must make necessary demands on the child, must be willing to demand that the child accept responsibilities as they arise and not postpone them. They must help him to arrive at a balance of giving and demanding. There is no evidence that children are born rebellious, neurotic, or psychopathic, but there is good evidence that they do have ungenerous neurotic parents.

During the period of development we have been discussing, the child has learned to give up infantile methods of expressing his instinctual desires and the use of body zones for that expression. As a result of this and other influences, his sex energy (if we may properly describe infantile affective tendencies in terms of adult sexuality) is directed away from oral and anal zones and toward the genitals.

The Genital Stage

The mother is the child's first love. To her have been directed all his feelings of affection. She is his one source of comfort and relief. Up to now, he has been able to obtain physical satisfaction from her and to do things physically to please her. The child attains adult sex feelings without the knowledge of what he feels or without the capacity to gratify them and the subject toward which his feelings are directed is his mother.

A later step in normal development will be further socialization in which the child will turn his sex aim away from his mother and extend his contacts from within the family group outward, expanding his capacity to adjust to society until he is a mature adult. This is a long process but its activities are a result of the earlier experiences.

The intensive love which the little boy has for his mother leads him to crave her undivided attention, interest, and caresses. He is balked in this desire by the fact that she shares her affection with other people — his siblings, and, notably, his father. He observes that his mother prefers to talk to his father, perhaps in privacy, excluding him, when he may be told to run off and play. His mother may go out in the evening with his father and leave him in someone else's care.

His father is his rival and a successful one. This disturbs the child.

He may brood over it, have hostile actions toward his father, and feel that his father will punish him if he learns of his thoughts. For the child's idea of justice is the primitive law of an "eye for an eye and a tooth for a tooth." So he attempts to curb his hostile aggressive acts toward his father. In place of desire for his mother, he develops a tender feeling for her. He replaces his hostility toward his father by tender affection. He is aided in repressing his hostility toward his father by the fact that he loves him as much as he hates him. This solution is the more successfully worked out when the father's personality is adequate and the child experiences his love and the gentle discipline of a strong character.

The ambivalence of love and hate is an aid in the solution and helps the child to repress his sexual feeling toward his mother, to turn his erotic instinctual energy away from members of his family to persons of the female sex outside the family. It helps him to repress his hatred of his father and to turn his aggressive energy away from the male members of his family, to use it in competition with male rivals outside the family, and in attacking the real difficulties of the world at large, changing his world to obtain satisfaction and happiness. So the father serves as the object for the development and outlet of aggressive instinctual energy and its gradual control. Various pathological and abnormal reaction patterns are formed in the absence of a father or when this development is prevented by a too severe or cruel or weak father.

The reaction patterns which the little boy forms to solve these difficult relations with his parents — and the little girl's development which is only slightly more complicated — serve as the pattern of all future human relations.

Period of Sexual Latency

After the resolution of this parental situation, the child enters a period of sexual latency which lasts from about the sixth year to prepuberty. During this period, he tends to play with children of the same sex. A boy will liberate his aggressive tendencies by playing rough and tumble games such as cops and robbers, whereas the girl tends to play dolls and keep house and thereby expresses her desire to replace her mother. Parents frequently unnecessarily traumatize their children by forcing them into each other's company during the latent period. Mixed parties for children are frequently arranged by parents during this latent period, much before the boys and girls are ready for it. Parents should wait until the children naturally seek each other's company before they force dating upon them. The latter part of this period is frequently considered as a normal homosexual period during which children of the same sex seek each other's company. It must be emphasized that this is a normal development and should, with the appearance of adolescence, lead to a proper heterosexual orientation. Having a "crush," or the development of an attitude of hero worship toward some admired figure, usually a teacher or clergyman, also frequently occurs during this period. This should lead to no difficulty if the adult is mature and well balanced. The "crush" usually passes very quickly.

Fixation is a term used to indicate a failure to advance to the next stage of development. For example, a child may become fixated at a homosexual level and fail to progress to a normal heterosexual adjustment. On the contrary, a child may advance to a stage of development and then, by a process of regression due to some traumatic episode, become fixated at a lower level.

Summary of Psychoanalytical Concept

This, in brief summary, is the psychoanalytical concept of the child's sexual development. It must be recognized that it represents only an hypothetical construction. It does, however, conform to certain observed facts. In general, boys prefer their mothers during their early years, whereas girls prefer their fathers. This is a matter of daily observation. Penis envy and castration fears are frequently recognized in psychiatric treatment. There is no doubt that in some cases these conditions do occur. There is, however, no proof that these concepts have universal application.

Sexual Characteristics of the Growing Child

There are certain sexual traits of children which, though normal, are a frequent source of concern to parents. The most frequent of these are:
1. Peeping
2. Exhibitionism
3. Cruelty
4. Masturbation
5. Homosexuality

Although these traits are considered normal characteristics of the growing child, their mismanagement may lead to sexual perversions in later life. Mismanagement in such cases usually consists of severe punishment when the child is caught in such conduct. This will usually drive the behavior "underground" because of the child's interest in what is forbidden. If such behavior is treated more gently, it soon ceases because the need no longer exists.

Peeping is the desire to see the nude body of either sex. In young children, it is usually the result of curiosity. This frequently is manifested in the "Doctor Game" played by many young children. In the course of the game, the children take turns being the "doctor" and performing a physical examination on the "patient."

The child has a natural curiosity about the bodily structure of others. Forcible repression of this tendency may lead in adult life to an intense sense of shame or horror when exposed to such sights. The normal adult sublimation of this tendency is in art, anatomy, or in certain forms of amusement as well as in normal sexual intercourse. The adult perversion equivalent is *voyeurism* or the so-called "Peeping Tom."

Exhibitionism is the reverse of peeping. It is the wish to display one's own body, especially the genitals, for the sake of deriving pleasure from the act. Children are natural exhibitionists and their apparent lack of modesty in running around nude is to be considered normal. This usually stops around the age of four or five and before this time children of opposite sexes may be allowed to mingle in the nude and to bathe together. Any severe repression of this tendency may result in an excessive sense of shame. The adult equivalent in perversion is exhibitionism, and its normal sublimation is pleasure in being looked at, as in the case of actors, models, and public speakers.

Cruelty is a normal characteristic of children to some degree. We have all seen children pull the wings off flies or throw the cat off the roof to see how he will land. Any sudden and severe attempt to suppress this tendency may result in a fear of one's self in competition with others and a reluctance to try to control a situation through fear of hurting others. The normal adult sublimation is in competition, in the struggle for existence, and in such medical specialties as surgery. The adult perversion equivalents are sadism and masochism. Naturally one cannot permit a child to display overt cruelty in his play, but, on the other hand, one should not respond to his childish cruelty with cruel methods of suppression.

Masturbation or self-induced sexual pleasure is not uncommon in small children. Many writers believe that the practice is universal, but there is no proof of this. It is more frequent in boys than in girls. In small infants, the process should not be called masturbation because it probably has nothing specifically to do with sex but is merely a part of the child's exploration of his body. He finds a part which is pleasurable when touched and consequently he tends to touch it repeatedly because of the pleasure involved. Genital play in small children is best handled by gentle admonition or by completely ignoring it. Forcible attempts at repression of masturbation may lead to thumb-sucking, nail-biting, tics, or other neurotic disorders, among which might be the development of compulsive masturbation. The treatment of compulsive masturbation is very difficult. Severe punishment never gives satisfactory cure. Masturbation occurring in older children and adolescents is best handled on moral grounds and by an appeal to their maturity.

Homosexual attitudes, as pointed out above, occur normally during the latent period of development. During early life (ages five and six) attraction to members of the opposite sex is not unusual. Parents should not become unduly alarmed if their male children want to play with dolls, because, under normal circumstances, the child becomes heterosexual as he grows older. Under certain circumstances, however, the child may become fixated at the homosexual level. For example:

1. A rejection by the normal heterosexual object, i.e., by the parent of the opposite sex.
2. Excessive care and attention by the normal homosexual object, e.g., the parent of the same sex.
3. A series of homosexual seductions by older children or adults or by the exclusion of the child from contacts with the opposite sex, as in prison or schools.

Pastoral Considerations

So far in this chapter nothing has been said about the religious implications of the psychology of childhood development. It is generally agreed that it is the duty of the parents to instruct the child in the facts of life. But instruction in the physical facts of life is not enough. The education of the child should not be purely naturalistic. It is also necessary to relate these "facts of life" to the supernatural. Even the little child can be trained in modesty by reminding him of God's presence and of the value of prayer. It may be necessary for the pastor to help the parents acquire understanding of the methods and objectives in this regard. He should help them to understand how to rear their children, so that they will want and work for and ultimately win eternal destiny. The parent must also know what to teach his child to help him be a true Christian. After this and as a secondary goal he should help the parent to help his child achieve a happy and successful life in the family and in society. In particular reference to the material just covered, he must help the parent guide the child in the way of modesty and chastity. He can tell them of the powerful influence of example given by the parents in the home. He can warn the parents in the spirit of Pope Pius XII's encyclical on the Christian Education of Youth, "not to descend to details, nor to refer to the various ways in which this infernal hydra destroys with its poison so large a portion of the world."

Pope Pius XII made many statements on this subject, none of which are more beautiful or more instructive than his allocution to the Italian Women of Catholic Action on the feast of Christ the King, October 26, 1941. This excerpt can be read with profit by both the pastor and the parents.

> . . . How joyous is the springtime of childhood, unruffled by wind or storm!
>
> But the day will come when the childish heart will feel fresh impulses stirring within it; new desires will disturb the serenity of those early years. In that time of trial, Christian mothers, remember that to train the heart means to train the will to resist the attacks of evil and the insidious temptations of passion; during that period of transition from the unconscious purity of infancy to the triumphant purity of adolescence you have a task of the highest importance to fulfill.
>
> You have to prepare your sons and daughters so that they may pass with unfaltering step, like those who pick their way among serpents, through that time of crisis and physical change; and pass through it without losing anything of the joy of innocence, preserving intact that natural instinct of modesty with which Providence has girt them as a check upon wayward passion. That sense of modesty, which in its spontaneous abhorrence from the impure is akin to the sense of religion, is made of little account in these days; but you, mothers, will take care that they do not lose it through indecency in dress or self-adornment, through unbecoming familiarities or immoral spectacles; on the contrary you will seek to make it more delicate and alert, more upright and sincere. You will keep a watchful eye on their steps; you will not suffer the whiteness of their souls to be stained and contaminated by corrupt and corrupting company; you will inspire them with a high esteem and

jealous love for purity, advising them to commend themselves to the sure and motherly protection of the Immaculate Virgin.

Finally, with the discretion of a mother and a teacher, and thanks to the open-hearted confidence with which you have been able to inspire your children, you will not fail to watch for and to discern the moment in which certain unspoken questions have occurred to their minds and are troubling their senses. It will then be your duty to your daughters, the father's duty to your sons, carefully and delicately to unveil the truth as far as it appears necessary, to give a prudent, true, and Christian answer to those questions, and set their minds at rest.

If imparted by the lips of Christian parents, at the proper time, in the proper measure, and with the proper precautions, the revelation of the mysteries and marvelous laws of life will be received by them with reverence and gratitude, and will enlighten their minds with far less danger than if they learned them haphazardly, from some disturbing encounter, from secret conversations, through information received from over-sophisticated companions, or from clandestine reading, the more dangerous and pernicious as secrecy inflames the imagination and troubles the senses. Your words, if they are wise and discreet, will prove a safeguard and a warning in the midst of the temptations and the corruption which surround them.[4]

The nervous disorders of children not dependent on errors of parental attitude are in the minority, especially with today's attitude of not wanting children. It must be emphasized and, in practice, admitted that the relations of the parents to the child are of maximum importance in the shaping of character; that the parents comprise the important environmental condition up to the time of adolescence when the individual begins to lead his own life and to acquire independence. The child's problem is usually at the surface of contact with the environment rather than deeper in the psyche. It is more often a question of direct frustration.

There are certain crises where the pathologic personality is apt to break down: puberty, leaving school, falling in love, disappointment in love, marriage, bearing or fathering a child, disappointment in vocational or financial life, loss of a loved person, and the involutional period. It suffices to point out that the adult neurotic person was already neurotic in his childhood and that his neurosis is largely the result of the way in which he was forced to alter the even course of his psychosexual development in order to adjust himself to the actual circumstances of his life. The adult whose childhood is normal is less subject to neurotic disturbance at critical periods than one whose childhood was difficult and unsatisfying.

---

[4] Quoted from *Clergy Review*, *XII* (New Series), No. 3, March, 1942, p. 136.

There are many practical lessons to be learned from the study of the psychology of childhood. There is no need to concern ourselves with such controversial subjects as the "Oedipus complex" to develop a practical knowledge of the subject. A little thought devoted to the above observation will be extremely useful to the pastor in the development of corollaries to the axiom, "As the twig is bent, so grows the tree."

CHAPTER XII

UNDERSTANDING THE TEEN-AGER

Columbus, viewing the new territory which he had come upon, undoubtedly experienced some of the emotions characteristic of the teen-ager. The teen-ager, in passing from childhood to adolescence, discovers an entirely new world. It is not so much that the world is new, but rather that the adolescent is seeing his old world from a new vantage point. No longer does he look upon it with the naïve, accepting eyes of a child, but with the self-conscious eyes of a puzzled youth. Small wonder then that the teen-ager is a creature of troubles and problems, of unrest and uncertainty, of wild hopes and terrifying fears. He daydreams and giggles; he is unreasonable, unstable, and unrealistic by turns. This child would indeed be intolerable if he were viewed as a finished product. But that is the whole point: he *is* only a child who is struggling to become a man or woman — the man or woman that is "me." He is dimly aware that something overwhelming is happening to him, but the constant changes within bewilder him. "How long does it take to find yourself — and to find your little niche in life?" was what a young girl once blurted out to me. Little did she know that she had put her finger on the very core of adolescence.

This double problem, dawning self-awareness and a vague sense of floundering in the outside world, is what is at the bottom of all that makes the teen-ager "difficult." He is pleasant today, and sullen tomorrow; co-operative and helpful now, stubborn and unapproachable next week. Or perhaps he is the gay, bubbling-over type for a time; and then suddenly he melts into the "pale and wan," persecuted, sensitive type.

He is not able to understand himself and wishes to hide this fact from others. His wish to remain obscure and mysterious, and the desire to further confound his adult "persecutors" leads him to develop a new jargon for communicating with his fellows. For example, he may express himself in the following phraseology:

> Most of the country's cool ones are convinced that only a slow-poke amoeba would get a large charge out of pounding the pad over anything as scaggy as brain food. Bugged by the square, they yen to cut out and send him to the dark side of the moon. Along the way, they are careful not to bug the fuzz by riding in a hot drag.[1]

Translated from the original teen-ese, this paragraph means:

> Most of the teen-agers contacted in a nation-wide survey think only an old-fashioned bookworm would find any fun in spending an evening at home with his homework. Angered by anyone so studious, they feel like telling him off and suggesting that he make himself less obvious. Along the way, they are careful not to antagonize the police by riding in a stolen car.

These characteristics do not occur in everyone to the same degree, of course, but there is no denying their existence in all teen-agers. This type of reaction can be quite tormenting to a parent who sees only the surface characteristics and who does not have the humility to take the sometimes rather harrowing treatment he receives from his "young jewels"! He thinks, at times, that he may be dealing with a group of split personalities. At other times he is convinced that his offspring are most unmannerly brats, unmindful of the deeper things of life. Neither of these conclusions is the true one. The teen-ager is simply testing, now one facet of his own personality, now another; or else he is expressing his anguished uncertainty — amid all the realities of life of which he is just becoming aware — now by a sham arrogance and boorishness, now by timidity. He longs for independence, and yet he is still afraid to accept it. With his new-found self, he loathes tradition and all laws on which he has not passed personal judgment; but at the same time he wants desperately to be accepted and approved and loved by the very society he ridicules. These characteristics may all be summed up in one phrase: the adolescent's deep sense of uncertainty.

This then, in quick outline, is the adolescent. Enigmatic though he may be, he is also intensely interesting, and entirely lovable: for he is the "springtime of a whole small universe, and the green years of a personality made to the image and likeness of the Divine."

---

[1] Eugene Gilbert, "Here's How They Talk in Other Parts of the Country," "Teen," *The Sunday Star*, Feb. 15, 1959, p. 5.

Physical Changes

Let us take a closer view of the teen-age. It is the period of transition from childhood to adulthood or maturity. It is generally thought to cover the period from twelve to twenty years of age. Physically, adolescence has commenced when an individual reaches the age of pubescence, i.e., the achievement of sexual maturity. The complete development of the body and its organs is continuous, but during adolescence there is a specific growth of those organs which relate to the capacity for reproduction. The mere fact that puberty, with its procreating capacity, inaugurates adolescence, does not mean that full maturity has been established. Body growth and differentiation continue long thereafter. Physical development is only part of the total process, but it is significant that the general growth produces definite changes in body form as well as in structure and function.

In many discussions of adolescence, the attendant physical changes, and especially the onset of puberty, are given the central significance. Certainly there can be no question that the physical changes are very striking. There is, for example, a spurt of bodily growth which starts between the ages of 10 and 15 years. This continues for about two years, after which the rate of growth declines until, at the end of about four years, it gradually comes to a halt. Intellectual growth increases rapidly between the ages of 7 and 13 years, after which there is a more gradual increase from 13 to 18 years. After this, there is a gradual leveling off until the age of 30.

In connection with the physical development there evolve secondary sex characteristics. These characteristics result in somatic changes which are typically masculine or feminine. In the boy, for example, there is a deepening of the voice, growth of hair on the face, in the pubic region and under the arms, and a broadening of the shoulders. In the girl, the breasts develop, menstruation starts, and her figure rounds. These changes are initiated by a hormone secreted by the anterior lobe of the pituitary gland, the gonadotropic hormone. It serves as a stimulus which causes the gonads to develop. The gonads then produce in turn their own hormones which bring about other changes. Along with these changes, there is the development of the primary sex organs and their accessory glands. As a result, there comes the ability to be sexually aroused and to feel sexual desires.

Associated with these changes is a great vitality and energy, a huge appetite, a rapid growth in height and weight, a rapid development of the muscles. The body begins to assume adult form and proportions.

Change Is Psychosomatic

The parent of the adolescent must attempt to understand the influence which these changes exert on the total adolescent personality. It is now generally recognized that there is a relationship between the spiritual and the physical which is so intimate that the state of one profoundly affects the state of the other. It is not surprising, therefore, that such a phenomenon as the rapid muscle development which takes place in an adolescent should occasion his very obvious feeling of awkwardness and lack of poise. Nor is it surprising that his physical sex development should cause him to awaken sexually. But it does not follow from these two instances of concomitance of physical and mental states that the mental change is explainable solely in terms of the physical changes. It does not even follow that the physical changes and their effects are the most important. Such a view is admissible only in the framework of philosophic materialism. Moreover, it is evident that human nature is much too complex to admit of such a simple explanation. These outward changes make the boy or girl feel disturbed and out of place. He feels all arms and legs and is very awkward. Self-consciousness brings about an over-awareness of his body.

Psychological Changes

In addition, there is, in the teen-ager, a tendency to change companions frequently. There is a preference for older companions. The boy is likely to give up long-time friends and may even drop out of groups to which he previously belonged, such as the Boy Scouts. His preference in play activities switches from informal games to organized teams. This preference may lead the adolescent to join groups which may be genuinely harmful. It is necessary to mention only the nonvirgin clubs and those which require criminal acts as part of their initiation.

The boy now begins to be aware of girls and later to enjoy their company. He likes dances and parties, but not in the home. He may express his new-found independence by smoking and being disrespectful. The youth may commit minor delinquencies with a suspicious and consciously independent attitude toward elders. He will usually resent direct demands or commands. His feelings of importance and physical pleasure help to cloud the rational choice of what to do and what not to do. He does not yet understand the moral issues involved. He is almost certain to resent adult direction and, if he can, he will circumvent adult-made rules and take pride in doing so. The adolescent often develops an aversion toward the customary or expected, as may be seen in his unconventional dress and manners. The new life he feels stirring within fills him with impelling desires before he has properly developed the mechanisms for their control.

The adolescent is emotionally unstable and yet his emotional reactions seem to be among the most important things in his life. He seems to enjoy his intense states of mind and is passionately fond of excitement. His drastically contrasting moods and inconsistencies are the result of his newly developing interests and his broadened outlook. His changes in outlook take place more rapidly than his habit systems can change or be developed. This naturally results in a high degree of unpredictability.

He may feel that life is too complex to be understood. There is a feeling of indefiniteness within his ego, with an attendant fear of adult responsibilities and hope that increased ability will come to him. He is easily discouraged; self-confidence is easily lost and energy may sink to a dangerously low level. The adolescent takes everything personally; his feelings are easily hurt. He is unwilling to face unpleasant situations, especially if they are of his own making. There is an overwhelming need for praise to sustain him and to inspire him to do his best. His moodiness results from self-consciousness and a tremendous longing for social approval. He has a desire to achieve, yet has misgivings about his ability to do so. The adolescent will frequently focus attention upon himself in an unhealthy way. He may become introspective and fall into habits of studying his own failures, dissecting his own motives, and, as a result, he is impressed with a sense of his own inadequacy. This tendency should be actively combated because it may lead to unhealthy thought patterns.

Since he is unstable, embarrassment, anger, excitement, and emotional responses to the other sex are touched off readily and are often more intense than the situation demands.

The teen-ager desires to act in a sophisticated manner and worries about his pubescent changes and self-conscious sex behavior. He is hesitant at times about expressing emotions, even though their expression may be perfectly acceptable socially.

A child's fears are relatively simple and personal; the adolescent's fears are complicated and social. He fears teachers, examinations, and reciting. The boy especially fears recitation because of his changing voice. Feelings of inferiority manifest themselves commonly in the adolescent because he underevaluates himself. Since variety dispels such moodiness, the need for excitement may lead to delinquency if some other outlet is not provided.

Sexual Awareness

In connection with his sexual awareness, purity seems to be the biggest problem. There is concern over impure thoughts and actions which are related to the fact that he is unsettled as to what is right and wrong. The teen-ager's sexual awakening seems to be a vague, undifferentiated response to many stimuli. The individual reacting to these experiences becomes excited, often without realizing fully what is happening to him. Mixed feelings accompany the new sensations. They are pleasant but may be disturbing if the adolescent feels that they are forbidden. Pervading these responses and his activity is a fundamental bewilderment.

The early awakening of sexual feeling is attested to by the appearance of sexual fantasy. Sex dreams are reported by a majority of adolescent boys. These may be associated with nocturnal emissions.

Sexual development is an integral part of his character and must be considered in relation to the many other changes that are occurring.

Environmental and cultural determinants are the important factors in psychosexual development. With the onset of puberty, members of the opposite sex become true sexual objects. New interests and attitudes begin to take shape, and basic needs, such as a desire to be loved, a fulfilling of the spirit of adventure, and finding acceptance, begin to develop in terms of this new orientation. These are novel feelings, concerning which he is inarticulate. With his increasing social participation, situations develop which bring members of the opposite sex into the orbit of his social interests and activities. Gang activities, dating, social dancing, heterosexual interest, growing realization of his part in the social scheme as a potential husband and father or wife and mother, thoughts of vocation, and moral and religious implications become part of his new sense of reality. Lack of proper sexual instruction may create further difficulties. Each sex is inclined to show off before the other. Boys tend to flex their muscles, and girls tend to be coy and flirtatious.

The psychological conflicts of the adolescent are not necessarily bad. It is through resolution of such conflicts that the individual achieves a level of integration and self-control that would otherwise be impossible. It is victory over contrary and dynamic impulses, not surrender to them, which leads to personal integrity and character. Most adolescents achieve such victory.

Spiritual Development

The final and most important phase of adolescent development is spiritual. There is a tendency for this phase to be overlooked in the hustle and bustle of the modern world. However, its importance cannot be overestimated. The development of a truly religious adult should be the aim of all persons charged with the guidance of adolescents. Religious training, although most important, is difficult to achieve. Religion is a basic need. The home is the first and should be the dominant influence in religious development. Adolescents who have had religious training throughout childhood will usually continue good religious practices. If this has not been so, there is good reason to wonder how the adolescent will fare.

Parents have the primary obligation in regard to the religious and moral training of their children. This obligation is a profound one because through this training the adolescents are being prepared for their future life. Guides other than parents should attempt to assist as much as they can by directing the adolescent's interests to spiritual and religious matters.

It should be borne in mind that adolescents will frequently be troubled with spiritual doubts. At such times, the guide will be most helpful if he aids the adolescent in a persistent, open-minded search for the truth.

In other respects, the home exerts a tremendous influence on the development of the adolescent. In the ideal home, affection is an even, mutual feeling that is present at all times; it does not ebb and flow, nor does it appear only when the one who is loved is particularly pleasing, or given as reward or withdrawn as a punishment.

Adolescent Complaints

Adolescents indict their parents on many scores. Their most common complaint is that their parents will not listen to them. They assert further that their parents do not trust them; that their parents treat them as children; that their parents interfere with their friendships; that their parents try to decide their futures; that their parents invade their privacy; that their parents complain too much; that their parents quarrel; in general, that there is a complete lack of understanding between them and their parents.

There is an underlying wholesomeness in the modern adolescent; he has a heart of gold, a willingness to do what is right, a frankness and lightheartedness and gaiety interspersed with fundamental goodness. As one writer expressed it, "The teen years are the wonderland of our life, the age of our mysticism, the years of ideals."

Pastoral Treatment

We have seen that the core characteristic of adolescence is uncertainty. This means that the most common state of mind of the teen-age child is one of anxiety: anxiety concerning the sort of self he is, anxiety about the kind of world in which he must live. Because he is young and spirited, this anxiety is less apt to manifest itself in cringing, cowering attitudes than in brash, rather crude defenses. Every adolescent "would rather die" than admit to others, and especially to himself, that he is afraid. He not infrequently will go to extravagant lengths to demonstrate his "self-sufficiency." Does this mean that the wild young things must be herded into line and made to walk the straight and narrow path more uncompromisingly than ever before (as some parents feel)? Definitely not! Actual moral evil can never be tolerated, of course, but what is often pounced on as "a bold, flippant, indifferent attitude" is very far indeed from moral evil. What then is to be done? — because obviously it is possible for an adolescent to remain an adolescent all his life if nothing is done. The answer can only be this: the proper intellectual climate must be provided.

> . . . for the upbringing during these years, far more love, tact, and selflessness are required than ever before. The word "selflessness" must here be understood in its literal sense; in seeking to influence young people, the upbringer must more than ever surrender himself.[2]

The adolescent stands at the crossroads of life. If the parent would win him, if he would help him be not merely a nominal, but a devoted and joyful Christian, he must be prepared to pay the price. He must

[2] Rudolph Allers, *The Psychology of Character* (New York: Sheed & Ward, 1933), p. 297.

accept with dignity, and without a flicker, some rather "rough" treatment from the unthinking cruelty of youth. He must make prolonged efforts to learn to know his children so that he will know how to approach them. He must take their point of view, sincerely consider their ideas and problems as seriously as they themselves do — because in no other way can he gain their confidence, and without this, he can do nothing at all for them. He must encourage when actually there is no more than a glimmer of hope.

This does not mean that the teen-ager may never be corrected or "disciplined." It does mean that correction and training must be conducted with intelligence and patience. The old maxim of St. Francis de Sales, that one can catch more flies with a teaspoon of honey than with a barrel of vinegar, is probably more applicable at the teen-age level than at any other. Only after the teen-ager's confidence and respect have been won can "pruning" be started, not before. Even then, because of his immense insecurity, it is better to inspire him with his great dignity as a child of God, and its concomitant responsibilities, than with his unworthiness, which he is sure to learn anyway. Above all, it is well to remember that infinitely more influence is exercised by not appearing to be influencing, than by constant preaching. The guide who is himself sincere can, by example, inspire young people with the desire to imitate him. The day will come when the guide must withdraw, but by then he will no longer be needed, for the foundation will have been laid.

Adolescence is not impressed with authority. It reveres only that authority which it sees vested in actual worth.

Too often the home resembles a battlefield: "Let's see how much we can get away with . . ." versus "Let's see how much I can drill into their heads." Now this sort of thing, in moderation, is not altogether undesirable. For the child, it is part of the time-honored fun of youth; for the parent, it is part of the challenge. But, to repeat, in moderation. The child must be taught where to draw the line, and the parent must know when to close one, or even both, eyes. As with all middles-of-the-road, this is not an easy one to find, much less to maintain, but it is imperative that the search for it never be abandoned, for on the parent-child relationship thus established, there often hinges the adolescent's whole future attitude toward authority. The teen-ager is still too much of a child to submit to authority simply because it is lawfully vested, but he is also too grown up to be bullied into conformity. Short of a direct intervention of God — which, on a minor scale at least, is not uncommon! — the teen-ager's parent must himself be mentally and morally mature if he is to exercise any influence. He cannot, of course, be impeccable, or infallible — but even this may be part of his child's growing-up. Someday there will be, for each adolescent, the jolting discovery that even persons highly regarded and dearly revered are not perfect.

Even when the adolescent's confidence has been won, the parent must know how to wait, to refrain at all costs from nagging or high-pressuring. The young sense immediately any lack of confidence in them and just as quickly withdraw their own confidence. The parent must have, above all, a deep, unwavering faith that the seed being sown through him is taking root, because, except for a few stray glimpses, he will never see the harvest. Human "popularity" is short-lived, indeed, and he will have been very foolish if he has made this the basis of his guidance.

There is a never ending possibility of advice to be offered by the pastor to the parents of teen-agers, but may I suggest as basic, for their own peace of soul, the following principles:

1. The difficulties of adolescence are not necessarily problems, but are normal phases of development.

2. The growth from childhood to adulthood is slow and a teen-ager is not an adult.

3. Rebellion is a normal characteristic of adolescence. Avoid making issues except over major matters.

4. Remember that hostility breeds hostility; guidance must be given with a loose rein.

5. Be quicker with praise than with blame when praise is at all justifiable.

6. Be patient; remember, "This, too, will pass."

7. Keep an eye out for the lighter side of things. A sense of humor is invaluable.

8. Be understanding. Every sullen mood, every disobedience, has an explanation; do not despair.

9. Be trustful; be affectionate; keep home a happy place, a secure place, a comfortable place, a place where one is welcome. Keep it truly a home.

10. Remember the family rosary. The family that prays together stays together.

Teen-Age Dating

Since we must start some place with the problems presented by adolescent rebellion, may I suggest that some return to previous dating habits be made. This will require parental co-operation. There is no doubt that dating customs have changed. Without giving any applause to the "good old times" which, on the whole, left much to be desired, there were then well-understood rules for dating. For example, in earlier times young girls were kept at home, especially after dark; going steady was a preparation for marriage; kissing was reserved for engaged couples; the male half of the date was one of the neighbor's children; the boy came to the house to pick up the girl and meet her parents; there was a definite destination for the date; teen-agers did not drive a car; drinking and smoking, especially by young girls, were taboo; petting and necking were sinful and not ladylike; nine o'clock was the hour for returning home; children obeyed their parents rather than the parents the children. These well-established rules are now in the discard because "nobody but squares ever get in by nine o'clock." What we need is a new set of customs which are established by the parents and not foisted on them by immature children who do not know what they want and who need guidance which can be given only by their parents. The pastor and the Sisters can talk, but only the parents can enforce the necessary discipline. Unfortunately, most modern parents are so afraid of their children that they will not establish or enforce the simplest rules of behavior. It is time for the parents to establish a few rules for the behavior of their children and then become that group of public opinion which says that "our will and not yours be done." If this were done, the children would be happier, the parents would be happier, and the juvenile courts would be less well attended.

In an effort to re-establish dating customs and to give parents a front on which to unite against their rebellious offspring, may I suggest the following basic rules for dating:

1. "Going steady" is a preparation for marriage and should not, therefore, be permitted to teen-agers. "Going steady" means going with one partner to the exclusion of others.

2. "Going steadily" is usually all right if it continues to be just that. "Going steadily" means that a boy and girl agree to go to more or less formal affairs together, but to go with others in between times.

3. No dating on school nights. When there is no school the next day, they should be in at a "reasonable hour." A "reasonable hour" is one long enough after the end of the function to permit the couple to get a bite to eat, if that is the local custom, and then get home.

4. The boy should come to the house to pick up the girl and meet her parents, at least on the first date.

5. No drinking should be permitted, and if it occurs it should be a reason for not permitting the continuance of the relationship.

6. When the couple leaves the house, they should have a definite destination and time of return. If not back on time, they should call the parents to explain.

7. No car driving should be permitted until the driver is old enough to get a driver's license. Unfortunately, many parents violate this rule.

8. Petting should be absolutely forbidden and not shrugged off as some parents are inclined to do. Petting is a preparation for sexual intercourse and should be restricted therefore to marriage. Parents should trust their children; they should not give them the third degree when they come in; they should, however, train them in what is proper and improper and then expect that they will conform.

9. Unchaperoned parties are a product of the present state of confused relationship between the sexes and should not be permitted.

10. Mixed parties for grammar school children are psychologically unsound and should be forbidden by the parents. This does not apply to formal dancing classes.

11. Solitary dating by grammar school children should be forbidden. This is especially true where a grammar school girl is allowed to date an older boy.

12. Grammar school children should not be out after dark unless accompanied by an adult.

In conclusion, urge parents to start early to train their children. Adolescence is too late. If a problem does arise in the teen-ager, try to understand his need for guidance. Attempt to lead rather than push. Offer guidance, but try it by indirect rather than by direct methods. Think of the teen-ager not as a finished person but as a rebellious intermediate between childhood and adulthood who needs your love and affection. He needs direction and will accept it if it is given kindly but authoritatively. Remember Shakespeare's words: "Youthful rashness skips like a hare over the meshes of good counsel."

CHAPTER XIII

THE PASTOR AND THE DIFFERENCES BETWEEN THE SEXES

Perhaps the biggest difference between the sexes is the question: *Should a wife obey her husband?* This thought is in bad repute today, but it seems clear by divine injunction, by nature, by innate psychology, and by tradition that the husband has been designated as the leader in the home with all of its prerogatives.

In the basic roles for which God created man and woman, man is better qualified to be the head of the family. He is by nature and tradition independent and aggressive. Woman is the helpmate of man in the process of creation. She is by nature and tradition dependent and passive.

This leadership of the husband and the need for obedience on the part of the wife was clearly defined by Pope Leo XIII in his encyclical on Christian Marriage:

> The husband is the chief of the family and the head of the wife. The woman, because she is flesh of his flesh, and bone of his bone, must be subject to her husband and obey him; not, indeed, as a servant, but as a companion, so that her obedience shall be wanting in neither honor nor dignity.[1]

Pope Pius XI in his encyclical *Casti Connubii*, after reaffirming this statement of his predecessor, continued:

> This subjection or obedience does not imply that woman is called upon to carry out her husband's request if it is unreasonable or contrary to her dignity as a woman. But it does forbid that false liberty urged by feminists who claim that the wife should have the same liberty as her unmarried sister.[2]

---

[1] Pope Leo XIII, *Christian Marriage* (New York: Paulist Press, 1942), p. 9.
[2] Pope Pius XI, *Casti Connubii*, Simplified Edition (New York: Paulist Press, 1944), p. 9.

American divorce statistics prove that heedless disregard of this wise papal advice in favor of the "You lead your life and I will lead mine" philosophy can mean only ruin of husband, wife, and family.

Before considering further this question of leadership in the family, we should define and describe the man and the woman who are husband and wife. A consideration of their biological, psychological, and spiritual characteristics may make more clear why the father should be the leader in the family.

Suppose you were asked, "What is a woman?" How would you answer? In Genesis, Adam spoke of her in these words:

> She is now bone of my bone,
> and flesh of my flesh;
> She shall be called Woman,
> for from man she has been taken.[3]

If you turn to literature, you would find quite a variety of descriptions of woman which are, however, more descriptive of particular women than definitions of "woman" as a group. For example, Whately comments: "Woman is like the reed which bends to every breeze, but breaks not in the tempest." Shakespeare, apparently less convinced of female stamina, has Hamlet say: "Frailty, thy name is woman!" Balzac more sympathetically states: "A woman has this quality in common with the angels, that those who suffer belong to her." Otway rather ecstatically eulogizes "woman" in these words:

> Oh woman! Lovely woman! Nature made thee
> To temper man: we had been brutes without you;
> Angels are painted fair, to look like you;
> There's in you all that we believe of heav'n
> Amazing brightness, purity and truth,
> Eternal joy, and everlasting love.[4]

Pope Benedict XV speaks more realistically of the women of his day:

> With the decline in religion, cultured women have lost with their piety, also their sense of shame; many, in order to take up occupations ill-befitting their sex, took to imitating men; others abandoned the duties of the house-wife, for which they were fashioned, to cast themselves recklessly into the current of life.[5]

---

[3] Gen. 2:23.
[4] Thomas Otway, Venus Preserved, Act I, Scene I.
[5] Pope Benedict XV, Letter Natalis trecentesimi, December 27, 1917.

Webster's Dictionary, a long-time standard, gives the following definition:

Woman:
An adult female human being, as distinguished from a man or child, sometimes any female person, often as distinguished from lady.[6]

If we were to ask, "What is a man?" we would get equally varied answers. Seneca described man as a reasoning animal; Pascal, as a reed, "but he is a thinking reed." Gavarni sarcastically stated, "Man is creation's masterpiece. But who says so? — Man!" Erasmus, in classical style, said, *Homo homini aut deus aut lupus* (Man is to man either a god or a wolf). Cervantes stated sorrowfully, "Every man is as God made him, ay, and often worse."

These definitions are clearly unsatisfactory because they deal only with certain aspects of men and women. They fail to take into account the spiritual aspects of husbands and wives.

Definition

It is obvious that men and women are more than these descriptions make them. In search of a better definition, I turned to the *Baltimore Catechism:* "Man is a creature composed of body and soul made in the image and likeness of God." For our purpose, we may include woman under the subject "man," in spite of a comment in a recent national magazine that a group of students in a Catholic university debated whether women had souls — all in good, clean theological fun, of course.

The catechetical definition goes beyond the physical, beyond "maleness" and "femaleness," and brings into focus new aspects of personality, the psychological and the spiritual.

Biological Aspects

If we were to consider further the purely biological aspects of woman as compared with man, we would see that man is endowed with greater strength and a natural ability in leadership and government. His fatherhood does not interfere with his duties in support of his family. The woman, on the other hand, is more frail, has a natural tendency to be

---

[6] Noah Webster, *New International Dictionary,* 2nd ed. (Springfield, Mass.: G. & C. Merriam Co., 1953).

dependent, and is necessarily so, at times, because of motherhood. Men are stronger to pursue; women more beautiful to attract. In this, woman has the advantage over her nonrational sisters; in the animal kingdom, it is the male who is more beautiful.

To fulfill their appointed task, men are stronger and more heavily built, are more muscular and have more heavily built skeletons. Women are physically weaker, more lightly built, and have a more fragile skeletal structure as befits what is naturally their less arduous life task.

The anatomical structures in which the woman differs most from the man are those related primarily to her reproductive function. The woman's sexual organs are constructed to receive and nurture; the man's sexual organs to give. The most important function of the woman is pregnancy. As Louis I. Dublin expresses it so well:

> Childbearing always will remain the central fact of life for women. It is the basic reason why women save themselves from overwork, protect their health, think subjectively, feel instinctively, react protectively and emotionally concerning their children, why they desire peace and wish to preserve the existing social structure. It is the basic reason why they are different.[7]

Biologically men and women complement each other. In marriage, they find the completion of their personalities. Woman's beauty is a foil for man's strength; her passivity for his aggressiveness. Even in the begetting of children this same relationship holds true. In the sex act the man gives, the woman receives.

In spite of man's greater physical strength:

> Females are more resistant to disease, the stress and strain of life. They are better operative risks, have fewer post-operative complications and continue to outlive males. In general their biologic existence is more efficient, preeminent than that of males. In brief, the human male with beard and functioning testes pays the higher price.[8]

The Psychological Aspects

Viewed by the psychologist, there are many differences between men and women. Psychologically, they complement each other, just as they do

---

[7] Louis I. Dublin, "Women Are Different," *The Reader's Digest* (Dec., 1950), p. 60. *Your Life* (Dec., 1950), Copyright by the Kingsway Press, Inc., New York.

[8] *M.D. Medical News Magazine* (M.D. Publications, Inc., 30 East 60th St., New York 22, N. Y.), p. 53.

biologically. This may be seen by a comparison of their psychological characteristics.

The woman is more perceptive, more feeling than the man. This does not mean that she is less intelligent, because there are no clear-cut differences in intelligence between the sexes. It is true that men excel in certain areas, women in others. This produces an unequal but equivalent status. Women talk earlier, and mature socially and sexually at an earlier age than men.

Women are less reasonable than men. They are guided by intuition, a fact commented upon by Shakespeare when he made Lucretia say: "I have no other but a woman's reason: I think him so, because I think him so." Being intuitive, woman has little use for logic. This characteristic seems to have impressed Kipling who wrote, "A woman's guess is much more accurate than a man's certainty." Since her conclusions are not attained logically, but rather by flashes of intuition, a woman easily arrives at unwarranted conclusions. Such conclusions are easily altered — "Vacillation," if we paraphrase Shakespeare, "thy name is woman."

Conversely, man may at times appear to be less adaptable than woman, but he is more consistent and follows a preconceived plan. Man is more secure and less possessive in his love relations. Women are less secure and are frequently overpossessive. Men are more realistic; women more idealistic. In speech, man says what he means; woman seldom does. Because of this, a man who tries to deal with his wife at the verbal level at which he would deal with another man is doomed to failure from the start. Man can laugh at himself; woman seldom does.

Woman does not take a comprehensive view of things, but is concerned with details. How frequently we hear the comment: "I'd rather work for a male boss; men don't pick up little things the way women do." Because of her less wholistic view, woman needs guidance in larger projects. Because of her narrower viewpoint, woman is biased in arguments; she sees only one side of the discussion. She is not only unable to accept opinions which differ from her own, but she tries to win over others to her own viewpoint. Led intuitively to her present opinion, she tries to impose her belief on others in the hope of increasing her own sense of conviction. Woman finds it difficult to deal in universal, theoretical, or abstruse concepts. Her interest is in the concrete, especially if it is living and particularly if it is human.

Woman is more emotionally labile and needs affection more than man.

She likes to have others depend upon her and attaches great importance to small things; she likes to be thanked. She is social-minded and seems to have a strong urge to confide in others, e.g., "I like men more than women. I feel you can trust men." She displays great curiosity in regard to the affairs of others. Women are more critical of other women than men are of each other. A woman is sorrowful over an unmarried male, whereas married men frequently congratulate him. Married men envy bachelors; married women pity spinsters.

> Man's love is of man's life
> A thing apart;
> 'Tis woman's whole existence.[9]

In these lines, Byron concisely states a notable aspect in the psychology of the woman. Love is the center of her life — to a woman, to love is as much a need as to be loved. She desires to be first in the affection of others. She likes others to be dependent upon her. To be loved is more important to a woman than it is to a man. The woman, therefore, needs a man more than he needs her. Because of at least an unconscious recognition of this fact, the woman is in constant need of reassurance. She needs to be told she is loved, a source of annoyance frequently to her husband whose attitude is: "I married you, didn't I?" Just because he does not always say so, a woman should not think that her husband does not love her. She should, however, if she can, make him say so. Because of her love, she is dedicated to her husband and children. Because of this dedication and her inability to take a comprehensive view of things, she feels a need of masculine guidance in the large issues of life. She cheerfully accepts this apparent subordination because she is devoted to her husband and to his creative work.

Father Stanford in his marriage preparation course adds these additional differences between the sexes:

Both men and women seek status. Men seek it through power; women through affection. Men become discouraged when they feel they are unimportant. Women crave affection. . . .
Men tend to be stern; women, tender. This can create problems in child-rearing.
Men face facts that are unsavory and annoying more readily than women.
Men want to lead; women, to be led.
Men tend to be soul-reticent (spiritually modest); women, bodily-reticent (physically modest).

---

[9] George Byron, *Don Juan*, Canto I, Stanza 194.

Men tend to be more content with the routine and colorless; women, with variety and the colorful.

Men tend to be more conceited; women, more jealous.[10]

Father Stanford then cites a good example of male-female difference. He points out the well-known situation in which man feels at home only when he is dressed like all the other men present. At a formal dinner, for example, all the men wear identical dinner jackets and ties, but each woman has on a different dress and "would die of embarrassment" if another woman present wore one which was similar to her own.

The Spiritual Aspects

But men and women are more than biological and psychological entities; they are also spiritual beings, in a true sense. The fall of mankind took place through the act of a man and woman, Adam and Eve; but our redemption also occurred through the co-operation of a man and woman, Christ and Mary. Perhaps it is because of the part she played in this redemption that woman excels man in her mystical and spiritual life. Perhaps it explains why she is more naturally religious than man.

Much of what we have said would seem to indicate that woman is more "earthy" than man. She is undoubtedly closer to nature, more sensual, more attuned to the universe because of the periodic nature of her bodily functions. In this respect, she may be said to be more carnal than man. But, on the contrary, she transcends man in her sensitivity to spiritual realities and values. She is quicker than man in interpreting the will of God. She is more quickly responsive in her religious role. She is more interested in unchanging spiritual values. Man studies the universe and tries to conquer it; woman is indifferent to these abstract and collective ideas but seeks only the God of love. Man deals with the finite, woman with the infinite. Men dedicate themselves to a cause; a woman dedicates herself to a person.

In this personal dedication, woman should not attempt to separate her role as wife and mother. One role does not take precedence over the other. She should think of herself as a wife-mother rather than a wife and a mother. No woman is completely happy until she has had a child. The primary expression of the love between a husband and wife is in the production of a new human being. What greater honor can there be

---

[10] Edward V. Stanford, O.S.A., *Preparing for Marriage* (Washington, D. C.: Archbishop Carroll High School, 1957), pp. 58–60.

than to co-operate with God in an act of creation. The beauty of the act of conception is too often overlooked. The co-operation of the parents with God in the formation of a new human being is not only a wonder of science; it is also a tribute to the majesty and power of God.

Thus we see that woman is a creature of many facets, each of which must be present in proper proportion if we are to have the "ideal woman" eulogized by poets and theologians. From a practical point of view, we should speak of woman as she is today. This "existent woman," in spite of her sublime mission, is frequently faced with false attitudes, frivolities, and perverse associations. Pope Pius XII commented on this:

> Woman, crown of the creation of which, in a certain sense, she represents the masterpiece . . . is still, despite a deceptive appearance of exaltation, frequently the object of disrespect and at times of positive and subtle contempt on the part of a pagan-like world.[11]

Although sensitive to moral values, the biological woman too frequently tries to measure up to and imitate the more sensuous image that man has of her. In doing so, she deserts her lofty status; she forsakes her trust. Throughout history, the moral status of woman has been an indicator of the rise or fall of a civilization, a sign of redemption or downfall. Woman represents a Mary or an Eve.

This is the way that nature and God designed the relations between the sexes. It does not mean that women are inferior to men, but it does mean that they are different. Man and woman are each designed for specific functions. When either steps out of his natural role, the order of nature is upset.

Scholastic Writers on Man's Leadership

Many of the scholastic writers have emphasized man's leadership and woman's dependence. Some of them went even further — Cornelius a Lapide, for example, taught that women were inferior to men.

The great Doctor of the Church, St. Thomas Aquinas, writes that the devil used Eve as a tool to "get to" Adam for two reasons: her weaker nature and the relationship she shared with Adam. Eve's sin, he states, brought punishment down upon woman on two counts. Because of it, she is united to man in the begetting of children and in the community of works pertaining to family life. God's wrathful pronouncement on

---

[11] Pope Pius XII, *Osservatore Romano*, October 15–16, 1956.

Eve — "Thou shalt be under thy husband's power" — defines the punishment she brought on woman as regards her role in family life. As St. Thomas so clearly explains, it is not the subjection of the woman to her husband that is her punishment, since even before the Fall man was head and governor of the woman, but it is her having to obey her husband's will *even against her own*.[12]

It seems clear, therefore, that divine injunction, nature, psychology, and the tradition of the scholastic writers are in complete agreement that man is designated as the head of the family.

Before I go any further, I want to make it quite clear that in no way are these arguments intended to indicate that woman is *inferior* to man. She is the equal of man — in intelligence, in opportunity, before God and before her fellow men, a fact of which she is perhaps too well aware in this "enlightened" age. In too many cases, today's modern woman is so preoccupied with the idea of her equality that she fails to see how this characteristic fits into the whole picture. She grasps for the straw and misses the real values. She may wear pants, but she loses sight of her esteemed position as the mother of man.

Father Has Abdicated His Position

Neither has the man of today escaped this myopic tendency. So far has he gone in accepting this whole-for-the-part concept of woman's independence, that to a large extent he has abdicated his position as head of the family. The children come to Father and ask for information, for a decision, for assistance. His reply is, "Ask your mother." It is here that most of the trouble arises. The child grows up thinking that the female sex is the strong sex — "After all, Father refers everything to Mother. All he knows is 'ask your mother.'" Mother is the one who knows and does things. If he constantly refers things to Mother he is telling the girls that they are expected to run things after they get married. The boys get the impression that the male role is a subordinate one. The father's retreat has left to the wife the active direction of the family and the raising of the children. Thus, the children are deprived of the paternal discipline which is so necessary for their complete development.

At the same time, this places the woman in a very unhappy position. It projects her into a situation which frustrates her natural need to be

---

[12] *Summa Theologica*, II–II, q. 165, Art. 2, reply Obj. 1; II–II, q. 164, Art. 2, Corpus.

dependent and passive. In assuming "head of the family" duties, she must assume the male qualities of independent action and aggressiveness. For this she is not prepared by nature.

It becomes a vicious circle.

Many factors have contributed to this unnatural change, such things as a change in the status of marriage, the emancipation of women, frustration of the woman's sexual needs, interference with the woman's maternal needs, failure of the husband as a leader, working wives, suburban living, and military necessity, among others.

As we all know, marriage is a sacrament which joins a man and woman in an indissoluble union. *This sacramental nature of marriage has long been under attack.* So now we see the absurd effects of this attack in the erroneous view held by many, that marriage is not a change of status, but merely an arrangement for companionship.

According to this line of reasoning, the husband is no longer head of the family; this position is shared by the husband and wife as equals, thus denying the traditional and biological fact that the father should be the head of the home. It leads, frequently, to the mother assuming matriarchal jurisdiction over the family.

The tendency toward *matriarchy* has already gone far in this country. In recent years, the majority of high school teachers have been women. This places the boy under the domination of women through high school and even into college. And when he gets a job his boss may be a woman. Because of this domination of women in both family and school life, a boy has no opportunity to learn independence of female domination. He accepts control and automatically obeys his female superiors.

The *emancipation of women*, long sought by militant suffragettes, has also made its inroads on family relationships. The freedom to participate equally with men, so eagerly sought by its advocates, now seems to have boomeranged, considering the dividends of happiness and sense of importance it was expected to pay. Perhaps one of its most easily observable results is the working wife. This may bring her equality of income but it cannot help having a detrimental effect upon the upbringing of the children.

Women have gained the right to wear pants, but they have lost much of their feminine appeal. The competition between the sexes socially and politically has greatly reduced the woman's feeling of security in her intersex relationships, including marriage.

It was not too long ago that almost every girl naturally assumed she would get married. Today's picture is quite the reverse. Many girls today feel that they will not get married unless they do something spectacular to attract and hold the attention of men. This has resulted in a greater exhibitionist tendency, absurd fashions, and lax morality. Virginity, once held in high esteem, is now sacrificed too frequently in payment for an evening's pleasure.

The so-called emancipation of women, it would seem, has brought more advantages to men than it has to women. As equals, women are often not treated with the honor and respect which was once theirs and which is due to them as potential mothers.

Frigidity as a Source of Frustration

We see another facet of this downward pattern in the fact that today a large percentage of American married women are frigid most of the time. Frigidity is not part of female nature, so this must indeed be a serious source of frustration. And its effects are all too obvious. Frustration leads to hostility. Hostility does not promote better marital relationships. This in spite of the fact that science itself has recognized only during the past century that the female has as much capacity for sexual arousal as the male. But in spite of this recognition, frigidity persists in large part due to the tradition perpetuated by so many mothers that women are primarily passive instruments for the sexual satisfaction of men. What girl can be expected to enjoy the intimacies of marriage if she is told by her mother that men are animals and that women in marriage have a duty to satisfy their animal needs?

Sex activity within the marital relationship is proper and good. Fortunately, much is being done to promote this idea by the premarriage instructions which are now being given. There should be more talk about the proper use of sex as contrasted to the immoralities connected with its illicit use.

Limitation of families is another factor that has given rise to frustration in women. No married woman can be completely happy if childless. Contraception is a grave source of psychological disturbances. No married couple can continually frustrate nature and not suffer. Feelings of guilt are a constant source of nagging frustration to these husbands and wives. As a result of efforts to limit families too stringently, unplanned pregnancy is considered a tragedy. Children of unplanned and unwanted pregnancies are frequently rejected and such rejected children do not have a fair chance in life. Their immature parents are unable or unwilling to give them the love and affection they need. Emotional security comes from love, nurtured in the early days of life by both parents.

Momism

In such parental rejection, frequently followed by overprotection, much of the trouble starts. The seeds of emotional insecurity are sown early under our matriarchal system. The father does not accept his proper role in the parent-child relationship. At the same time, the mother, not finding the strength she should in her husband, transfers the dependency she should have on him to her children. Then, when the time comes for the children to be liberated from the maternal nest so that they may lead an independent life, she may more or less consciously refuse to let them go. However, liberation of the children from parental control is a sacrifice which every mature parent must make, if the children are ever to be mature.

Tragic are the consequences when this liberation does not take place. The immature woman, because of her dependent needs, develops a neurotic attachment to her child which too often binds the child in psychic slavery. She ties her child to herself by a symbolically intact umbilical cord. This is the "silver cord" on which the immature mother plays a soothing tune, and like the Pied Piper of Hamlin lures her unsuspecting child to his emotional downfall.

Evenually, of course, the child must face the world alone. The realization that he cannot have everything he wants, when he wants it, comes to him as a sudden shock. Thus frustrated, he will find himself overwhelmed by feelings of self-depreciation mixed with hostility for the mother. This hostility is frequently transferred to his marriage partner. This same pattern, it might be added, is just as applicable to immature fathers, and produces the same tragic results.

Carried into the marital relationship, this continuing pattern of childish self-gratification leaves little room for the real purpose of marriage — the begetting and raising of children. The practice of contraception leaves a deficit which may only be recognized when the woman is past the child-bearing age. Then it is too late.

The Present Situation

Let us look again at what is causing this imbalance in the present-day marriage relationship, namely, the failure of the male to assume his responsibility as head of the family.

The modern concept seems to be that the father is responsible only for the financial support of the family. How many times have we heard: "Don't you think I'm doing enough? I'm supporting this family — what more do you want?" A great deal more, if he would know the truth about his parental responsibilities. The father has an obligation to contribute more than money to the upbringing of the children. His wife needs him to be dependent upon. How many wives today cry out: "If my husband would just help me make decisions. He always says, 'Do what you please; it's all right with me.' This is not enough. I need his help. I'm not capable of making these decisions." These wives do need help which the inadequate, dependent men of this generation are too frequently unwilling or unable to supply.

When a man abdicates his responsibility in the home, he forces his wife into a position of leadership for which she is not prepared. At the same time, the male children are deprived of paternal supervision. This too frequently results in weak, passive males inadequate to take over the leadership in the home because they never learn independence of female leadership. The female children also suffer because it is from the father that they learn about men. It is his example which sets the pattern for the girl's future response to men.

Just as surely as if she had administered a physically crippling injury at birth, the immature mother, with her "silver cord" domination, has produced a neurotic, frustrated male, incapable of thinking and acting for himself, much less for those under his care.

Obviously, this situation is not true of every family, or we would have complete chaos. Perhaps my own views are colored by the fact that I am a psychiatrist and work only with neurotic people. However, we need only to look at the rejection rate for psychiatric misfits by the draft boards of World War II to get an idea of the extent of this problem. Even in peacetime, the neuropsychiatric rejection rate is high. The military services, which have always prided themselves on the feeling that they made men out of boys, have yielded to "Mom's" pressure. The enlistee is coddled. Respect for authority is necessary for mature development. But

Mom's immature offspring, overprotected in their growing years, have contempt for law and order. This disdain does not lead to respect for the marriage contract.

If Dad's position has now descended to that of a figurehead, worse yet is the plight of the children if the mother also deserts the family. This leaves the children in the hands of hired help who cannot provide the type of tender loving care they need.

Perhaps such a mother thinks a few words over the telephone during the day, if her job allows, will suffice, or spending all day Sunday with the children will make up for her week's absence. But it will not make up to them for the regular routine of week nights when she returns home too tired and worn after the day's work to be bothered to give them the maternal love and affection they need, there and then.

The wife who is a homemaker and stays at home pays dividends not only in the greater maturity of her children, but in the saving to the family budget. Statistics prove that the average wage-earning wife contributes only about $1,000 a year to the family income, whereas the busy housewife contributes in saving at least twice that amount.

Suburban living is another factor, which few husbands and wives realize frustrates their parental role. They may think that moving from crowded city conditions to semirural areas is a real contribution to their children's welfare. It can, on the contrary, make the children psychological orphans. Longer traveling time to and from the job and school allows little time for the family at home. Late working conditions may prevent the father from seeing his children for days on end. Suburban life can indeed be a great disrupter of family life.

Is it any wonder then that under these frustrating conditions, so many people do not wish to mature emotionally? Add these to the group who are not allowed to grow up by immature parents. Over the years we will have an enormous number of husbands and wives included in this category. Here are the ingredients of a major, if not catastrophic disaster.

Pastoral Considerations

What, then, can pastors do about this serious situation? As a start, it would be best to estimate the extent of the problem. There are very few people who are completely mature. And the degree of emotional maturity that is necessary for a successful marriage has never been estimated.

If we are to break the vicious circle of immature parents, immature offspring, more immature parents, and so on unto the fourth and fifth generation, we must find out who those parents are. "Let's make mature parents out of immature parents" — this is easier said than done, but there must be a starting point. Immature parents must be given insight into their condition. Lack of insight keeps them from seeing themselves in a true light. How many of us would be willing to admit our own immaturity? On the other hand, how many of us would be willing to seek a diagnosis of our own immaturity. The pastor should keep these questions at hand if he wishes to determine quickly just how mature his parishioner is in his family relations:

1. Do you look to your children for sympathy when you do not feel well?
2. Do you have temper tantrums?
3. Do you seek your children's sympathy when either of you (husband or wife) have a serious quarrel?
4. Do you select your children's clothes without regard to their wishes?
5. Do you consider it your right to know the details of your family's private affairs?
6. Do you find yourself having greater sympathy for the child who most resembles you?
7. Do you usually blame your children's school troubles on the teachers?
8. Do you use tears to get your way with your child?
9. Do you criticize your husband or wife to the children in order to get their sympathy?
10. Do you think your nine-year-old child too young to spend a vacation away from home, even though under proper supervision?
11. Do you follow a just punishment you have administered to the child with sympathy or reward to him?
12. Do you worry excessively about your child possibly falling ill or getting hurt?
13. Do you tell your children how to handle their problems, rather than teach them the principles by which they can solve their own?
14. Do you give them the third degree when they return from an outing, or do you give them a chance to tell you about it?
15. Do you brag about how early you trained your children in toilet habits?

If the answer to any of these questions is "yes" it is an indication of immaturity and "smother love." The more "yeses," the greater the degree of the immaturity. If the parishioner is in the "no" category, then, to make his analysis a more thorough one, the pastor should check him against these qualities of *emotional maturity*. Being *emotionally mature* means:

1. Being comfortable with one's self.
2. Being free of unpleasant emotionally induced symptoms.

3. Being able to get along with others, both in society and in business.
4. Being able to accept authority.
5. Having the ability for independent thought and action.
6. Being tolerant.
7. Being patient.
8. Being adaptable.
9. Being pliable.
10. Being self-understanding.
11. Being dependable.
12. Being persevering in seeing a job through.
13. Being able to handle hostility in a socially acceptable way.
14. Being able to love someone other than oneself.
15. Being able to accept others as they are, with interest and without annoyance.

Such perfect maturity is seldom achieved, but the closer one comes to the fulfillment of these character qualities, the less likely is he to become a problem spouse or parent. Being mature means acting maturely. We must permit ourselves to grow up.

Next on the list of corrective treatment of this serious problem must be the father's resumption of his role as head of the family. He must be more than a provider. He must arrange to be at home to help in family planning, to help instruct the children in household duties, to partake in family recreation. He must participate in the discipline of the family, that of the boys, especially.

Stricter discipline of children is necessary. We know all too well that in many homes, and schools, discipline has become very lax. Self-expression is the rule of the day. Too much self-expression can mean self-destruction. I certainly do not advocate crushing the child's spirit but, for the good of the individual and of society, it is imperative that more respect for authority both at home and in the community be observed.

There is too much of a tendency today to find the easy way out. Because it is easier to acquiesce, parents enforce few rules. Consequently, they cover their own feeling of guilt at this laxity by protecting their children when they should be punished. When the police arrest juvenile offenders, the parents frequently are more offended with the police than they are with their own children. Many of today's immature parents are afraid of their aggressive offspring.

Good training consists of frequent small frustrations, yet how many parents are willing to frustrate their children? Boys especially need strong discipline if they are ever to achieve their proper masculine role in the family. I have been horrified to see suggestions made that boys be helped to unlearn masculine traditions "because this is no longer a frontier where masculine strength is necessary." Masculine strength should be more than physical. It should be spiritual, religious, and ethical; it should include knowledge, integrity, courage, and the ability to love and please others. It should enable the individual to accept his proper role in the community as a good citizen and as a good father.

Conclusion

In summary it may be said that woman is not equipped by nature to be the head of the family. The man must accept this responsibility for which he was designated by God and nature. If the father will resume his rightful role as head of the family constellation, the mother can then assume her proper place as his helpmate. The children can then receive their proper training in a happier atmosphere. This will allow the whole family to grow to a greater emotional maturity. In this way the vicious circle of immaturity can be eradicated.

Consider the words of St. Paul in his first Epistle to the Corinthians:

> When I was a child, I spoke as a child, I felt as a child, I thought as a child. Now that I have become a man, I have put away the things of a child.[13]

The pastor is in a strategic position to help his parishioners "put away the things of the child."

INTERESTING FACTS CONCERNING THE SEXES[14]

LIFE EXPECTANCY (1949–1951) IN CONTINENTAL UNITED STATES

	At birth	At age 25	At age 65
White males	66.3	44.9	12.8
Nonwhite	61.1	41.0	12.9
White females	72.0	49.8	15.0
Nonwhite	65.9	44.8	15.3

Each year over 200,000 more men than women die. There were 7,700,000

---

[13] 1 Cor. 1:13–11.
[14] These facts were assembled from a variety of sources, principally:
   a) Statistical Abstracts of the United States, U. S. Department of Commerce, Bureau of the Census (1959, U. S. Government Printing Office, Washington, D. C.).
   b) M.D. Magazine, March, 1958, pp. 53, 93.
   c) What's New, "Longer Live the Married," 1957, No. 200, pp. 7–9.
   d) Medical Science, "Longevity and the Sexes," Feb. 10, 1958, p. 170.

widows in 1956. This greater longevity of women is due to a decline in their mortality since 1900, not due to an increased mortality in men.

The stillbirth rate is 12 per cent higher for males, and for deaths which occur within 24 hours of birth the male rate is 30 per cent higher.

The death rate for diabetes mellitus is 35 per cent higher in women.

In 1955 the death rate for nonwhite males exceeded that for nonwhite females by only 30 per cent. Among whites this figure was 60 per cent. If present trends continue, by 1975 there will be 3,250,000 more women than men over age 65.

ACCIDENTS (100)
Male 33.1   Female 22.9

Fatal accidents cause more than four fifths of the excess male mortality in the age group 10–24, and nearly three fourths at ages 25–34 years. The male excess is greatest, 500 per cent between these ages, i.e., from years 20–24.

FIRST ADMISSIONS TO MENTAL HOSPITALS (1956)

	Male	Female
Total:	58,165	44,270
Psychotic Disorders	14,082	18,148
Schizophrenia	10,625	12,292
Personality Disorders	13,462	3,077

The discrepancy between the incidence of personality disorders in men and women is hard to explain.

HOMICIDES AND SUICIDES (1957)

	Male	Female
Homicide	5,739	1,902
Suicide	12,951	3,681

Women make suicidal attempts much more frequently than men, but with less success.

INDIVIDUALS CONFINED IN STATE AND FEDERAL PRISONS (JANUARY 1, 1957)
Male — 182,190   Female — 7,375

EDUCATIONAL FACTS (1957)
a) Cumulative level of schooling completed by age 25 or over (1957)

	Total population 25 years or over (1000)	Less than 8 yrs.	8 yrs.	4 yrs. h.s.	4 yrs. college
Male	46,208	23.2	74.6	38.8	9.4
Female	49,422	20.3	78.1	42.6	5.7

b) Faculty of Institutes of Higher Learning (1956)
Male   230,342
Female   68,568
c) Earned Degrees Conferred (1957)
Bachelor and 1st

	Professional degrees	2nd level degrees	Doctorate
Male	222,738	41,332	7,817
Female	117,609	20,623	939

Biological Factors

a) Chromosomes

A female cell contains two X chromosomes, the male carries an X and a Y; the Y chromosome is considerably smaller than the X. Quantitatively, the male possesses less chromatin material in every cell than the female. Presumably it has fewer genes.

The ovum is capable of being fertilized by either type of spermatozoon.

Sperm X plus ovum X — male offspring (XX)
Sperm Y plus ovum X — female offspring (XY)

b) Sex ratio

It is generally established throughout the world that the sex ratio at birth is between 105 and 106 males to 100 females.

c) Brain

Average weight of the male brain: 1360 gm.; female, 1250 gm.

d) Fat

After puberty, women have about 1.75 more fat than men.

e) Heart

Average weight in men: 312 gm.; in women: 255 gm. But the heart is 0.53 per cent of body weight in women and 0.43 per cent in men.

f) Temperature Range

Within a range of 82.4 and 87.8 degrees F., the nude male body can easily maintain a balance between heat loss and heat production, without sweating or shivering. For women the range is broader: 80.6 to 91.4 degrees F. In a cold environment, the heat loss of the female body is 10 per cent less than in men. Women thus have a more efficient thermoregulatory mechanism than men.[15]

---

[15] For full details see Journal of Obstetrics and Gynecology of the British Empire, February, 1958.

Men, Women, and Bath Temperature.

Few men can enter their wives' baths without scalding; women can endure, or indeed enjoy, water temperatures consistently five degrees or more higher than the male can tolerate. At the same time, in spite of a generally more adequate *panniculus adiposus,* women seem hypersensitive to cold. The female range of working temperatures, in fact, is permanently set at a higher level.[16]

g) *Hearing*

Women have a superior sense of hearing until age 65; after that it is equal in both sexes.[17]

Psychological Factors

a) A "skeptical psychoanalyst" says:

Men walk from the knee, while women walk from the hip. Men strike matches towards themselves, while women strike away. Men dress to look like other men, while women dress to look unique within the current fashion. Men look at their fingernails by cupping their palms and bending their fingers towards themselves, while women look at their nails by straightening their fingers palms outward. Men spit flecks of tobacco off their tongues; women pick them off. Men nag their wives for what they do. Women nag their husbands for what they don't do.[18]

b) Mark Twain in *Huckleberry Finn* wrote of two feminine characteristics in an instance which is probably well known to most readers. The hero was masquerading as a girl when put to a test by a suspicious woman. She threw a ball at him and in attempting to catch it Huckleberry put his knees together, a thing which no girl accustomed to skirts should do. She would throw her knees apart. The second test to which Huckleberry was subjected was that of threading a needle. The author observed that everyone knows that a girl pushes the thread through the eye of the needle, while a boy holds the thread steady and attempts to push the needle eye onto the thread.[19]

Intellectual Differences

Louis I. Dublin, statistician of the Metropolitan Life Insurance Company, after making a study of the subject had this to say:

Age for age, boys and girls average the same intelligence potential. However, test-makers have noted that in certain subjects girls excel, in

---

[16] Lancet, 2:1226 (1957).

[17] *M.D. Magazine,* March, 1958, p. 53.

[18] Kenneth M. Colby, *A Skeptical Psychoanalyst* (New York: Ronald Press, 1958), quoted by *Current Medical Digest,* Aug., 1959, p. 63.

[19] Mark Twain (Samuel Clemens), *Huckleberry Finn* (New York: Dodd, Mead).

others boys are ahead. The favored feminine areas, in preschool children, are color-matching, paper-folding, buttoning, tying bows; in grade school they are reading and language. Boys are better in sense of direction, in anything mechanical, in arithmetic, nature study; later, in history and the sciences. Though girls and boys come out about even in I.Q. tests, their skills and potentials are still not the same. Here, as elsewhere, the two sexes are not equal but equivalent; neither is superior or inferior; they are just different.[20]

In tests of *manual dexterity* women are superior. According to J. P. Guilford,[21] these differences are as follows:

Males excel in tests of:
1. Spatial aptitudes
2. Mechanical aptitude
3. Intelligence
4. Mechanical comprehension
5. Numerical reasoning
6. Arithmetic reasoning
7. Ingenuity

Females usually begin to talk earlier and mature socially and sexually at an earlier age.

In tests of the following women excel:
1. Dexterity
2. Speed and accuracy of computation
3. Clerical aptitude
4. Speed and accuracy of perceiving details
5. Verbal or linguistic ability
6. Speed of reading
7. Naming opposites
8. Analogies
9. Sentence completion
10. Disarranged sentences
11. Learning another language
12. Code learning
13. Memory

Girls of preschool age have a larger vocabulary than boys. Speech disorders such as stuttering disabilities are less frequent in girls. Females also excel in scholastic achievement and have fewer behavior problems.

Wives

There are more wives than ever in the United States. In 1956 there were approximately 40 million, i.e., two thirds of all women over thirteen years of age.

Of women between ages 25 and 34 years, 87 per cent are married.

---

[20] Dublin, op. cit., p. 58.
[21] J. P. Guilford, *Fields of Psychology* (New York: Van Nostrand Co., Inc., 1950), p. 390.

In nine out of ten households husbands and wives live together. Only 2.8 per cent were separated because of marital discord.

In four fifths of families in which the wife is 25 to 34 years of age there is at least one child.

In fifty-six per cent of all households there are children under eighteen years of age.

There are over a third of a million children under eighteen in families in which the wife is 65 years of age or older.

In about one family in four both husband and wife work. The wife is the sole support in only 1.2 per cent of families.[22]

Pregnancy

Dr. Carrel in *Man the Unknown* stated:

> Females, at any rate among mammals, seem only to attain their full development after one or more pregnancies. Women who have no children are not so well balanced and become more nervous than the others. In short, the presence of the fetus, whose tissues greatly differ from hers because they are young and are, in part, those of her husband, acts profoundly on the woman. The importance to her of the generative function has not been sufficiently recognized. Such function is indispensable to her optimum development. It is, therefore, absurd to turn women against maternity.[23]

Father Cervantes concluded:

> All of our evidence seems to lead to the uniform conclusion: Religiously, women are superior to men.[24]

A *feminine ending* in poetry is an extra unaccented syllable at the end of a line of verse, e.g., in lines 1 and 3 of the following:

> With rue my heart is laden
> For golden friends I had,
> For many a rose-lipt maiden
> And many a light-foot lad.[25]

Myths

According to *M.D. Magazine,*

> Superstitions concerning menstruation persist to this day in many parts of the world. Menstruating women are not allowed to work in some French

---

[22] "The American Wife," *Metropolitan Life Insurance Company Statistical Bulletin*, 36:1 (October), 1955.

[23] Carrel, *Man the Unknown*, quoted by Lucius F. Cervantes, *And God Made Man and Woman* (Chicago: Henry Regnery Co., 1959), pp. 68–69.

[24] Lucius F. Cervantes, *op. cit.*, p. 140.

[25] A. E. Housman, *Schropshire Lad*, Stanza 1.

flower-processing plants; in some rural districts they are believed to have the power of "measling" meat; innumerable cases are reported of menses breaking the strings of cellos and harps, shattering glasses, stopping clocks. To this day the belief persists among countless women that the menstrual flow is the elimination of "bad blood" and that the whole process is shameful and unclean.[26]

Womanhood After Fifty

Many misconceptions and false fears surround the menopause. From the mystic past come beliefs that women are entitled to be nervous or unstable, and that they often lose their minds at this time in life; that there is a loss of sex interest; that a menopausal pregnancy will result in a feeble-minded youngster or a genius; that heavy and irregular bleeding naturally accompany the climacteric period; and that a gain in weight is inevitable with middle age. There is a faint background of truth in most superstitions, but fortunately none of the above fears is founded on firm facts. Fear-provoking attitudes toward the menopause are decreasing with freer, more intelligent understanding of this phase in the life cycle.[27]

Crime

Some 84 per cent of all crimes of violence committed in Paris by women were during the premenstrual and early menstrual phases of the cycle. In a clinical study at a large woman's prison in the United States, 62 per cent of the unpremeditated crimes of violence were committed during the premenstrual week and 17 per cent during menstruation. Commented one clinician: "From what some of my patients tell me (both the ladies and their husbands) I am surprised that the incidence of crimes of violence is not even greater in the premenstrual period."[28]

---

[26] M.D. Medical News Magazine, loc. cit., pp. 91–92.

[27] John Parks, M.D., "Womanhood After Fifty," Medical Arts and Sciences, Second Quarter, 1959, p. 69.

[28] M.D. Medical News Magazine, loc. cit.

PART IV

THE PASTOR AND MENTAL ILLNESS

Facts About Mental Illness*

1. It is estimated that about 17,000,000 Americans (1 in every 10) are suffering from a mental or emotional disorder requiring psychiatric treatment.

2. One out of 10 children born each year will sometime during his life need to go to a mental hospital. (This estimate of expectancy is based on current rates of hospitalization and actuarial tables.)

3. On any one day of the year, there are about 750,000 patients in our mental institutions. This is as many as in all other hospitals combined.

4. More than 300,000 people will be admitted for the first time to a mental hospital this year. In addition, about 125,000 will return this year to a mental hospital as re-admissions. Thus, a total of about 425,000 patients will be admitted to our mental hospitals this year.

5. Over 1,000,000 patients are treated in the course of a year in our mental hospitals. In addition, it is estimated that 1,500,000 adults and children are seen each year in psychiatric clinics and by private psychiatrists.

6. Each year, about 23% of all new admissions to state mental hospitals are patients with schizophrenia. Because these patients are relatively young and often remain in mental hospitals for long periods, they make up half of the mental hospital population.

7. Senile psychosis and cerebral arteriosclerosis (psychoses of old age) account for about 25% of all new patients admitted each year.

8. About 6% of new admissions are patients with involutional psychosis; about 5% with manic-depressive psychosis; and about 13.7% with severe mental conditions brought on by alcoholism.

9. Personality disorders account for about 15% of new admissions and psychoneuroses make up almost 6% of our public hospital's new patients.

* National Association for Mental Health, 10 Columbus Circle, New York 19, N.Y.

CHAPTER XIV

THE PASTOR AND MENTAL HEALTH

About two years ago, an article on the subject of "Psychiatry and Religion" in the *Ladies Home Journal* mentioned the fact that there was a guild of Catholic psychiatrists. In response to this simple statement of fact, there arrived in the guild headquarters over 1100 letters, most of which expressed the same thought — "How can there be such a guild? We did not know that a Catholic could go to a psychiatrist, much less be one!" I wish I could say that this response was a surprise. Unfortunately, it was not. It was, however, a mass demonstration of an all too obvious fact; the fact that many individuals, even among university graduates, have a distorted view of psychiatry, especially in its relations with religion and morality. It is not unfair to say that there has been and perhaps still is a real feeling of prejudice on the part of many people toward psychiatry and toward psychiatrists, and to a lesser extent toward psychologists. How much of this is a defense reaction is hard to say. By rejecting psychiatry, an individual may be unconsciously putting aside his own conflicts.

Jokes about psychiatry are numerous. This may also be a defense. Some wag described psychiatry as: "Observation of the Id by the Odd." And people, dealing with some psychiatrists, conclude that mental disease must be contagious: it seems to brush off the patient and catch on the doctor. Others, again, are convinced that the subject is an immoral one: psychiatrists have altogether too much to say about sex.

Distorted views on the role of the psychiatrist are not new. This is unfortunate because, as long as such opinions persist, they will deter the psychically disturbed patient from seeking and obtaining help to get relief from needless suffering.

Historically, this feeling, though irrational, is not hard to understand. We can say, broadly, that too many persons have false notions about the origin and constitution of mental disorders. It is too frequently asserted (and often by people who should know better) that psychiatric disorders are the result of sin or culpable weakness on the part of the patient.

This notion is somewhat reminiscent of those friends in the Book of Job who explained to the hero of that story that his evils and infirmities resulted from a transgression of his own, which he had forgotten but which was fresh in the mind of God. It is far from true that in every case the patient is directly responsible for his psychiatric illness. If anything, the contrary is true, at least in regard to the development of symptoms. But until we can eradicate that widespread belief, the emotionally disturbed patient will be reluctant to let anyone know that he is in need of psychiatric aid.

Mental Illness Once Considered Subject of Theology

According to Zilboorg, the acceptance of psychiatry was hindered because it dealt with a subject which many authors considered as the sole domain of theology.[1] After a review of the historical development of psychiatry, however, he concluded: "It would . . . be a mistake indeed to assume the view that it was the church and theology which militated against the scientific development of psychology; it was man and man alone who was responsible."[2] Moreover, there was a reluctance on the part of some philosophers to admit defective activities in the mind, since it was believed that what was mental was of the *strictly* spiritual nature of man. Descartes, for example, states this in the following:

> And, therefore, merely because I know with certitude that I exist, and because, in the meantime, I do not observe that aught necessarily belongs to my nature beyond my being a thinking thing, I rightly conclude that my essence is only in my being a thinking thing (or a substance whose whole essence or nature is merely thinking). And although I may, or rather, as I will shortly say, although I certainly do possess a body with which I am very closely conjoined; nevertheless, because, on the one hand, I have a clear and distinct idea of myself, in as far as I am only a thinking and unextended thing, and as on the other hand, I possess a distinct idea of body, in as far as it is only an extended and unthinking thing, it is certain that I (that is, my mind, by which I am what I am) is entirely and truly distinct from my body, and may exist without it.[3]

[1] Gregory Zilboorg, M.D., A History of Medical Psychology (New York: W. W. Norton & Company, 1941), pp. 128, 228, 294, 467, 508.

[2] Ibid., p. 247.

[3] René Descartes, The Method, Meditations and Philosophy of Descartes, trans. John Veitch (New York: Tudor Publishing Co., 1901), pp. 269–270.

Today we realize that the mental sphere includes more than will and intellect. It includes other elements as well. The term "mental" as used in this frame of reference refers to all the psychic functions of a human being. That is to say, it refers to those of intellect, will, external senses, internal senses, and emotions. Since certain mental illnesses may at times reveal highly distorted judgments, and since the judgment act is essentially that of the intellect, there was argument among some writers that since the intellect was capable of operating apart from the matter principle, then the intellectual power itself could not be directly involved in an illness subject to treatment by a physician because a physician was capable only of curing bodily defects.

Furthermore it seemed that many mental illnesses were of preternatural origin because, so far as laymen were concerned, there did not seem to be any kind of physical change in the mentally ill person. He seemed to be "taken over" by some other influence.

Let me answer this objection. The basic reason given by the psychologist whose interest is primarily in the philosophical aspects of psychology for rejecting the psychogenic origin of mental disorders is that the soul is an immaterial entity and that there can be no defect in a spiritual being. To some, the presence of a neurosis seems to indicate that some power or another of the soul has been actually destroyed. But a power of the soul cannot be *destroyed*, if by that we mean *disintegrated* (as the tissue in the body can disintegrate). The power itself continues to exist, but it is misdirected. It may be conditioned by bad habits to operate too readily toward its own goal without regard for the other operations of the human person (for example, excessive eating, or excessive use of the sex function, or readiness to anger, etc.). On the other hand, the power may be conditioned by habit and circumstances so that it does not operate as readily as it should (for example, when the power of will is not actuated to exercise its control over other functions).

The potentiality for operation remains in the powers of the soul of the neurotic or psychotic. But the powers of the soul are not integrated so that they accord with the total good of the whole human person.

Mental Illness and Preternatural Influences

Zilboorg also states that the acceptance of psychiatry was delayed due to the old and deeply rooted belief that disorders of the mind were the manifestation of preternatural influences.[4] This notion had to be destroyed before mental aberrations could be studied as problems of natural things. Another reason for delay came from medicine itself. Medicine had long been shackled by a tradition that all disease was organic in origin. This belief had arisen because of the way in which medicine developed as a healing art. The physical phase originated when patients realized that they were sick and went to get help. Medicine thus came to be out of a demand for help on the part of the patient. But patients with psychogenic illness frequently do not recognize it as an illness. In these cases, more often than not, it was the doctor who had to go seek out the patient. Another reason why psychiatry has not received a more cordial welcome in recent years is probably because the most significant of all developments in the field was the work of an atheist who introjected his materialistic philosophy to support his psychological findings. This was Sigmund Freud, of whom more will be said later. There is still prevalent the uneasy suspicion that all psychiatrists are materialistic psychoanalysts, and that anything even remotely connected with psychoanalysis is atheistic.

These conclusions are more easily accepted if we look briefly at the history of medical psychology and see the vicissitudes suffered by the mentally ill and those who have tried to help them. Our survey, because of limitation of space, must be brief. But even a brief look is sufficient to bring home the conviction that psychiatry was, until recently, the stepchild of medicine.

From even the earliest days, the mentally ill were looked upon as witches. The Code of Hammurabi mentions them and declares that the most severe punishments should be meted out to them. No attempt was made to determine the causes of "madness." "Mad people" as a whole were simply mad, they reasoned, and they did disgusting things. No attempt whatever was made to consider whether the misfortune might be an illness.

Diabolical Possession

Many of those who were mentally ill were considered by the average citizen as having some kind of diabolic possession. Some humanitarians objected to the torments inflicted upon the mentally ill and the neurotic,

---

[4] *Ibid.*, pp. 24, 153, 155, 212.

but the practice continued. A belief in witchcraft was rampant. And witchcraft was not an easy problem to solve. In view of the fact that possession was, and still is, a possibility, it had to be considered. Its occurrences are, and were, however, more rare actually than the popular mind held them to be. As Father Herbert Thurston says:

> The question of the reality of witchcraft is not one upon which it is easy to pass a confident judgment. In the face of Holy Scripture and the teaching of the Fathers and Theologians, the abstract possibility of a pact with the devil and of a diabolical interference in human affairs can hardly be denied, but no one can read the literature on the subject without realizing the awful cruelties to which this belief led and without being convinced that in 99 cases out of 100, the allegations rested upon pure delusion. The most bewildering circumstance is the fact that in a large number of witch persecutions the confession of the victims, often involving all kinds of satanistic horrors, have been made spontaneously and apparently without threat or fear of torture. Also the full confession of guilt seems constantly to have been confirmed on the scaffold when the poor sufferer had nothing to gain or lose by the confession.[5]

I think we have the answer to Father Thurston's last observations. Such delusional confessions of guilt are not unusual in schizophrenic patients. Even today they state that they are possessed by the devil and demand that they be punished, even killed, because of their imagined transgressions.

Many historical misconceptions continue into the present and have been revived in recent years. There is no real conflict between psychiatry as a science and true religion.

Prejudice and Psychiatry

Psychiatry has been under suspicion for too long. This cloud should be lifted. It would be lifted if physicians and laymen alike would put aside the false notion derived from centuries past that the psychiatrist is a new-fashioned witch doctor, who in a mysterious and frequently immoral way has the ability to cure mental illness by some occult power. Such a description sounds silly, but it is not too farfetched as may be seen from comments and ideas expressed both by physicians and patients.

Everyone should realize that there is nothing mysterious about psychiatry; that although it still has a lot to learn, it has available technics which are frequently successful, if given enough time. They must also realize that psychiatry as such does not recommend any immorality,

---

[5] *Catholic Encyclopedia* (New York: The Encyclopedia Press, Inc., 1914).

although certain psychiatrists may. Patients should be warned against such psychiatrists.

Prejudice arises from ignorance. The clear light of day brightens the dark corners and takes away the frightening shadows. Knowledge of the facts makes it clear that psychiatry is a science, not merely an art. Do not misunderstand me. There have been problems. Some psychiatrists are atheists. They act and believe whatever atheists believe. Other psychiatrists are immoral and act as one would expect immoral people to act. But most psychiatrists are not atheists, and most psychiatrists are not immoral. Difficulty arises in psychiatric practice because, although in general the religious belief or moral conduct of a scientist does not alter the science of which he is a professor, this is unfortunately not true in psychiatry. An immoral mathematician can correctly add a column of figures and an atheist would get the same result. So would a believer. In psychiatry, however, which is still somewhat of an art, treatment is on an individual basis. The psychiatrist, in order to treat an individual successfully, must treat the whole person, not just one facet of the personality. He must consider all factors uniting to form the total individual — body, soul, beliefs, ideals, religious convictions, etc. For this reason, a thorough knowledge of religion and philosophy is a necessary part of a psychiatrist's education, for the study of medicine alone will not give him the background to understand the complete individual effectively. The beliefs of the psychiatrist frequently "rub off" on the patient. It is for this reason that it would be better to refer a patient to a competent psychiatrist of another faith than to refer him to an equally competent psychiatrist of the same faith who, however, is poorly oriented in his religion.

Knowledge of the true facts about psychiatry would, I believe, clarify most of the difficulties that the clergyman has in regard to this subject. At the risk of being offensively elementary, I would like to start with some definitions because I feel that simplicity is desirable. If we get the elementary facts correct it will avoid confusion later.

Definitions

Psychiatry may be defined as that branch of medical science which treats of the tendencies, development, characteristics, care, and cure of people afflicted with mental disorders.

A *psychiatrist* is a *doctor* of *medicine* who specializes in the diagnosis, prevention, and treatment of mental disorders.

Alexander defines *psychoanalysis* in these terms:

> Psychoanalysis, in common usage, is both a practice and a theory; it is concerned with techniques and with principles. From the microscopic study of many individuals under psychoanalytic treatment, a theory of personality development has been devised — a theory which, as in every science, is constantly changing with new discoveries. These principles of the dynamics of personality have wide application. They are not limited to the practice of psychoanalysis, nor yet to the wider field of psychotherapy in general. They extend to many fields, to every sphere of activity in which the human being is an object of study.[6]

As a means of therapy, psychoanalysis aims at the redistribution of psychic energy and goes much farther in its scope than the usual short-term psychotherapy. It aims at eliciting unconscious conflicts and interpreting these to the patient. The method of psychoanalysis includes the use of free association, dream interpretation, and the manipulation of the transference phenomenon. As a general rule, the therapist remains passive throughout the therapy and interprets the findings at appropriate intervals.

The psychoanalyst of today generally employs techniques from one or more of the following schools of thought or disciplines designed for analysis of the psyche: (1) psychoanalysis (Freud), (2) analytical psychology (Jung), (3) psychobiology (Meyer), and (4) individual psychology (Adler). Each school, however, has its own strict adherents.

The Difference Between a Psychiatrist and a Psychoanalyst

One very important thing to know about a psychoanalyst is that some of those who practice psychoanalysis are not doctors of medicine. In the usual meaning of the term, a psychoanalyst is a psychiatrist who analyzes, that is, resolves a whole into its parts. He differs from the average eclectic psychiatrist in the microscopic nature of his dissection and the length of time required for his analysis.

While the term *psychoanalyst* has its generic meaning, today it usually refers to those who adhere to the psychoanalytic formulations of Freud. Most nonanalytic psychiatrists are eclectic; i.e., in their therapy they would select their methods of treatment from what they considered the

---

[6] Franz Alexander, M.D., and Thomas Y. French, M.D., *Psychoanalytic Therapy* (New York: Ronald Press Co., 1946), p. 4.

best from all other fields of psychiatry. A psychoanalyst, however, is not so free. He obviously may choose as he wishes but, as I have noted above, most analysts follow a particular school of thought. In many cases, this adherence is so rigid that it becomes cultlike.

Most psychiatrically ill patients have no need for psychoanalysis. This is a specialized form of psychotherapy suited to only certain types of disorders. The choice of patients for this treatment is too complicated to be discussed here and should be left to specialists.

There are in the United States about 12,000 qualified psychiatrists. Of these, a few over 1000 are qualified psychoanalysts.

Psychosomatic medicine is that branch of medicine which studies somatic symptoms which occur because of, and as a conversion manifestation of, emotional and mental disturbances.

Emotional disturbances may enter the clinical picture in three ways: (1) as the whole cause of the illness, (2) as an emotional response to the presence of organic disease, and (3) as a fear of the consequences of serious physical disease. The first type is most representative of the psychosomatic group of disorders.

Psychotherapist is a term which designates an individual who gives psychotherapy. Anyone can do this: the butcher, the baker, the candlestick maker. *Psychotherapy* is the art of treating mental diseases or disorders. It is any measure, mental or physical, that favorably influences the mind or psyche. Usually, however, the term is applied to measures that are associated with the amelioration or removal of abnormal constituents of the mind.[7]

This is a very loose term and it would be well to inquire more deeply into the qualifications of those who proclaim themselves merely as psychotherapists.

A *clinical psychologist* is one who applies psychological data and techniques to the diagnosis and treatment of mental and emotional maladjustments. His procedures may be carried on either in private practice or (as is more usual) in clinics or mental hospitals. The clinical psychologist is not a doctor of medicine. Those fully qualified have a doctor of philosophy degree. The training of a psychologist varies widely, but it usually includes applied psychology, methods of testing, and some supervised clinical experience. The psychologist deals with a wide variety of

---

[7] Leland E. Hinsie, M.D., and Jacob Shatzky, Ph.D., *Psychiatric Dictionary* (New York: Oxford University Press, 1953), p. 450.

problems: vocational guidance, counseling on personal and marital affairs, speech defects, school maladjustment or failure, child behavior, and many others. Since he has no training in the diagnosis and treatment of disease and no medical training, he should work only under the supervision of a psychiatrist when treating emotional and mental disorders.[8]

The Difference Between a Psychiatrist and a Psychologist

The basic difference is that the psychiatrist is a doctor of medicine and the psychologist is not. The psychologist, not being a doctor of medicine, should limit himself to the areas of his own competence, which do not include the diagnosis and treatment of disease. There are many unqualified individuals who call themselves psychologists. The best evidence of qualification is membership in the *American Psychological Association*. There may be qualified psychologists who do not belong to this group, but the burden of proof is on them.

In considering the psychiatrist, his most important and tangible evidences of qualification is membership in the *American Psychiatric Association*, and the fact that he is a diplomate in Psychiatry of the American Board of Neurology and Psychiatry.[9]

Mistaken Notions

There are two mistaken notions concerning the ministrations of the Catholic priest and of the psychiatrist. One of these centers about the idea that confession, being a cure for the soul, must also restore full

---

[8] James E. Royce, S.J., *Personality and Mental Health* (Milwaukee: The Bruce Publishing Co., 1955), p. 289.

[9] American Board of Neurology and Psychiatry, Inc.:
Executive Secretary
David Boyd, Jr., M.D.
102–110 2nd Avenue, S.W.
Rochester, Minn.
There are approximately 12,000 members of the American Psychiatric Association, of whom 6,815 are certified as specialists by the American Board.
The American Catholic Psychological Association:
Executive Secretary
Rev. William C. Bier, S.J.
Fordham University
New York, N. Y.
The American Psychological Association, 18,215 members:
Executive Secretary
John G. Darley, Ph.D.
1333 16th Street, N.W.
Washington 6, D. C.

mental health; the other affirms that a return to mental health also assures a return to spiritual well-being. Neither of these ideas is correct. The priest, in restoring spiritual health, may also, in a secondary or accidental manner, assist in restoring bodily or mental well-being. This, however, is not his principal purpose. The soul in the state of sin is not necessarily mentally ill. Confession is not a substitute for psychotherapy; neurotic guilt is not real guilt. Guilt, as it is dealt with by the priest in confession, refers to objective reality. It is guilt that arises from an actual transgression of the moral code. The psychiatrist, however, is concerned only with feelings of guilt which are delusional and distorted and not based in objective reality. The guilt feelings which are dealt with in psychopathology may not be experienced by the individual as guilt at all, but may manifest themselves as a feeling of insecurity or as overt anxiety. The depressed person accuses himself of all sorts of sins which he has not committed but for which he feels a tremendous amount of guilt. A great gulf, therefore, exists between guilt based on actual deeds and feelings of guilt based on unconscious conflicts. It is the latter, the neurotic sense of guilt, with which psychiatry is concerned.

As the ministrations of the priest do not have for their prime purpose the restoration of mental health, so the treatment given by the psychiatrist does not, of itself, restore the soul to spiritual well-being.

As in every successful undertaking the individual must have a suitable standard or goal toward which to strive, so also the psychiatrist must have an ideal which he wishes to see fulfilled in his patient at the culmination of treatment. His concept of the human person will determine the type of individual he wishes his patient to become. It is most important, therefore, that the ideal which he wishes his patient to achieve be in accord with the correct concept of life and its purpose. These concepts cannot be derived from psychiatry alone, however. They must be taken from religion, philosophy, and ethics, for it is through the latter that the meaning of life and its purpose can be explained. The words, "I am the Way, and the Truth, and the Life," provide a clear ideal for both clergyman and psychiatrist to follow.

We are constantly confronted with the statement of psychiatrists that they are not concerned with value judgments. Scientific facts, it is true, are neither moral nor immoral — they are amoral, but a scientist approaching a problem is concerned with morality in at least three ways:

1. The purpose of the study,

2. The methods to be employed in the study,

3. The use to which the results are to be put.

A psychiatrist, therefore, cannot avoid making some type of moral judgment. He is not, however, required to point out to his patient the immoral nature of his behavior. Still he may not condone it. Father White speaks clearly on this point:

> It does therefore seem to me unscientific to contend that, in the name of science, psychotherapy can and should disregard religious and moral issues. Even from the purely therapeutic standpoint it seems that a patient's religion and moral principles cannot be regarded by the practitioner as a tabu, a constant which can remain unchanged throughout the process. And I would further venture to contend that the psychotherapist who supposes otherwise is of all the most to be regarded with suspicion, for he is of all the most unconscious of his responsibilities, of the principal factors and of the inevitable outcome of any effective treatment he may give. Moreover, an analyst who is so minded will be unaware of, and so incapable of transforming, the religious and moral transferences which the patient will be all the more likely to project upon him.[10]

The following comments of Father O'Doherty, which were made in the course of his remarks before a Psychiatric Congress in Dublin, Ireland, are apropos:

> One must never forget that psychiatry is a branch of medicine, using natural means to cure natural ills. This is in no sense the nature of religion. Both are concerned with human betterment, but in different, sometimes complementary but not in opposed ways. Should it ever appear to a psychiatrist that he might achieve the desirable result of his patient's return to mental health through some means which conflicted with his patient's religious belief or moral code, he would do well to remember the awful warning of our Divine Lord to those who scandalize His little ones; and the patient would do well to remember the question: "What doth it profit a man to gain the whole world, and suffer the loss of his own soul?" For the universal ethical principle holds in psychiatry, as everywhere else: It is never lawful to use an intrinsically unlawful means to attain a result however desirable it may appear. I should like to point out at once, however, that there is nothing wrong, nothing immoral, in the recognized techniques of good therapists: analysis, hypnosis, narco-therapy, shock treatment, leucotomy, and so on. But again because these things are not understood as they ought to be, one finds a certain malaise in the popular mind concerning them.[11]

---

[10] Rev. Victor White, God and the Unconscious (Chicago: H. Regnery, 1953), p. 146.

[11] Rev. Eamonn O'Doherty, "Religion and Psychiatry," The Catholic Medical Quarterly, Vol. III (XXI), No. 3, April, 1950.

Summary

An attempt has been made in this chapter to establish more clearly some of the differences which have arisen between some clergymen and some psychiatrists and psychologists. Obviously, this treatment is not exhaustive; it merely high-lights some of the issues. The next chapter will attempt to compare the individual clergyman with the individual psychiatrist. This is of special importance in pastoral work when, because of overlapping areas of interest, there must be a close co-operation between the pastor and the psychiatrist or psychologist.

CHAPTER XV

RELATIONSHIP OF THE PASTOR AND
THE PSYCHIATRIST*

In November of 1956, Dr. Finley Gayle, Jr., in his presidential address to the annual meeting of the American Psychiatric Association in Chicago said:

> Regardless of our own individual religious or non-religious commitments or attitudes, as psychiatrists we need to be accepting of our patients' religious situation as of any other significant area in their lives.[1]

These comments were undoubtedly prompted by his recognition of the fact that the relationship of religion to psychiatry, although at present quite accepting, was not always one of friendly co-operation. It was also recognition that over the years religion and psychiatry have attained a state of peaceful coexistence. In concluding his talk Dr. Gayle stated that the time had come for clergymen and psychiatrists to move closer together in a confident spirit of positive mutual co-operation. In his own words:

> It is my conviction that we are ready to move gradually from a status of peaceful coexistence to one of active cooperation.

In so speaking Dr. Gayle showed clearly that in his opinion there is no conflict between psychiatry as such and religion as such. He recognized that there has been conflict between some psychiatrists and some religious leaders. He exhorted psychiatrists to "gain an understanding of religious functioning in both its healthy and pathological manifestations." Espe-

---

* This section was prepared with the assistance of Rev. Ramon A. di Nardo, to be read to the section on "Religion and Psychiatry" of the American Psychiatric Association at its annual meeting in San Francisco, May, 1958. What is said here about the pastor and the psychiatrist applies as well to the pastor and the clinical psychologist.

[1] R. Finley Gayle, Jr., M.D., "Conflict and Cooperation Between Psychiatry and Religion," reprint from *Pastoral Psychology*, Nov., 1956.

cially since the time of Freud, psychiatry and religion, in certain areas, have gone through stages of hostile rejection, cold indifference, and finally cautious acceptance. Some psychiatrists, it is true, accepted religion as a psychological fact of some indeterminate significance to the patient. In the process of moving closer together, it becomes necessary for each discipline to take a positive stand on the question of the other and its significance, not only in psychotherapy, but in human living. Mental suffering often brings the patient face to face with basic issues that have a religious involvement.

Relationship of Pastor and Psychiatrist

It is in this area where the mental illness takes on a religious coloring that the roles of the clergyman and psychiatrist especially need clarification. Co-operation between the two professions requires of each a proper understanding of the role the other must play in the care of the patient. The clergyman must realize that where religion is helpless, "because the twisted soul is a defective transmitter of the Divine," psychiatry can help heal it, integrate it, release it "to participate in religious experience." The psychiatrist too must recognize that the clergyman has a legitimate field of responsibility in the care of the mentally ill. Before attempting to assign a role to each discipline the basic training of each should be considered.

Training of Clergyman and Psychiatrist Differ

Clergymen and psychiatrists have so much of their training in similar areas that they should find it easy and satisfying to work together. Each, however, has such obvious gaps in his training that co-operation is in many cases a necessity if the best results for the patient are to be obtained. Both are possessors of an incomplete knowledge of one of God's infinite mysteries, that of the human personality. Both have a broad and intelligent view of that personality, but from different vantage points.

The clergyman sees in a person a supernaturalized human nature with faculties, organs, and powers directed toward the Infinite. These, he recognizes, are indeed, subject to natural laws, but they also involve a higher life of grace. He knows the nature of man in terms of ultimate causes. He knows it in terms of why it exists, who made it, what is its ultimate end. The clergyman, like the physiologist, views the organs of the body as parts of an organic whole; and, like the psychiatrist, he goes further to view the psychic structure of the human person. The clergyman goes even more deeply — he sees the human person as organized by a more fundamental principle which he calls the human soul. This soul is not of course directed merely to natural ends.

The clergyman has at his hand the pragmatic and empirical knowledge gained by the church in years of directing the human personality. From his ministry and with the grace of ordination he knows the human emotions in a way that few others do. Yet with all this, his knowledge of the person is incomplete. The wisdom of the ages is always valid, but its correct application to circumstances and persons is not guaranteed by the mere fact of possession. The clergyman sees man in his relation to God, as the beloved, the created, the child, the heir, and the image of the Almighty. He sees other things too, such as man's human frailties and his virtues which are but aspects of his dependence on his Creator. He has the theological view, which should never be excluded from the practical knowledge of man, but he must recognize that it is not the total view of man.

There is another aspect of man, that seen by the psychiatrist as a scientist. The psychiatrist should likewise know man as something more than material and should be conversant in some degree with the theological and philosophical point of view demanded by the needs of his profession. But his is essentially another view, another emphasis of the subject. The psychiatrist deals with causes which the philosophers would call "secondary and accidental." In the technical language of philosophy and theology that is what they are. But in practice and for the normal welfare of persons (to use common language), these causes are quite "primary" and "necessary" for the diagnosis and treatment of the psychic ailments of man. The psychiatrist is trained and experienced not so much in the "why" of man as the "how." It is important to know the basic faculties of man and the purpose of their function. But it is also necessary to know all about the organs upon which they depend and through which they function. Here the medical training of the psychiatrist becomes significant and it is a field about which the clergyman ordinarily knows little. In the intimate relation between body and soul the psychiatrist is a specialist from a different point of view. The psychiatrist, without rejecting the supernatural in man, has a deeper knowledge of man's physical nature upon which the supernatural rests.

The clergyman as a hospital chaplain is in a position to co-operate with the psychiatrist and must depend in great measure upon the practical and scientific knowledge of his colleague. This is so, because the clergyman's knowledge of anatomy, physiology, psychopathology, and other branches of psychiatric science is of necessity very cursory. He needs some orientation with regard to his part in this co-operation. For each case, and even at times for an ability to recognize a need for psychiatric treatment, he must depend on the practical knowledge of the psychiatrist. He needs some warning concerning the most obvious and elementary pitfalls in this work.

From this brief description it is readily apparent that the services of the psychiatrist and of the clergyman are not interchangeable but complementary. But, you will say this applies especially to mental hospital chaplains. What of clergymen in general? Regardless of his training, just where does a clergyman fit into the psychiatric team?

Is there any intrinsic difference between a chaplain in a mental hospital and a pastor of a city church? In the case of the hospital chaplain about 90 per cent or more of his parishioners are emotionally or mentally ill and know it; in the case of the city pastor the percentage will be far less, but, on the other hand, his parishioners may have less insight. Unless the clergyman takes complete medical and psychiatric training he can never hope to be more than a pseudo disciple of Aesculapius. We may as well dismiss this possibility, because if the clergyman did take such training he would become a psychiatrist as well as a clergyman and he could then wear his hat either "fore or aft" as he saw fit.

Short of such complete training, what should be the aim of pastoral psychiatric training? Should it be to give a clergyman a necessary and desirable orientation in psychiatry so that he may more efficiently perform his spiritual ministrations, or should it prepare him, as some have suggested, to perform psychotherapy "in certain cases"?

It is our belief that the training of the chaplain should not be in the direction of diagnosis or of treatment but toward a recognition of where he must not trespass. Active co-operation does not mean that the clergyman should become a "junior therapist" whose assignment is to be made by the psychiatrist. The pastor certainly should receive enough psychiatric training to be dynamically oriented in his understanding of mental illness. He should be empathic and understanding, but his primary orientation should be spiritual and not psychiatric. The clergyman on the psychiatric team should, threfore, retain his supernatural orientation while the natural orientation should be left to the medical specialist, the psychiatrist. The pastor's training in psychiatry is only to provide a background for his pastoral practice.

Here is another observation on this point:

> Yet there seems to be a movement among the younger preachers to use psychiatry in their counseling. It can be dangerous, if preachers dabble with the emotional health of their parishioners without the need to be responsible to some one. *Many clergymen have installed couches in their studies and have regular office hours.* Armed with a few volumes of Freud, they attempt to delve deeply into the lives and emotions of their people. In no field can a little knowledge be more dangerous than in psychiatry. Clergymen who, without academic training, attempt to psychoanalyze their parishioners can be as guilty of malpractice as if they were attempting to heal a respiratory or cardiac infection. The role of the clergyman as a counselor is important, but the importance of the job emphasizes the need for adequate training. The invasion of the health field by untrained clergymen should be of deep concern to both religious and medical leaders. I am not implying that clergymen have no right to bring the healing forces of their religion to people in trouble, but caution must be exercised in tampering with health problems that require intensive knowledge to solve and heal.[2] (*Italics* added.)

Privileged Communications

Before considering further the area of co-operation between the chaplain and the psychiatrist we should give thought to the type of privileged communication given to the clergyman and the physician. Communications to both are, of course, privileged. The patient, however, expects the psychiatrist to record his findings. Hospital records are known to exist, and the patient is aware that they contain confidential facts. But what he says to the clergyman he considers to be in a different realm. He does not feel that his affairs of conscience and his moral indiscretions, which he traditionally has thought were bound in the utmost secrecy, may be the subject of discussion at staff meetings if the clergyman becomes a therapist. Of privileged communications most patients would consider those offered to the clergyman as more privileged than those given to the psychiatrist. If the clergyman becomes a therapist it is likely to have a seriously detrimental effect on patient-clergyman communication.

---

[2] George C. Anderson, "Current Conditions and Trends in Relations Between Religion and Mental Health" (New York: Academy of Religion and Mental Health, 1960), p. 8.

Place of Pastor on Hospital Clinic Team

Bearing in mind that being properly placed on the therapeutic team, the clergyman and the psychiatrist have separate functions, let us give thought to the areas in which they each function best. The fields in which difficulties arise and in which the co-operation of physician and clergyman is most fruitful are in the area of sin and forgiveness, conscience and guilt, responsibility, the problem of evil, human destiny, and man's relationship with God. Another area in which the chaplain has traditionally given assistance is the area of alcoholism. Obviously all these conditions cannot be discussed in the short space of one chapter but both disciplines should keep them in mind as a road map for co-operation.

There is one important area where special attention is needed. Probably the most common clinical condition which the patient is likely to present first to the clergyman is the condition known as religious scrupulosity, more properly known as an obsessive-compulsive reaction with a religious content. Traditionally this condition has been treated by members of the clergy. The success of the psychiatrist has been no greater in this area than that of the clergyman. Both find the condition resistant to treatment. Although authoritative treatment as given by the clergy has been helpful and at times effective, the greatest relief for many of these unhappy people is insight therapy. The clergyman must be alert in these cases because such a symptom is often seen as an early manifestation of schizophrenia. In such cases the clergyman's ministrations are not likely to be helpful. Cases which grow worse under pastoral counseling should be referred for psychiatric consultation to determine whether a more malignant process is present.

Human behavior at any particular instance is the resultant of many determinants: conscious and unconscious, free and determined, rational and emotional, natural and supernatural. The normal person is one who enjoys a reasonable integration within his own personality on all these levels, and in relation to his environment and to an objective hierarchy of values. The mentally ill person is one who suffers some measure of threatening disintegration in these relationships, and therapy must concern itself with the restoration of a total unit to the human person. Obviously, then, there is need for a comprehensive approach to the problem of mental suffering, such as is operative in the joint effort of psychiatrist and clergyman.

The psychiatrist, functioning strictly as a scientist, will be reluctant to make value judgments. Yet the patient will introduce ethical questions into therapy, and will come eventually to the clergyman for a moral evaluation of his behavior. On the question of sin, the psychiatrist will find himself at a disadvantage, and it is to the pastor that the patient will come for forgiveness. The pastor, in turn, must take into consideration the emotional factors and unconscious motivations that are the concern of the psychiatrist, and which concern him only insofar as they may lessen imputability. In the very difficult cases of scrupulosity, it is still the clergyman whom the patient will expect to assist him to separate his religious symptoms from a genuine, underlying faith. This gives support to the therapist, who, in turn, disposes the patient toward a more fruitful reception of the benefits of religion, through the removal of emotional obstacles.

The psychiatrist is hampered in the areas of the problem of evil, the meaning of life, human values, ultimate destiny, and God, for these are the areas of value judgment, and it is to the clergyman that the patient prefers to turn for reassurance and explanation. Without attempting to treat symptoms, the clergyman nevertheless supports the efforts of the psychiatrist, while at the same time carrying out his primary function as a spiritual director. A part of this spiritual direction is to urge the patient to co-operate with both the psychiatrist and the clergyman, and patients do generally respond to this recommendation.

In the area of responsibility, the psychiatrist may simply assume its existence, at least potentially, and hope that somewhere in the course of therapy it will begin to function normally. He cannot, however, require it of the patient. But in the relationship of patient to clergyman, the patient generally freely offers whatever responsibility he is able to muster up. This places the clergyman in a position to encourage it, and he does so within the limits of the patient's capabilities. Confession is the most frequent example of this, for the patient himself is the first to act on whatever responsibility he may have, by the mere fact of his coming to confession to evaluate his own behavior.

The pastor encounters many instances of the fact of religion as an integrating factor in the process of personality development, and frequently a person who is quite ill psychiatrically may be well oriented religiously. A few examples will illustrate the important position of religion, even in mental illness. A certain catatonic schizophrenic speaks only when he comes to confession; a disturbed person quiets down and speaks courteously when the chaplain appears; a patient who is "on critical" and utterly confused will reach out and kiss the cross on the stole of the priest who has come to administer the Last Rites; and a patient in a coma will revive long enough to complete a familiar prayer the priest has begun to whisper in his ear. There are many such evidences that religion is often the last hold that a patient may have on reality, and hence the importance of co-operation between psychiatrist and clergyman for the total welfare of the patient.

Conclusion

I would like to conclude this chapter with the following suggestions to the psychiatrically oriented clergyman. These suggestions I feel will be helpful toward the very desirable active co-operation which is needed between the clergyman and psychiatrist.

1. Remember that the services rendered to the patient by the clergyman and psychiatrist are complementary, not interchangeable.

2. Remember that the clergyman is responsible for the spiritual welfare of the patient, and although therapeutic benefit may flow from his ministrations this is not the primary purpose of his ministry.

3. Remember that the confidential relationship of clergyman-patient is different from that of the psychiatrist- and psychologist-patient relationship and should be carefully guarded by the clergyman, especially in matters of conscience.

4. Although some of the information received outside the sacrament of Penance by the clergyman during his patient contact may, of course, be transmitted to the therapist, the pastor should nevertheless contribute little or nothing of the patient's mental content during group conferences.

5. Anxiety of the patient in regard to religious disturbances which are of a delusional nature is not a proper subject of treatment by the chaplain. If, for example, the patient speaks to the pastor about having committed "the unpardonable sin" the clergyman should be only reassuring and explanatory. He should not, in other words, attempt to treat symptoms.

In conclusion, then, we feel that the psychiatric team of the clergyman and psychiatrist will function most smoothly and most fruitfully if each confines his major effort to the professional field in which he has been trained. This is, furthermore, the field in which the patient is most likely to accept him.

The call, then, is for the psychiatrist to treat the emotionally and the mentally ill, and the priest-counselor to be prepared to advise on the fears, anxieties, and other normal, perplexing problems which arise in the everyday lives of his parishioners. The art (and a certain necessity) comes in knowing who can be helped by pastoral counseling and who needs to be referred for expert treatment.

As Dr. Braceland says:

> Although I am a strong believer in the use of counseling in pastoral work, I emphasize equally strongly that such counseling should always be kept subservient to over-all religious and pastoral goals.[3]

[3] Francis J. Braceland, M.D., "A Psychiatrist Examines the Relationship Between Psychiatry and the Catholic Clergy," *Pastoral Psychology*, Feb., 1959, p. 13.

CHAPTER XVI

CONTEMPORARY SCHOOLS OF PSYCHOLOGY

"In every affair consider what precedes and what follows." These words of Epictetus are the keynote of this chapter. An attempt is made here to condense the findings of those students from the past who have contributed to our present knowledge. Some of their ideas may seem undeveloped and crude, but at the time they were pronounced they were new and frequently startling. Some authors might have chosen different names to discuss, others might have given a different emphasis to those chosen. My only apology for those selected is that they seem to me to be most important. Each pastoral counselor may find a new meaning for himself in the teachings of these founders of the modern psychological science. Each may find something useful. Each may develop new insights. This is what it means to be eclectic. Choose that which best suits yourself and that from which you can gain new insights either into yourself or your clients. Remember, "The past is prologue."

BREUER

Modern psychopathology may be traced to the work of Viennese general practitioner, Josef Breuer (1842–1925), who made use of hypnosis with his neurotic patients. One of these was a young woman suffering from hysteria. Under hypnosis she could speak without restraint about things she could not mention in her normal waking state. She accompanied these revelations with impressive outbursts of emotion, and when she was brought out of the hypnotic state she would find her condition improved.

Similar experiences with other patients suggested to Breuer new concepts as to the causation and significance of hysterical manifestations. He was, therefore, led to believe that a neurosis results from failure to express the affect of a past psychic trauma. He concluded that the affect had been repressed but came forth in the form of symptoms, and that the condition could best be relieved by hypnotizing the patient, bringing about a recall of the initial trauma, and at the same time helping him to abreact (work off) the associated emotion. Breuer's work would probably have received little attention except for his association with Freud, who developed Breuer's germinal idea. Breuer eventually disassociated himself from Freud after the deluge of criticism following publication of their joint works.

FREUD

Sigmund Freud was born of Jewish parents on May 6, 1856, in a small town in Moravia. At the age of four, he was taken to Vienna, where he remained until 1938. In that year he moved to England because of the German invasion of Austria. He died in London in 1939.

Freud studied medicine at the University of Vienna, which he entered in 1873. Here he spent six years concentrating on the histology of the nervous system in the laboratory of Brüche. His intense interest in this field caused him to neglect other phases of medical studies, and for this reason he did not receive his degree until 1881.

Freud began his professional life as a research worker and later as a lecturer on neurological diseases at the University of Vienna. At this time, according to his *Autobiography*, he understood absolutely nothing about neuroses, but in 1885 he went to Paris to study with Charcot who was already famous for his use of hypnosis in the treatment of hysteria. Trained in neurology, like Freud, Charcot sincerely believed that the ultimate explanation for hysteria would be found in neurological research.

In the following year, on his way back to Vienna, Freud stopped off at Liébault's clinic in Nancy. Liébault was a country doctor who employed hypnosis for the treatment of certain illnesses. Freud said that from what he observed in Liébault's clinic, he "received the profoundest impression of the possibility that there could be powerful mental processes which nevertheless remained hidden from the consciousness of men." Freud did not realize at the time how much his own work would be an outgrowth of Liébault's experiments in hypnosis.

When he returned to Vienna, Freud entered private practice as a specialist in nervous diseases. He first tried electrotherapy but soon gave this up. He then decided to try the method suggested to him by Breuer, whom he had met originally in Brüche's laboratory.

When Freud put his patients under hypnosis he found, like Breuer, that the patient would recall and reveal contents which he seemed unable to recall in normal awaking states. The recollection and expression of this hidden content was accompanied by outbursts of emotion. Since the patient felt purged after he was brought back to consciousness, Freud called this the "Cathartic Method." He realized that he and Breuer had discovered a previously unrecognized factor in mental life — what is today called the "unconscious." This was Freud's greatest contribution to psychiatry.

> This was the first time in the history of medical psychology that a therapeutic agent had led to the discovery of the cause of the illness while attacking or attempting to remove this cause. This was the first time in the history of psychopathology that the cause of illness, the symptoms generated by the cause, and the therapeutic agent revealing and removing the cause were combined in one succession of factors. It is doubtful whether the full meaning of this historical fact has as yet been properly appreciated.[1]

Free Association

Freud soon discovered that hypnosis was not necessary in order to delve into the newly found unconscious. In fact, Brill says that Freud eventually found it a hindrance.[2] Instead of employing hypnosis, all Freud had to do was to tell the patient to speak at random, expressing everything that came into his mind and not censoring any emotion or idea no matter how shameful or painful it might appear.

This new method of pursuing random thoughts to explore the unconscious was what we now call "free association." The process of free association was not something new. Since the time of Aristotle philosophers had known that the human mind tends to bring back its images in a definite order. Aristotle (De Memoria et Reminiscientia) had asserted that the contents of mind succeed one another by relations of

1. Similarity, or
2. Contrast, or

---

[1] Gregory Zilboorg, A History of Medical Psychology (New York: W. W. Norton and Co., 1941), p. 486.

[2] Sigmund Freud, Selected Papers on Hysteria and Other Psychoneuroses, trans., A. A. Brill, Nervous and Mental Disease Monograph Series No. 4 (New York: Nervous and Mental Disease Publishing Co., 1920).

3. Contiguity in space and/or time.

To illustrate, suppose someone thinks of George Washington. He may next think of

1. Abraham Lincoln, who was also a great president

    or

2. Benedict Arnold, who was a traitor rather than a patriot

    or

3. Mount Vernon or the American Revolution, one of which is associated with him in space, the other in time.

These three relations are called the "laws of association."

Certain medieval philosophers, most notably St. Thomas Aquinas (1225–1274), wrote commentaries on Aristotle's short treatise and generally accepted his formulation of these laws. So too did Juan Luis Vives in his *De Anima* (1528). David Hume (1711–1776) also discussed the laws of association. Hume's treatment differs from that of his predecessors. He combined the three Aristotelian laws into two and added a third which he called the law of "Cause and Effect."

Freud's significant contribution was his use of the laws of association. He discovered that by using these laws he could bring into consciousness a chain of mental associations linking the neurotic symptoms of a patient with certain data repressed in the patient's unconscious.

Freud's Theory of Psychic Structure

As he pursued his studies, Freud tried to visualize the structure of the human mind in order to understand exactly what was occurring in the minds of his patients. Parts of this theory are common talk in modern culture. The notions of the Ego, Superego, the Id, Oedipal Complex, for example, have been adopted by historians, literary critics, educators, and others.

Freud modified his views on mental structure throughout the course of his medical career, but his general theory can be outlined as follows:

The contents of the human mind may be likened to an iceberg. Only a small part shows above the surface. The greater part of the iceberg is below the surface of the water. In the case of the human mind, only a small portion of its contents are in the field of consciousness; most of its contents are below the surface of consciousness. The unconscious part of the mind may be divided into two parts: (1) the Preconscious (Pcs.) and the Unconscious, properly speaking (Ucs.). Contents of the Preconscious are said to be unconscious in so far as the individual at that time is not directly aware of them. However, these contents can be brought into consciousness by the individual if he makes an effort to recall them. On the other hand, the contents of the Unconscious proper (Ucs.) cannot be recalled by the individual's own efforts but only through the aid of special techniques such as the use of free association. It is the Unconscious (Ucs.) that is significant in Freudian theory. This Unconscious contains repressed emotional experiences which an individual has undergone previously in his life. It contains also psychic material inherited by an individual from his ancestors. Freud insists, however, that these racial residual contents are less important than the individual's own experiences (see p. 224).

The Ego, Superego, Id

Freud looked at the psyche in another way. He divided it into the Ego, the Superego, and the Id. The *Ego* is the center of consciousness. It is the mediator between the individual's consciousness and his own unconsciousness. It also mediates between the individual and the world outside of him. The *Superego* is a collection of rules, customs, admonitions, and prohibitions which an individual has unconsciously incorporated from parents, teachers, and other authoritative figures in his environment. Eventually, the Superego takes over the function of "judging" an individual's actions. The *Id* is a "seething cauldron" containing the most primitive biological and emotional drives. Freud asserted that the Ego mediates between the wild irrational impulses of the Id and the strict norms for behavior imposed by the Superego. Whenever an individual's Ego is unable to resolve a conflict between the demands of the Superego and the Id, repression occurs. This, in turn, may lead to a neurosis.

Repression

Freud described his theory of repression as "the pillar upon which the edifice of psychoanalysis rests." He explained the process of repression as follows: A mental conflict occurs between a particular impulse or instinct which craves satisfaction and the moral standards of the individual. A solution of the conflict would be reached if the individual were to consciously and deliberately decide whether he would satisfy or repudiate the impulse. But in a conflict which leads to repression the patient cannot tolerate the primitive impulse and refuses to consciously deal with it. Since the patient cannot admit to himself in consciousness that the impulse exists, he does not, therefore, resolve the conflict. Consequently, the unaccepted impulse retains its full energy charge. Since the impulse cannot be resolved through channels of consciousness, it will seek its discharge and substitutive gratification through some other kind of symptom formation, just as a stream of water which is blocked by some obstacle will overflow its banks and seek a new outlet.

Opposition to Freud

Freud's new theory that deep in the human mind were contents not immediately accessible to consciousness was first treated with general antagonism. There were many reasons for such opposition: (1) First of all, the discovery of these hidden recesses was obtained by means of hypnosis which was still generally looked upon as the practice of charlatans. (2) Psychology was still dominated by the philosophical outlook of Descartes and Locke, both of whom equated the term *mental* with the term *conscious*. (3) The man in the street objected to Freud because if he were to admit Freud's new theory he would have to acknowledge the presence within himself of a vast influence of which he was only partly aware. (4) Freud's principle of psychological determinism was extremely disturbing to moralists because it first looked as if it were totally opposed to the notion of free will. (5) Freud was opposed because of his emphasis on sex in mental disorders. (6) Lastly, Freud was opposed by the majority of physicians who took it for granted that every kind of illness had to be bodily in origin.

The opposition to Freud was intensive enough to exclude him from privileges in many hospitals. As a consequence, he withdrew from academic life. He stopped attending medical society meetings and for ten years devoted himself to the treatment of private patients with neurotic complaints. During this ten-year period of isolation Freud continued developing his theories. It was at this time that he gave up the use of hypnotism and developed the process of free association which, in time, he described as the "*via regia* to the unconscious."

Concepts of Sexuality

Freud was impressed by how frequently his patients' recollections had sexual significance. The more he investigated these, the more he was led to the belief that neurotic manifestations were due to conflicts between sexual impulses and resistance to the acceptance of these impulses. Freud's study of the reasons for the repression of sexuality led him back to very early childhood, and he concluded that early sexual traumata formed the basis of later neurotic disturbances. He published these findings in 1905 under the title *Three Contributions to the Theories of Sex*.

Since the Freudian concept of sexuality, particularly his ideas on the oedipal situation, forms such an important basis of present psychiatric thought, it must be discussed in some detail. Freud separated the concept of sexuality from the close association it previously had with the genital organs. He felt that it included "all of those merely affectionate and friendly impulses to which usage applied the exceedingly ambiguous word 'love.'" He considered pleasure as the goal of the sexual function and felt that this function exists from the beginning of life. These sexual feelings, he stated, are at first diffuse and their object is the subject's own body (autoerotic). These feelings later become localized in certain erotogenic zones, the first of these areas being the lips. He considered that the pleasure which the infant gets from sucking (oral stage) was sexual in nature. Later the erotogenic zone shifts to the anus where the sensation arises first in the pleasure of giving feces (anal-erotic stage) and later in withholding feces (anal-sadistic stage). The next shift is to the genitals where it is at first unorganized (phallic stage) but later develops into the adult or genital stage.

To explain certain neuroses, Freud stated that the libido (the energy of the sexual instincts) does not move smoothly along with the course of development, but that, as a result of a traumatic experience, it may become fixated at any level of development, or if the individual has progressed beyond a phase of development, he may regress to any previous level where pleasure was obtained. The stage of libido fixation determines the choice of the neurosis. This mechanism of fixation he also used to explain the various sexual perversions which he felt merely represented either fixation at, or regression to, the appropriate childhood level of sexuality.

He further stated that the first love object in both sexes is the mother.

This relationship he described under the title of the oedipus complex, which was one of his most disputed concepts. This concept forms a basic part of the Freudian theory and since it has been adopted in some measure by many subsequent writers, it warrants a fuller description.[3]

The Oedipus Complex

According to the Freudian psychoanalytic school, the male child's first love object is the mother upon whom he is at first entirely dependent. He craves her full attention, her interest, and her caresses. He becomes disturbed when she shows interest in any others, but he becomes especially disturbed over any interests she may show in his father, of whom he is jealous. He regards his father as a rival for the mother's love. He feels that his father may be successful in his attempt to win his mother and, as a result, he wishes to kill his father. He discovers about this time that some people have no penis and wonders why. Could this be as a punishment (castration fear), he asks himself. If so, perhaps he had better curb his hostile feelings toward his father so that he will not be punished. He, therefore, relinquishes his sexual feelings toward his mother and develops tender feelings instead toward both parents and turns his erotic feelings toward females, and his hostile feelings toward other males, outside of the family group.[4]

The *female oedipus complex*, sometimes referred to as the Electra complex, is, according to Freud, at first the same as that in the boy, inasmuch as the girl's first love object is the mother, and she wishes to destroy all rivals for her affection. She also discovers that some people have a penis and wonders why. She feels that in some way her mother has failed her and is hurt (penis envy). Because of this, she turns from her mother to her father in the hope that he will give her a penis. This hope does not materialize and she finally realizes that she cannot have a penis, but hopes that the father will give her a baby instead. The father continues to favor the mother and this increases the child's hostility, but she soon feels that the mother may retaliate and therefore turns her hostile feelings toward others outside of the family and develops tender feelings toward her mother. Freud felt that the female oedipal situation

---

[3] Patrick Mullahy, *Oedipus, Myth and Complex* (New York: Hermitage Press, 1948), pp. 16–30.
[4] *Ibid.*, p. 29.

was not as well worked out as that in the male. He also stated that it is resolved much more slowly and complete solution may not occur.[5]

The Oedipus Complex (male)

1. Mother First Love Object (child has been entirely dependent on her).
2. Craves her individual attention, interest, physical caress.
3. Bothered because of her attention to siblings, but especially to father.
4. Jealousy arises because of interest of mother in father.
5. Father is regarded as a rival and a successful rival.
6. Wonders why — he wishes he could kill father.
7. Becomes curious about body structure and learns that some people have no penis, wonders why this occurs.
8. He decides that it is result of punishment (they were castrated).
9. Decides to curb his aggressive acts and thoughts against his father so that he will not be punished.
10. No longer does he dare to cherish sexual thoughts toward mother but develops tender feelings for her in their place.
11. Ambivalent attitude toward father helps in repressing hostility and helps to develop tender regard for him.
12. Turns erotic instinctual energy to females outside of family and his aggressive instinct to males outside of family group.
    Sudden suppression of ambivalent attitude may leave child ambivalent for rest of life.

The Oedipus Complex (female)
(Electra Complex)

1. In oral and anal stage same as boy.
2. Loves mother and hates and wishes to destroy rivals for mother's love.
3. Discovers that some human beings have a penis.
4. This is a blow to her pride.
5. Develops idea that reason for her failure to have a penis is that her mother has failed her.
6. In fury wants to retaliate — decides to hate mother because of this failure.
7. Turns to father whom she desires and who will give her a penis if she loves him.
8. The penis does not grow and she becomes annoyed and disappointed with father.
9. Finally realizes that she cannot have a penis — decides maybe he will give her a baby.
10. This increases hostility to mother whom father favors but soon fears that mother may retaliate.
11. Turns aggressive energy to competition outside of family and develops tender regard for mother.
12. Solution does not take place quickly.
    May be frigid until after first child.
    Possibility of unsublimated heterosexual trends.

---

[5] Ibid., p. 27.

Repression, according to Freud, accounts for the fact that these ideas are not only forgotten but seem so fantastic to us as adults. That such situations occasionally occur is undoubtedly true; so also do cases of "penis envy" and "castration fear." These cases, however, are very much in the minority and there is no scientific basis for asserting them as a universal concept. That there is a strong emotional bond between the child and its parents is generally admitted and can be easily demonstrated. The idea of Kraines in this respect is probably much nearer the truth. He feels that the child, never having learned emotional independence, early in life identifies with the parent of the same sex. The boy learns that he is masculine "like his father" and that marriage may occur with girls "like mother." The boy's thought then would run somewhat as follows: "Boys marry girls; I am a boy and when I grow up, I will marry a girl just like mother, since she is the nicest girl I know."[6] (See Chapter XI.)

Early Students

At first, Freud's studies received very little attention from psychiatrists or the medical profession, but beginning in about 1902, a few students began to study with him in Vienna. At about the same time in Zurich, Switzerland, Eugen Bleuler (1857–1939), Carl G. Jung (1875–1961), and others began to apply psychoanalytic teachings to their treatment of psychotic patients. In 1906, Jung published his well-known work on *The Psychology of Dementia Praecox*[7] in which he used analytic interpretation in explaining the symptoms and thought content in cases of schizophrenia. In 1907, Freud received his first public recognition when he was visited by men from the Zurich clinic. Later a meeting was arranged by Jung in Salzburg, Austria, where ideas were exchanged and the first journal devoted to psychoanalysis was founded. This was to be published by Freud and Bleuler and edited by Jung. Abraham A. Brill, who had been a student at the Zurich clinic, learned there of the work of Freud and became his enthusiastic disciple. It was Brill who introduced Freud's works into the United States and translated most of them into English.

---

[6] Samuel H. Kraines, *The Therapy of the Neuroses and Psychoses* (Philadelphia: Lee and Febiger, 1941), p. 423.

[7] C. G. Jung, *Psychology of Dementia Praecox*, Authorized trans. with an introduction by A. A. Brill (New York and Washington: Nervous and Mental Disease Publishing Co., 1936), Vol. 3.

About four years after this meeting (1911–1913), the first disagreements appeared among the original group and two major dissenting groups were formed, one under Alfred Adler (1870–1937) and the other headed by Jung. Adler, who had been active in psychoanalytic work for ten years, developed his school of "Individual Psychology" and Jung developed another which was called "Analytical Psychology" at the insistence of Freud, so that it would not be confused with his school of psychoanalysis.

Discussion of Freudian Psychoanalysis

Much of the terminology found in psychoanalytical literature was originated by Freud. The terms *foreconscious* or *preconscious, unconscious* as well as *id, ego,* and *superego* were first used in their present sense by him. Freud deserves great credit, however, in spite of the excesses of which he was guilty at one time or another in his overly enthusiastic application of some of his theories.

He was an atheist and a materialist; he was primarily a neurologist and not a psychiatrist. He was neither an anthropologist nor a philosopher. It was inevitable that his teachings would be seriously influenced by his personal beliefs.[8] It is out of the teachings of Freud and his followers that most of the disagreements between psychiatry and religion have occurred.

Freudian psychoanalysis was infected with materialism. It postulated complete evolution, it denied the freedom of the will, it overemphasized sex, it incorrectly explained the origin and development of morals. In addition, Freud failed to differentiate between sense and rational knowledge and denied the divine origin of religion. It is thus evident that much of the philosophy of Freud is unacceptable to us. In spite of this, there are certain aspects of his technique which are useful and acceptable. In spite of some who feel otherwise, I believe it is possible to divorce the philosophy from the technic of Freud. It is therefore possible for a Catholic in good faith to practice psychoanalysis.[9]

It is neither necessary nor desirable to prove all these points against the Freudian theory at this time. It is sufficient to say that, in its pure form,

---

[8] A good discussion of this view is found in Ira Pogroff's *The Death and Rebirth of Psychology* (New York: The Julian Press, 1955). Pogroff asserts this is true not only for Freud but also for Adler and Jung.

[9] John R. Cavanagh and James B. McGoldrick, *Fundamental Psychiatry* (Milwaukee: Bruce, 1953), p. 100.

Freudian psychoanalysis is unacceptable to Catholics. Please note that I have said in its *pure* form. The technic can be separated from the philosophy. The methods of Freud are used in some form by all psychiatrists.[10]

ALFRED ADLER

Individual Psychology

Alfred Adler lived from 1870 to 1937, a resident of Vienna, Austria. He joined Freud and his group in 1902, but his studies in organ inferiority eventually forced him to conclusions incompatible with Freud's theories. Therefore, in 1907, he began to secede from that school and to establish his own school of "Individual Psychology." He had assisted Freud in the development of a concept of the ego but was forced away from him when his studies led him to place greater emphasis on the ego as against the libido. He also believed that Freud was overemphasizing sexuality.

The psychology of Adler is based on the "masculine protest" which he seems to have derived from the "will-to-live" of Schopenhauer and the "will-to-power" of Nietzsche. His reason for calling the "protest" of the neurotic "masculine" is based on the concept that the "male" man has always been taken as the criterion of complete human potency, whereas the feminine aspect of the individual has always been relegated to an inferior position.

One important aspect of this "masculine protest," according to Adler, resulted from an inherited inferiority of bodily organs and the nervous tissues controlling them. This inferiority led to attempts at compensation by either the organ itself, its paired mate, or organs elsewhere. If, for example, one kidney was damaged or inferior, the opposite kidney would compensate for it. The enlargement of the heart in hypertension is a familiar example of this type of compensation. This organ inferiority might in turn give rise to psychic manifestations which would reveal themselves clinically as feelings of inferiority. In compensating for these feelings of inferiority and his sense of inadequacy, the person achieves a sense of importance or dignity sufficient to balance his sense of weakness or frustration. Man is guided by some goal (directive fiction) or end connected with his desire for superiority. It is in his inability to achieve this goal, Adler states, while still conducting himself as a member of society, that a neurosis begins.

---

[10] See Pope Pius XII, as quoted in *Catholics in Psychology*, by Henryk Misiak and Virginia M. Staudt (New York: McGraw-Hill Book Co., Inc., 1954), p. 291.

As Adler amplified this system, he paid less attention to organic defect and more attention to feelings of inferiority and inadequacy and the urge toward compensation. Murphy sums up Adlerian psychology in this way:

> [He] regards all mental illness as derived either directly or indirectly from humiliation and a sense of failure and believes that every patient aims at the removal of such humiliation and the acquisition of a sense of power or prestige.[11]

As Adler's psychology finally developed, it had little in common with psychoanalysis. In fact, Adler repudiated some of the basic postulates of Freud; e.g., he denied the importance of repression; he rejected his theories of infantile psychosexual development; he ignored the latent content of dreams; he paid little attention to the role of the unconscious and ascribed little or no driving power to the emotions.[12]

Adlerian psychology was the first dynamic theory of personality and, although incomplete and thought by many to be superficial, it is, nevertheless, an important contribution which emphasized an aspect of personality previously underestimated. Clinically, the system has considerable value in understanding the behavior problems of children, but, as pointed out by Moore, it is not a complete psychology:

> Adler seeks the origin of neurotic conditions in the degree to which an individual has been well or ill-prepared to meet and solve the problems of life. This lack of preparation may be traced back to the earliest years of childhood. It is a matter not so much of the conscious or the unconscious, as to the lack of understanding. . . . We cannot trace all neurotic conditions back to a faulty education of the child for meeting the difficulties of life.[13]

Adler also failed to distinguish clearly between the striving for rational and irrational power. As pointed out by Mullahy:

> He did not see clearly between the striving for irrational power — the striving for power over people — and the sense of adequacy, competence, and power which comes from self-respect and respect for others — a ra-

---

[11] Gardner Murphy, A Briefer General Psychology (New York: Harper & Bros., 1935), p. 509.

[12] Cf. Alfred Adler, Understanding Human Nature (New York: Greensburg Publishing Co., 1927); The Neurotic Constitution (New York, Dodd, Mead Co., 1930); The Practice and Theory of Individual Psychology (New York: Harcourt, Brace and Co., 1932); Study of Organ Inferiority and Psychical Compensation, Mental Disease Monograph Series No. 24 (New York: Nervous and Mental Disease Publishing Co., 1917), passim.

[13] Dom Thomas V. Moore, The Nature and Treatment of Mental Disorders (New York: Grune & Stratton, 1943), p. 68.

tional feeling of power. Hence, he was not able to see that it is the manner in which human potentialities are given a chance to develop, or thwarted, or distorted, which is the essential point.[14]

In his work, *The Practice and Theory of Individual Psychology*, Adler has attempted to apply his concepts to clinical psychiatry and, although his work contains numerous clinical cases with statements in regard to etiology, he gives very little scientific evidence for his statements.

---

[14] Mullahy, *op. cit.*, p. 325.

CHAPTER XVII

CONTEMPORARY SCHOOLS OF PSYCHOLOGY
(Continued)

CARL GUSTAV JUNG

Analytical Psychology

Carl Gustav Jung was born in Basel, Switzerland, in 1875. He died there in 1961. He early developed an interest in abnormal psychology and psychiatry, which he studied in the Zurich School of which Eugen Bleuler was the chief. In 1905, he was appointed lecturer at the University of Zurich and later became a senior member of the Zurich group. While Freud was working with neurotic patients in Vienna, Jung was using similar technics with psychotic patients in Zurich. As previously noted, Jung was one of the original group which collaborated with Freud in 1907, but, as in the case of Adler, it was soon apparent that they were using different methods of research and that they had little to contribute to each other. In 1913, he discontinued his work with Freud while still remaining president of the International Analytical Association. This displeased Freud, who, with some of his followers, became very critical of Jung. They not only were critical of his work, but also accused him of anti-Semitism.

Some of Jung's work is well known, although his connection with it is frequently overlooked. For example, Jung, before his association with Freud, introduced the association test which has since become an integral part of clinical psychology. The purpose of the test is to discover, by means of free association, the presence and nature of hidden complexes. For this purpose Jung prepared a list of 100 common words which were read to the patient one at a time. The subject was then asked to give his first association to each word. Any delay, unusual emotional response, or unusual association, was regarded as a "complex indicator" and was used as a basis for further clinical investigation. Two other terms in common use — introversion and extroversion, were coined by Jung and have been widely accepted as part of psychological terminology. Jung is, perhaps, best known for his work on the psychoanalytic interpretation of dreams.

Jung's system is difficult to present in brief form because it is quite complicated. It is rooted in many sources, and it reverberates in many fields. Moreover, he maintained that he had never crystallized his thinking so that no exposition of it can be called definitive. The best way to approach it is to outline his theory of psychic structure.

Psychic Structure According to Jung

First of all, in this system the psyche is considered as a sphere. It is then said to consist of two hemispheres possessing contrary properties. One hemisphere can be called "the conscious"; the other can be called "the unconscious" (see diagram). These two hemispheres are not always exactly half conscious and half unconscious. The boundary may shift so that in the same psyche there may sometimes be more of conscious and less of unconscious elements, or vice versa (see diagram).

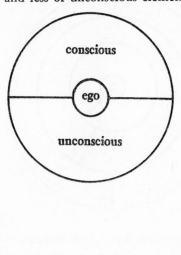

At another time this same psyche may have a balance as follows:

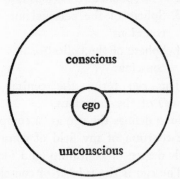

Although the properties of each hemisphere are contrary to each other, they do not cancel each other out. They supplement, complement, and compensate each other.

The total psyche consists of a number of *systems* (functioning units) which, although they are clearly distinguished from each other, nevertheless interact.

Besides the systems there are:

1. The ego
2. The personal unconscious with its complexes
3. The collective unconscious with its archetypes
4. The *persona*
5. The *anima-animus*
6. The shadow
7. The *attitudes* of
   a) Introversion
   b) Extroversion
8. The *functions* of
   a) Thinking
   b) Feeling
   c) Sensing
   d) Intuition
9. The self

The accompanying diagram shows another way in which some parts of the psyche may be indicated:

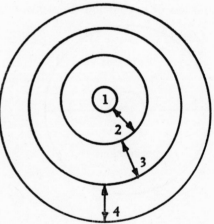

1. The ego
2. The sphere of consciousness
3. Sphere of the personal unconscious
4. Sphere of the collective unconscious

The ego forms the central "core" of the conscious.

Jung defines the ego as "a complex of representations which constitutes the centrum of my field of consciousness and appears to possess a very high degree of continuity and identity."[1]

The ego is the *subject* of consciousness. Consciousness is "the function or activity which maintains the relation of psychic contents with the

---

[1] C. G. Jung, *Psychological Types*, trans. by H. Godwin Bayhes (London: K. Paul, Trench, Trubner & Co., Ltd., 1946), p. 540.

Ego."[2] Consciousness is only a very small part of the psyche.

Beyond the sphere of consciousness the contents of the psyche are unconscious. The unconscious part of the psyche may be further subdivided into two main spheres: the sphere of *The Personal Unconscious*, and the sphere of *The Collective Unconscious*. The first sphere encountered in the depths of the Jungian psyche is the sphere of *The Personal Unconscious*. This is comprised of two parts:

1. Contents which are not at the time in the field of consciousness but which can be called back readily into consciousness. (These contents correspond to the contents of Freud's preconscious.)

2. Contents which are repressed, subliminally perceived, thought, or felt.[3]

Much of the content of the personal unconscious is grouped in complexes.

The Complexes of the Personal Unconscious

A *complex* is a constellation of feelings, thoughts, percepts, or memories organized around a "nuclear element" which attracts other unconscious psychic experiences to it. Complexes are incompatible with the habitual consciousness of the individual and they function arbitrarily and autonomously. They are split off from the rest of the personality. This split often comes as the result of a psychic trauma.

Everybody has complexes. They need not be actual deficiencies in the person's make-up; they may indeed be stimuli impelling the individual to higher achievement. Complexes, therefore, can be either healthy or unhealthy. The complex *as a whole* is unconscious but at different times one part or other, even the nucleus, will show up in consciousness.

The Collective Unconscious

Beyond the sphere of the personal unconscious lies the sphere of the collective unconscious. Whereas the personal unconscious contains "forgotten, repressed, subliminally perceived thought and emotive matter," the collective unconscious possesses mental contents which did not arise from the individual's own ego, but are inherited by the whole human race and possibly even the whole animal world. Jacobi remarks that the contents of the collective unconscious are "precipitates" left over from

---

[2] *Ibid.*, p. 536.
[3] *Ibid.*, p. 616.

humanity's typical forms of reacting since the beginnings of the race.[4] The reactions of which these are residual forms are the reactions under situations of fear, danger, struggle against superior force, relations of the sexes, relations of children to parents, reactions of hate and love, reactions to birth and death.

The racial experiences as such are not inherited; but as a result of the experiences of preceding generations, human beings are born with predispositions according to which they tend to react in a selective way. In other words, just as a man is born with the capacity to see in three dimensions (but does not at birth actually see in three dimensions) and develops that capacity, so, too, a man is born with the capacity to think and feel according to definite patterns and contents. All the psychic data acquired by an individual as the result of his own individual experiences is influenced considerably by the contents of his collective unconscious.

The Persona

Persona is a Latin term signifying the mask which actors wore on the Roman stage. In Jung's psychology it is defined as the whole system of relations through which the inner psyche reveals itself to the outside world and keeps the core of the psyche shut off from the outside world. In his Two Essays on Analytical Psychology,[5] Jung asserts that the persona is a compromise between the demands of the extramental world and the necessities of the individual's own inner world. An individual who is well adjusted to both the outer and his own inner world will have a persona which can adapt itself to both these worlds.

Functions

Jung defines a function as a certain form of psychic activity that remains theoretically the same under varying circumstances and is completely independent of its momentary contents.[6]

There are four functions:

| 1. Thought | 3. Sensation |
| 2. Feeling | 4. Intuition |

1. Thought is the psychic function which seeks to understand and

---

[4] Jolande Jacobi, The Psychology of C. G. Jung, revised edition (New Haven: Yale University Press, 1951), p. 12.

[5] C. G. Jung, Two Essays on Analytical Psychology (London: Bailliere, Tindoff and Cox, 1928), p. 165.

[6] Psychological Types, p. 547.

adjust to the outside world by forming conceptual relations and logical deductions.

2. *Feeling* is the function which seeks to understand and adjust to the outside world by evaluating things as pleasant or unpleasant, desirable or undesirable.

3. *Sensation* is the function which perceives things simply as they are in themselves without reference to other things.

4. *Intuition* is the function which perceives the inner meaning, the possible relations one thing may have with another thing.

Thought and *feeling* are called the *rational functions* because they make use of reason, judgment, abstraction, and generalization. Both of them are concerned with evaluating and discriminating. *Thought* evaluates in terms of cognition. *Feeling* evaluates in terms of emotions. *Sensation* and *intuition* are called the *irrational functions* because they take no account of judgment, abstraction, and generalization, but deal rather with the concrete, particular, and accidental. The irrational functions are more impulsive than the rational.

Every human being possesses all four functions but he develops one more than the others. That which is better developed than the others is called the *superior function*. The opposite to the superior function will be the *inferior function*. The superior function is always in the field of consciousness. The inferior function is entirely outside consciousness and outside control by the individual's will.

In addition to the superior and inferior functions, an individual will develop an *auxiliary function*. When the contrary of the auxiliary function is brought up into consciousness it will bring with it influences it has received from the inferior function. In this way the auxiliary function can act as a mediator with the unconscious because, whenever contents of the inferior function are brought to the surface by deep probing, they bring with them contents of the unconscious. It is the primitive, archaic, infantile, instinctual content of the inferior function which explains otherwise inexplicable behavior in persons.

If the superior function is overdeveloped it may create significant conflicts especially around the time of middle age. If an individual does not adjust to the world by what is *naturally* his superior function, he will develop a kind of rigid and stereotyped character and he may even develop a neurosis.

Attitude: an attitude may be defined as the general tendency an individual has to orient himself toward conditions of the outer world or toward conditions of his own inner world. An individual whose reactions are determined predominantly by reference to the objective world is called an *extrovert*; whereas one whose reactions are determined predominantly by reference to his own inner world is called an *introvert*.

Archetypes: there are psychic dispositions found in all men. They are permanent residues accumulating from repeated experiences of many human generations. They are *patterns of behavior* which will actually manifest themselves in the psyche of an individual during his mental life. The most common archetypes are those of birth, rebirth, the child, God, the old wise man, the demon, the hero, the earth mother, the animal, death, and magic. There are other archetypes, such as the siren, the nymph, Helen, Venus, the Three Graces, Atlantis, the daughter of the Erlking, etc. Archetypes usually show up in a long series of dreams, or in psychotic symptoms. They may also be found in myths, dreams, rituals, and works of art. Certain of the archetypes have become so fully developed in the human race that they act like wholly distinct systems. These are especially the *persona*, the *anima-animus*, the *shadow*, and the *self*.

The *persona* has already been discussed.

The *anima-animus* is concerned with a fact well established in psychology today: every male has both masculine and feminine psychological characteristics, although the masculine predominate. The converse is true for the female. The *anima-animus* can lead to difficulties between the sexes because a male, for example, may evaluate some particular woman according to the unconscious notion of a woman that is present in his own psychological make-up.

The *shadow* is the pattern of psychic behavior which is a residue of those animal instincts man has retained as the result of his evolution from lower animals. The shadow has to be controlled, but if it is held down too forcefully it will erupt with violence.

The *self* is the very center of a human personality. The self is the integrated goal toward which all the systems of the personality are tending. Christ and Buddah are perfect examples where the self has been achieved.

Between the primitive beginning and the ultimate achievement of the self there is a lifelong process of integration which Jung calls "individuation."

Individuation is the psychic process of development as a result of which an individual becomes fully developed and possessed of a total personality (i.e., achieves the *self*).

The Unconscious of Jung

Woodworth's description of Jung's concept of the unconscious is both valuable and brief:

> Jung regarded the unconscious in the same significant fashion as Freud and, if anything, made more of it. In addition to the personal unconscious there is another which is more important and which he calls the racial unconscious or the collective unconscious, out of which both the conscious and the unconscious life of the individual develop. Only rarely does this deepest unconscious show itself in dreams or in the neurosis, but the phantasies of really insane persons sometimes bring to the surface weird ideas and ways of thought which have never been experienced before, that seem like vestiges of the primitive thinking of the race. The collective unconscious is inherited, just as everything else is, by way of the structure of the organism. Inherited brain structure disposes the individual to think and act as the race has been habituated to think and act through countless generations of primitive life. This collective unconscious consists of instincts and archetypes. The instincts are primitive ways of acting. The archetypes are primitive ways of thinking. The collective unconscious does not contain ideas exactly — nothing as clear-cut as that. But it contains natural ways of thinking, lines of least resistance, tendencies to gravitate in our ideas toward primitive modes of thought. In dreams, nightmares, hallucinations and delusions of the insane, and even in our waking life when we are caught off guard by something for which we are totally unprepared such as an earthquake, our recently won scientific conceptions of natural processes drop away and we think animistically or have vague primitive notions of magic and spirits, fairies, witches, dragons and the devil.[7]

Differences Between Jung and Freud

Jung differed with Freud over more than his theory of psychic structure:

1. *Jung's theory of libido differed radically from that of Freud.* Mullahy summarizes this difference:

> In [Jung's] The Theory of Psychoanalysis, the concept of libido is altered so that it is made synonymous with undifferentiated energy. In this sense, the meaning of libidinal or psychical energy is analogous to the meaning of energy in physics, which may be considered as manifesting

---

[7] R. S. Woodworth, *Contemporary Schools of Psychology* (New York: The Ronald Press Co., 1931), pp. 176–177.

itself in various forms; potential, kinetic, etc. Due to evolutionary change, the libido, which was originally to a large extent of a primarily sexual character, became desexualized. So the libido is considered to be manifested in various activities and forms, in nutrition, in play, sexual feeling and love, etc. For Jung the real value of the libido theory lies not in its sexual definition, as he put it, but in the "energic" conception of it. "We owe to the energic conception," says Jung, "the possibility of dynamic ideas and relationships, which are of inestimable value for us in the chaos of the psychic life." In other words, psychical "energy-processes" are life-processes.[8]

2. Jung used *dream analysis* as did Freud, but he interpreted dreams as not simply revealing old repressed sex wishes, but as indicating the patient's unconscious attitude toward his present problems.

3. Jung differed with Freud regarding the role of family life in shaping the child's later development. While Freud claimed that it was most important to hold that the oedipus complex was completely sexual in nature, Jung held that, although this was important, the *attitude* of the parent toward it was more significant. He believed, as many since have believed, that problem parents make problem children and both must be treated.

4. The concept of psychotherapy resulting from Jung's psychopathology is radically different from the analytic technic of Freud. Moore describes this difference in these words:

> The psychological treatment [of Jung] must not only destroy an old, morbid attitude, it must also build up a new, sound attitude. But for this a reversal of vision is needed. Not only shall the patient see from what beginnings his neurosis arose, he shall also be able to see towards what justifiable aims his psychological tendencies are striving. One cannot, as though it were a foreign body, simply extract the morbid element, lest one remove with it an essential piece, which, after all, is destined to be lived with. This piece must not be weeded out, but must be transformed, until it attains that form which can be included in a way that is meaningful to the whole of the human psyche.[9]

5. According to Jung, the importance of religion, or at least a religious attitude, cannot be overestimated as an element in the psychic life.

6. *Psyche* as used by Jung is more akin to our concept of soul, and the term is used as referring to an immaterial substance which he describes as characterized "first of all by the principle of spontaneous movement and activity, secondly by the property of free creation of images

---

8 Mullahy, op. cit., p. 133.
9 Moore, op. cit., p. 63.

outside of sense perception, thirdly by the autonomous and absolute manipulation of these images."[10]

7. The psychology of Jung although less materialistic than that of Freud, is still heavily tainted by it. In some places it becomes quite mystical.[11] There is no proof of his concept of a collective unconscious, and, on the basis of our present knowledge of heredity, it seems unlikely that such ideas could be inherited.

ADOLF MEYER

The Psychobiology of Meyer

One of the most influential figures in modern American psychiatry was Adolf Meyer (1866–1950).[12] His contribution was not so much in the realm of theory as in the realm of practical technic. Essentially, psychobiology is a practical, common-sense method of dealing with the integral individual as acting. Normal, as well as abnormal, people must be viewed as psychobiological units. Meyer defines his system as a study of the total integrated and functioning personality of the individual resulting from the biological and mental forces at work and these in relation to environment.

To obtain such an understanding of the functioning individual, it is necessary to have a complete picture of the individual as acting. This is the composite picture formed as a result of a careful study of the individual's past, and an understanding of his dominant interests, traits, difficulties, handicaps, social activities, ambitions, failures, etc. A complete physical and mental examination is required. Anything and everything is utilized to give a complete picture. All theories are eschewed; the facts of the case are the all-important thing. A single factor is seldom, if ever, considered the only cause of a disorder. It is most generally considered to have been brought about by a cluster of factors.

There is much virtue in this popularly accepted technique. It capitalizes

---

[10] C. G. Jung, *The Psychology of the Spirit*, trans. by H. Nagel (New York: The Analytical Psychology Club of New York, Inc., 1948), pp. 7, 18.

[11] Cf. C. G. Jung, "The Question of the Therapeutic Value of 'Abreaction,'" *Brit. J. Psychol. Med. Sec.*, 2:22, 1921, *passim; Contributions to Analytical Psychology*, trans. by H. G. and Cary F. Baynes (London: Routledge and Kegan Paul, Ltd., 1948), *passim; Psychology of the Unconscious*, authorized trans. by Beatrice M. Hinkle (New York: Moffat Yard, 1916), *passim*.

[12] Wendell Muncie, *Psychology and Psychiatry* (St. Louis: The C. V. Mosby Co., 1939), Preface.

on common sense. It is predominantly interested in facts. It painstakingly employs every device to acquire the necessary knowledge of the patient. It fully comprehends the tremendous complexity and diversity of clinical cases.

Sadler[13] thinks that Meyer's philosophy and technic are "too scientific and thorough-going." This criticism is hard to understand. He also says that Meyer's concept is "too common-sense," his terminology "too involved." The latter remark has much merit. Many would want further enlightenment on the charge that psychobiology is "too common-sense"; but whatever validity these criticisms may enjoy, they are secondary in importance. The strongest criticism of Adolf Meyer's theory and work is that it is predicated upon a materialistic concept of man and human life. Mind is matter. Anything like a superorganic life is unknown. If this materialistic concept of man and human life is true, then psychobiology offers much indeed. If materialism is false, psychobiology loses much of its value. None of Meyer's many followers have as yet presented a view of psychobiology expurgated of materialism. Even though it is not a philosophy but rather a technique, it cannot be forgotten that, as presented by Meyer and his followers, the system is predicated upon and takes for granted the typical psychology of the materialist.

BEHAVIORISM

This school of psychology enjoyed a tremendous popularity in the first part of the twentieth century, and even though it has ceased to be a dominant school of thought, it continues to exercise some influence, especially on psychotherapy in Russia. As its name indicates, behaviorism insists that the study of psychology should be that of behavior, and not of consciousness. John B. Watson[14] was the chief exponent of this system. All conduct, according to behaviorism, is a matter of conditioned reflexes; mind, will, personality do not exist. Training and education are to be achieved by controlling the reflex and are entirely a matter of stimulus and response.

---

[13] Cf. William S. Sadler, *Theory and Practice of Psychiatry* (St. Louis: The C. V. Mosby Co., 1936).

[14] J. B. Watson, *Psychology From the Standpoint of a Behaviorist*, 3rd edition revised (Philadelphia and London: J. B. Lippincott Co., 1924).

Behavioristic psychology is really physiology. Other materialists make some pretense of salvaging the intellect and will, but the behaviorist makes none. The system has been condemned by materialists themselves as being ultramaterialistic and mechanistic. The conditioned reflex is an important fact in physiology, but behaviorism hopelessly exaggerates its significance and, in general, contributes very little to the understanding, treatment, and prevention of mental illness. The materialism of the system renders it well nigh useless for the understanding of psychic data.

CONSTITUTIONAL PSYCHOLOGY

According to Draper, constitution is defined "as that aggregate of hereditarial characters, influenced more or less by environment, which determines the individual's reaction, successful or unsuccessful, to the stress of environment."[15] The possession by each individual of a factor of personal identity which marks him as a unique specimen is a basic belief of constitutional medicine.

Dr. George Draper founded the Constitution Clinic at the Presbyterian Hospital in New York in 1916. Since that time, he has continued his researches and is the recognized leader in the field.

For the sake of convenience in study, Draper divided the personality into four main categories or panels: "The use of the term panel arose from the conception of a Japanese screen composed of four panels, across which was painted a complete picture; any one of the panels of such a screen alone would signify little, for upon it would be found but one phase of the whole." The four categories which he selected for study were: (1) morphology; (2) physiology; (3) psychology; (4) immunology. Draper's work represents a marked advance over the work of Kretschmer and others who attempted to classify men within specific types. This type of study of man is inadequate and, as pointed out elsewhere, without a firm scientific foundation. Draper attempted to study man in his entirety, and his work furnished a spearhead in the development of psychosomatic medicine, for, in 1928, Draper's first paper, "Disease, A Psychomatic Reaction" appeared.[16] His emphasis on the unity of the

---

[15] G. Draper, *Human Constitution, A Consideration of Its Relationship to Disease* (Philadelphia: W. B. Saunders Co., 1924), p. 24.

[16] G. Draper, "Disease, A Psychomatic Reaction," *J.A.M.A.*, 90:1381–1385, April 21, 1928.

organism is credited by both Cobb[17] and Braceland[18] for the present-day awakening of the profession to the concept of psycho(so)matic medicine.

KAREN HORNEY

A brief description of the work of Karen Horney is presented to show the extent to which this newer school of psychoanalysis has deviated from the original postulates of Freud. Horney, as do many other recent writers, placed much more stress on environmental influences than on childhood trauma. This difference may be stated in her own words:

> I do not believe that any conflict between desires and fears could ever account for the extent to which a neurotic is divided within himself and for an outcome so detrimental that it can actually ruin a person's life. A psychic situation such as Freud postulates would imply that a neurotic retains the capacity to strive for something wholeheartedly, that he is merely frustrated in these strivings by the blocking action of fears. As I see it, the source of the conflict revolves around the neurotic's loss of capacity to wish for anything wholeheartedly because his very wishes are divided, that is, go in opposite directions. This would constitute a much more serious condition indeed than the one Freud visualized.[19]

In her study of neurosis, Horney points out, with others, that the essential factor common to all neuroses is anxiety and the defenses built up against it. She describes a neurosis as "a psychic disturbance brought about by fears and defenses against these fears, and by attempts to find a compromise solution for conflicting tendencies."[20] As to the source of this anxiety, she feels that it arises from hostile impulses of various kinds.[21]

She feels that underlying all neuroses, regardless of their variety, there is a "basic anxiety" which she describes as a feeling "of being small, insignificant, helpless, endangered, in a world that is out to abuse, cheat, attack, humiliate, betray and envy." This "basic anxiety" gives rise to three basic attitudes which cause the individual to move (1) toward people, (2) away from people, and (3) against people. In each of these

---

[17] S. Cobb, Psychosomatic Medicine, in R. L. Cecil's Textbook of Medicine, 7th ed. (Philadelphia: W. B. Saunders Co., 1947), p. 1646.

[18] F. J. Braceland, "The Practice of Psychiatry," Quarterly Bulletin, Northwestern University Medical School, 22:312, 1948.

[19] Karen Horney, New Ways in Psychoanalysis (New York: W. W. Norton & Co., 1939), p. 38.

[20] Karen Horney, The Neurotic Personality of Our Time (New York: W. W. Norton & Co., 1937), p. 15.

[21] Ibid., p. 63.

attitudes one of the elements involved in basic anxiety is overemphasized: helplessness in the first, hostility in the second, and isolation in the third. It should be understood that all three attitudes may be present in any one individual; one attitude, however, predominates. Based on this predominance, Horney describes three types of personality: (1) the compliant type; (2) the aggressive type; (3) the detached type. Moral problems play an important part in neurosis, according to Horney — this being a further departure from Freud who felt that morality was not a question for scientific consideration.[22]

Horney presents a theory of neurosis which avoids Freudian misconceptions and faults. She has particularly eliminated the libido theory which was one of Freud's most contested ideas. Her own theory, while well worked out at some levels, is not very clear in its fundamentals.

EXISTENTIALIST THERAPY

The differing theories already presented in this chapter indicate that there are several possible ways in which the counselor may look at his patient. He may consider him as the product of instinctual drives, of his will-to-power, or as a product of his inherited racial unconscious. Furthermore, the counselor may use one of these outlooks exclusively in handling all his clients, or he may adopt an eclectic viewpoint depending on the particular symptoms manifested by a particular client. The very fact that he can use several different technics to treat the same symptoms or that he can adopt different outlooks to treat different symptoms has caused counselors to wonder whether they are truly seeing the client as the client himself really is or whether they are simply projecting certain preconceived theories on the client. Once they have asked this question, counselors ask another: Is it possible for the counselor to determine whether or not he really does see the client as the client sees himself? In other words, can the counselor set up such a relation with the client that the counselor "lives," as it were, inside the life of the patient? Flaubert, the French nineteenth-century novelist, tried to do this with the character of Emma Bovary in his novel Madame Bovary but he gave up the attempt. Yet the counselor has to have some kind of contact with the inner world of the client if he is going to help the client rid himself of the "rotten timber" in his psychological struc-

---

[22] Cf. Karen Horney, Our Inner Conflicts (New York: W. W. Norton & Co., 1945).

ture and construct a more solid foundation for living a freer and more wholesome life.

These questions have given rise during the past thirty years to a new group of psychotherapists collectively called the Existential Therapists. This group is reluctant to be called a distinct school for several reasons: First, the group has more than one leader. It arose spontaneously in several countries of Europe. The most notable leaders have been Ludwig Binswanger of Zurich and Viktor Frankl of Vienna. A second point of difference between the Existential Therapists and previous groups is that the existentialists do not present their views in opposition to other theories, but rather to supplement already-existing theories. In other words, they have not come "to destroy the law but to fulfill it." Frankl, for example, maintains that perhaps only 12 per cent of the cases seen at his clinic require treatment according to the new outlook.

It would be incorrect to draw too close a parallel between Existentialist Psychotherapists and Existentialist Philosophers but there are some points where similarities can be found. Both, for example, maintain that a man is responsible for what he becomes, and both maintain that a man may be overwhelmed with a dread (Angst) of this responsibility. Existential psychiatrists believe that certain clients manifesting symptoms of anxiety may be suffering from this kind of Angst of which the philosophers speak. To illustrate these points more clearly, let me present a brief and by no means comprehensive outline of some relevant aspects of existentialist philosophy.

Existentialism as it is known today arose during the nineteenth century. It is usually attributed to the Danish Lutheran theologian, Soren Kierkegaard (1813-1855), who protested against the dominant philosophical trend of dichotomizing the elements within man himself and dichotomizing man from his immediate environment. If we accept Descartes as the father of modern philosophy, we can say this dichotomizing has been characteristic of all modern philosophy.

When Descartes separated the mental from the physical and put emphasis on the conceptualizing activity of the mind, he arrived at the conclusion that "mind" is essentially "conscious thought activity" and "man" is essentially a mind. Consequently man, as Descartes defines him, is a thinking thing which is attached to a body; or, as someone has remarked, "an angel driving a machine." Cartesian man is explained in terms of thought; the body has no direct influence on that thinking mind which is called man. As a result of his outlook on man as a thinking being who is not directly in contact with things of the world about him, Descartes, like Plato before him, established the human mind in a world of abstract principles and universal essences. A mind like the "Cartesian mind" can lose contact with what people ordinarily call "the objective world," because a mind confined to its own activities of abstraction and judgment may construct all kinds of logical relations, which in themselves are absolutely necessary but which may not correspond directly with any actually existing extramental objects. For instance, suppose we accept the definition of a triangle as a three-sided plane figure; we can assert immediately that a triangle cannot have four sides. In order to make this assertion we do not have to consider at all whether triangles do actually exist outside our minds. Let us take another illustration: we can formulate the concept of humanity, and we can talk about humanity; but humanity as such does not exist outside the mind. What exists outside the mind are human beings from whom the mind may abstract the idea of humanity. This tendency to treat reality almost exclusively with reference to concepts and definitions without referring these to the extramental world was one of the main difficulties of Cartesianism. It led to a position where the mind knows all kinds of logical relations but has no guarantee that there really are actually existent things in which these logical relations are objectively fulfilled.

Kierkegaard protested against this tendency in European thought. He asserted, for example, that humanity as such does not exist, but that individual human beings are the only existing reality. "What is important," he would say, "is that, here and now, I, Soren Kierkegaard, a human being, am actually existing. I have been 'thrown' into existence and must sink or swim. Moreover, I have an awesome responsibility: I must bring to fulfillment the potentialities with which I have been endowed. Unlike lower animals, I am self-determining. I am always in a state of becoming; and because I am always becoming, at any instant I can be in crisis."

One of the most graphic descriptions of the condition humaine as the existentialist views it today can be found in the writings of a French philosopher, Blaise Pascal, who lived two hundred years before the father of modern existentialism was born:

> When I consider the brief span of my life, swallowed up in the eternity before and behind it, the small space that I fill, or even see, engulfed

in the infinite immensity of spaces which I know not and which know
not me, I am afraid, and wonder to see myself here rather than there:
for there is no reason why I should be here rather than there, now rather
than then. . . .[23]

Another fundamental point about any existentialist philosophy is its
recognition that, whereas many beings may be considered abstractly as
having the same kind of essence, each existing thing exists as something
absolutely unique. For example, there are many beings whom we call
human beings but no one human being can be another human being.

Now, let us apply these principles to existentialist depth psychology:
The realization that this human being alone can be himself, that no
other person can do his existing for him, creates in some men an
intolerable feeling of anxious responsibility: (1) they are "thrown" into
existence with potentialities which they must fulfill; (2) they alone can
individually fulfill their own unique potentialities. As a result, a man
may withdraw from this "challenge"; he may refuse to "make a commitment of himself to existence." He can do this in many ways: (1) he
may repudiate his unique existence by becoming a conformist (and
this is one of the most common escapes in Western culture today);
or (2) he may detach himself from his own existence by treating
himself as an object to be studied (for example, he may talk about his
problems without ever doing anything about them). In other words,
he makes no commitment of himself to reality. He refuses to make a
decision.

Rollo May expresses the existentialist position in reference to psychotherapy in a rather striking fashion:

> Man [or *Dasein*] is the particular being who has to be aware of him-
> self, be responsible for himself, if he is to become himself. He also is
> that particular being who knows that at some future moment he will
> not be; he is the being who is always in a dialectical relation with non-
> being, death, and he not only knows he will sometime not be, but he
> can, in his own choices, slough off and forfeit his being.[24]

Existential psychotherapy looks upon a neurosis as something that
is impeding a man's capacity to bring his being to fulfillment. Anxiety,
as the existentialist sees it, occurs when a human being finds himself
face to face with some new potentiality. This new potentiality is a source

---

[23] *The Thoughts of Blaise Pascal,* trans. by C. Kegan Paul (London: George Bell
and Sons, 1890), p. 28.
[24] Rollo May, *Existence* (New York: Basic Books, Inc., 1958), p. 42.

of anxiety because it will upset the present security of the individual by changing his status quo. The individual faced with this new anxiety may try to alleviate it by destroying the new potentiality he encounters. But if he destroys the new potentiality he will find himself with feelings of guilt. Guilt in this case will be objectively real as well.

In order to meet the patient on his own grounds, the existential analyst recognizes that he must see the patient in the patient's own unique world. By world is meant here *the structure of meaningful relationships in which a person exists and in the design of which he participates.* This "world" includes all the past events which have conditioned the existence of the patient and all the coexisting influences which here and now are determining the patient's existence. This "world" includes not only the events themselves, but the events as the patient relates to them.

Existential analysts distinguish the patient's world into: *Umwelt, Mitwelt,* and *Eigenwelt.*

The *Umwelt* is the biological world. It includes biological drives, needs, instincts. It is the world in which beings react automatically without any consciousness of themselves.

The *Mitwelt* is the world in which one human being acts with other human beings in interpersonal relationships. In this world, when one human being encounters another, both human beings are changed.

The *Eigenwelt* is that world in which the patient relates objects to himself.

Existential therapists maintain that if any one of these predominates over the other two, the patient loses contact with his own unique existence-in-itself, as-related-to-others, and as related-to-himself. They hold that classical Freudian theory really accounts for only *Umwelt,* that certain interpersonal theories account for *Mitwelt,* but that existentialism alone truly accounts for *Eigenwelt.*

Existentialists maintain, then, that the important thing about man is that he is a being who is not completely subjugated to the strictly deterministic principles governing the world of matter, but that he is, in short, a being possessive of what we may call spiritual traits as well since he can be self-determining. But a man may try to escape his responsibilities for self-determination by repressing the spiritual element in him. One of the chief aims of the existential therapist is to bring up into consciousness those spiritual values which the patient may have repressed in his anxiety about fulfilling his existential responsibilities.

In addition to Binswanger and Frankl, some of the more noted European proponents of the existentialist technics have been G. Bally, M. Boss, F. J. Buytendijk, I. Caruso, R. Kuhn, J. J. Lopez-Ibor, E. Minkowski, A. Storch, J. H. Van Den Berg, V. E. von Gebsattel. In the United States the movement has been associated with Ernest Angel of the Institute For Motivational Research, Henri F. Ellenberger of the Menninger Clinic, Rollo May of the William Alanson White Institute of Psychiatry, and Erwin B. Strauss of the University of Louisville Medical School.

PART V

THE PASTOR AND RESPONSIBILITY

CHAPTER XVIII

THE PSYCHOLOGY OF PERSONAL RESPONSIBILITY

The psychology of personal responsibility is, for all practical purposes, the psychology of the unconscious and of the will. We must answer these questions: Is man free in his conscious choices to act or not to act as he chooses? Are his acts merely influenced or are they coerced by his unconscious?

The current trend in psychiatry is to consider that there are no criminals, no sinners, but only sick people. The conclusion is, therefore, that no one has responsibility for crime or sin. A typical example of this trend is demonstrated in this quotation from the Group for the Advancement of Psychiatry:

> He [the criminal psychopathologist] cannot accept the concept that the criminal is normal and sane, because he sees that the criminal is guided by much the same unconscious forces as the neurotic and psychotic, the criminal act being in the nature of a symptom, the manifestations of which the criminal cannot control and the basic reasons for which escape his insight.
>
> Neither can it longer be maintained that the criminal is a sane person, a responsible agent who can profit by punishment, but instead one must look for the motives behind the criminal deed and recognize that these motives are entirely unconscious, and therefore cannot be reached by punishment.[1] (Italics added.)

We must reject these extreme opinions. Before considering the subject further, let me define the meaning of the term responsibility as it appears at least to this psychiatrist.

The concept of personal responsibility depends upon the recognition by the average man that he is answerable to a higher authority, whether

[1] "Criminal Responsibility and Psychiatric Expert Testimony," formulated by The Committee on Psychiatry and Law of the Group for the Advancement of Psychiatry; Report No. 26, Topeka, Kans., May, 1954, p. 2.

it be a parent, the city, the state, or God, for approval or blame. Such answerability has no meaning unless the individual is capable of earning reward or meriting blame; in other words, unless he possesses a free will. Responsibility depends on free will as an effect depends on a cause.[2] All men at all times have recognized that culpability for a free act is a reality. Responsibility does not mean punishability, as some have claimed. It means only that the individual, whose responsibility is under examination, at the time he performed a certain act or acts was in such a state of mental health that he was able to act freely on the basis of a *subjective* evaluation of his act or acts. To be culpable, the individual must be able to distinguish *subjective* ideas of right and wrong from the *objective* reality of right and wrong. In other words, a person may judge subjectively that he is doing right, whereas objectively he is doing wrong. This establishes the familiar difference between material and formal sin. Formal sin, therefore, requires knowledge that the act is wrong and freedom of the will.

The word *responsibility* has a different meaning for many of those who use it. Sir James Stephen, for example, points out that to the lawyer it may mean one thing; but to the priest, the physician, and the average layman, who makes up juries, it may mean something entirely different. For many the concept has lost its original meaning. One of these is Frym, who states: "Therefore, our medieval concept of responsibility no longer can be defended effectively."[3] Frym is not the only one to express this thought. Such denials of responsibility for the acts which we commit may offer some degree of comfort for those who wish to have their cake and eat it too, but the idea of responsibility is not merely a gratuitous assumption. This is demonstrated by the fact that the laws of all countries accept it and, in practice, many schools of philosophy, even the determinists, at least implicitly admit it. It seems clear that without responsibility there could be no law to direct and harmonize the social body and no reason for punishing crime. Wharton somewhat reluctantly agrees with this opinion. He says: "No matter what may be our speculative views as to the existence of conscience or of freedom of action we are obliged when determining responsibility to affirm both."[4]

---

[2] St. Thomas Aquinas, *Summa Theologica*, Ia, Qu. 83, art. 1, c.

[3] Marcel Frym, "*The Criminal Intent*," 31 *Texas Law Review*, 260–278 (1953).

[4] Wharton, quoted by J. S. Cammack, *Moral Problems of Mental Defect* (New York: Benziger Bros., 1939), p. 13.

Free Will

There is no agreement among scientists or philosophers concerning the precise meaning of free will. In fact, most psychiatrists would even deny its existence and, in doing so, would deny responsibility. What is clear, however, is that most people act as if they possessed freedom of action and the power to make free decisions. A typical psychiatric opinion on this subject is that of Diamond:

> . . . Each act of will, each choice presumedly made on a random basis, turns out to be as rigidly determined as any other physiological process of the human body. Yet all of us continue to live our lives, make our choices, exercise our free will, and obey or disobey the law as if we actually had something to say about what we are doing. Criminal law could not exist were it not for this posit that each normal person intends to do the act which he does do and that such intention is based upon the exercise of free will.[5]

Doctor Diamond is apparently unable to accept his own conclusion that such a concept as free will is necessary.

Jones, a Freudian psychoanalyst, concludes that:

> Psychoanalysis of the unconscious shows that, whatever the conscious attitude towards the matter may be, there exist in the deeper layers of the mind the strongest, and probably ineradicable, motives creating what may be called the "sense of free will," closely connected with the sense of personality itself and retained so long as this is retained, i.e., until insanity, delirium or death dissolve it. That from the point of view of scientific objectivity this belief is illusory, is irrelevant to the fact of its existence, and in a way to the necessity of its existence.[6]

In spite of such apparently uncompromising opinions, Klein points to the inconsistency of these deterministic psychiatrists in the position they take:

> As a matter of fact, even the staunchest psychiatric advocates of determinism are not hesitant to use the concept of freedom in their professional work. . . .
> What is more, even an ultradeterministic psychiatrist wants to be left free to choose the course of action he deems best for his patients, and sees no incongruity in talking about his responsibility for their welfare. In

---

[5] Bernard L. Diamond, M.D., "With Malice Aforethought," *Archives of Criminal Psychodynamics*, Vol. 2, No. 1, Winter, 1957, p. 27.

[6] Jones, quoted by Diamond, op. cit., p. 28.

his professional role he wants to be regarded as a free agent capable of making intelligent choices, and willing to assume responsibility for what he prescribes.[7]

Forester, in *Faith of an Agnostic*, says: "If we give up free will, then we must give up moral responsibility with it. And this in practice we cannot do. We are bound to assume that men are free agents and responsible for their actions."[8] Responsibility, therefore, presupposes the liberty of the agent and implies the consciousness of his obligation to account for his actions. It is "accountability for conduct in the case of an agent possessing knowledge of the [moral] law with power to govern conduct in harmony with such law."

Psychic determinism is often confused with the denial of the freedom of the will. Father Donceel explains this clearly:

> According to this hypothesis [psychic determinism], psychological phenomena, as well as physiological or physical phenomena, have definite causes, from which they follow with absolute necessity. Forgetting a name, dreaming a certain dream, experiencing a mood or an emotion, manifesting a neurotic symptom — all these are psychological phenomena. . . . Philosophically there is no objection to the principle, provided we except the free decisions of our will. Only man's will, in its deliberate and conscious decisions, escapes the law of psychic determinism. Freud, of course, does not mention this exception.[9]

This distinction must be made. Man is only free in those acts which follow deliberation. He is not free in his choice of his symptoms or his disease. When we state that the symptoms have value for the patient, we do not mean that he has made any deliberate choice of his particular symptoms. For example, the physical symptoms resulting from psychological conflicts result from disturbances in the physiological mechanisms of the person. These are not under the control of the will. One individual who has a marital conflict may get a backache, another anxiety, and yet another may develop an obsession. This statement concerning the determined nature of symptoms gives rise to the statement occasionally seen in articles to the effect that the neurotic individual is not free. This does not mean that he has lost his freedom to act in a responsible way, but refers only to his lack of choice regarding his symptoms. The following discussion of the psychosomatic unity of man may help to place the will in its proper relationship to the other faculties.

---

[7] D. B. Klein, *Abnormal Psychology* (New York: Holt, 1951), pp. 142–143.

[8] Forester, quoted by Cammack, *op. cit.*, pp. 13–14.

[9] J. Donceel, S.J., "Second Thoughts on Freud," *Thought*, Vol. XXIV, No. 94, p. 468.

The Psychosomatic Unity of Man

For descriptive purposes the personality must be described piecemeal, but it should not be pictured as a compartmented structure. It is actually functioning as a unit with a constant frictionless interchange between its component parts. It is as if each component was a mirror which by its reflection activates the other components. As long as each mirror reflects its proper degree of light in the right direction and with proper intensity there is a normal interchange. If something happens to one or more of the mirrors it will disturb the whole mechanism. So it is with the component parts of the mind.

The *structure of the personality* as usually described by the scholastic philosopher shows how intimately each aspect of the individual is affected even by small changes in its component parts. Although this material is undoubtedly familiar to the pastor counselor it is repeated here to illustrate how disturbance in any part affects all the others.

Phase One

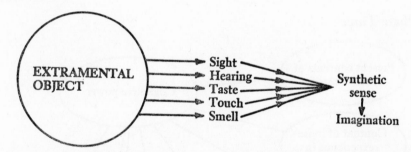

Cognition starts with the perception of an object in external reality. The *external senses* pick up the qualities of the external object. Since some of these qualities are restricted to one particular sense — for example, sight alone picks up light qualities; hearing alone picks up sound qualities; taste alone picks up sweet, sour, bitter, and salt; touch picks up hot, cold, etc. — the object may be said to be "broken up" by the external senses when it is received by the one. These "fragmented" data, as received by the external senses, are reunited into one unified sense object by the *synthetic sense* which, at the same time, actuates the imagination. The *imagination*, once actuated by the synthetic sense, retains the data. Under the right conditions, the contents of imagination may be withdrawn and made available to the knower when he wants to relate one sense experience to another sense experience as stored in the imagination (see Phases Two and Three).

Phase Two

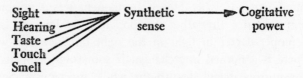

The *cogitative power* is said to "scan" the contents of the synthetic sense and pick up certain sense qualities which are not directly acquired by the external senses nor directly presented to the synthetic sense. Such qualities are time-relationships, relative benefit or harm of an object, etc.

In the adult human knower, the cogitative power *fully* determines this relative benefit or harm of an individual material object by comparing the sense data then present in the synthetic sense with related data summoned from the imagination and the memory.

Phase Three

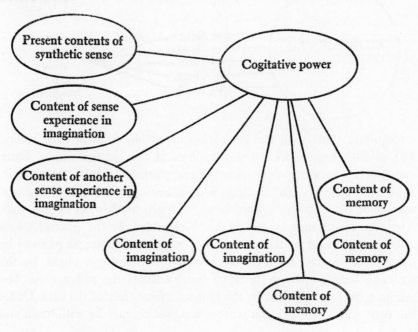

As a result of the collation of the present sense experience with other sense experiences previously stored and now summoned from imagination and memory, the human knower formulates what is called a sense *insight* (sometimes called an *experimentum*) into the presently sensed object. By "sense insight" we mean that the knower recognizes the "value" of the external object for him, the knower.

As a result of this, the knower may have a surge of emotion. . . . (How the object is evaluated will determine what kind of emotion arises.) At the same time as an emotional surge arises, the intellect is working on the data of the object and deriving its own data.

Phase Four

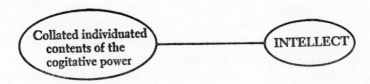

As a result of this, the intellect formulates a knowledge of the object which knowledge understands the object under its aspects of universality.

As a result of the act of the intellect, the object can be viewed under its universal aspect of goodness, either under its positive aspect of being a desirable object or under its negative aspect of being a less than infinitely desirable object. (We might say, in this latter case, that the object is viewed as comparatively undesirable.) Therefore, the will may react to the object under one of two aspects:

1. In so far as the object is desirable;
2. In so far as the object is lacking in desirability compared to the infinitely desirable.

It can be seen that the readiness of any one of these knowing powers to react or the force with which these powers individually react will determine the balance in which the cogitative power is affected by the contents of the other sense powers. It will be equally true that the intellectual outlook will be affected by the sense content as presented to the intellect. All of these, plus the readiness of the emotional faculties themselves to act, will determine eventually the balance (or imbalance) of conditions which will ultimately influence the choice of the will.

Man, a Unitary Being

Man is a unitary being composed of body and soul. In his soul are rooted proximately and ultimately the faculties of intellect and will. All the other faculties of living activity are rooted ultimately in the soul but proximately in the soul-body composite. Those rooted proximately in the soul-body composite include the activities of sensation (e.g., seeing, hearing, tasting, imagining, remembering, etc.) and emotion (love, anger, joy, desire, etc.). The soul-body composite is also the proximate source of the vegetal operations (i.e., nutritive, growth, and generative functions).

All these activities of both the sensile and vegetal powers of man have their own proper goals toward which they naturally tend. Achievement of any of their own limited goals results in an accompanying effect called pleasure. The intellect and the power of will also tend toward their natural goals which are more universal than the objects of the sensile and vegetal powers. Therefore, the operations of the intellect and will achieve their own analogous kind of pleasure as well.

The appetitive power on the intellectual level of man is called the will. It is the will which, when correctly trained, chooses objects which the intellect recognizes as serving the good of the whole man and as helping him toward his final end.

From what I have said up to this point, you can readily understand how there could arise a conflict within the total human person: Each of the faculties is bent on its own goal with its accompanying pleasure. But if each of these faculties achieves its own end with no regard for the total person, then the individual will fail to achieve his ultimate good. There is a constant struggle between the sensile and vegetal appetites which are seeking their own limited goods and the rational appetite (will) which is seeking the universal good.

In the development of this conflict, the *intellect* acts upon the data presented to it by the senses (primarily through the cogitative power) and picks up the universal aspects to be recognized in the external object (or situation). The *intellect* evaluates the object (or situation) on the level of universality, whereas the cogitative power evaluates the object as *individuated*.

The person who possesses practical intellect and cogitative power judges that this object, in these circumstances, is in some respect or respects good or evil, and therefore should be chosen or rejected by the *will*. In fact, the very functioning of the intellect and cogitative power will occur only if the will allows them to function. Metaphysically, the will must choose an object as good, or reject it as evil. The will cannot choose evil as such or reject good as such, and the good or evil of an object which moves the will to choice or rejection must be presented to the will by the intellect.

The will then is presented with the object. The person possessing the will makes his choice through the will. The practical intellect may present to the will a judgment that a given object, as it exists in a concrete situation, is good or evil with reference to qualities apprehended by, to list just a few of the cognitive faculties, sight, hearing, taste, touch, smell, synthetic sense, memory, imagination, cogitative power, or intellect itself.

The total presentation, in a given case, may be weighted in favor of the qualities apprehended as good by one or more of the powers named. If the person has developed one of these powers by habit, for example, to the detriment of certain other powers, this habit may serve as an *influence* upon a more ready choice by the person toward some particular good rather than another. Similarly, emotion may influence the choice of a good related to one power or another.

Or the person may maneuver certain of his sense powers by intermediate acts of the will before he comes to his practical judgment. For example, in evaluating a concrete situation, the person may refuse to let memory carry out its full role. In such a case, the full contents of memory would not be available to the cogitative power in collating data for the experimentum. Then the data of the experimentum, and the practical judgment based thereon, would be distorted to the extent that the contents of memory were refused by the will. A constant refusal would develop an habitual reaction which in turn contributes its influence.

Even after the practical judgment has determined that a given object in its present situation should be chosen or rejected by the will, the will is not necessitated to follow the counsel offered. If the counsel does not accord with the person's inclination, the will can direct the intellect to consider some other aspect of the situation. This would then be another judgment determining that, despite the judgment of conscience, it is more suitable to pick this action. This is the mystery of sin. By emotion and habit, principally, the will is inclined to choose some particular sorts of good and to reject others.

The will must be considered under two aspects. In the ultimate act of choice, the will accepts or rejects the object — in this act, one cannot speak of *degrees* of choice. In a dynamic sense — considering the entire process by which choice is made, and not its ultimate act alone — the will may be considered as affected by many factors both conscious and unconscious (such as memory, imagination, habits, etc.). In this dynamic sense there may be *degrees of choice* which would result in varying degrees of responsibility. It must be emphasized that man is responsible only for his free acts. If there is no freedom there is no responsibility.

The Will and Neurosis

To some, the presence of a neurosis seems to indicate that some power or another of the soul has been actually destroyed. Philosophically considered, however, a neurosis is not the result of a *destroyed* psychic power. The neurosis is rather a defective application of a power and does not indicate any intrinsic defect in the power itself. A power of the soul cannot be *destroyed*, if by that we mean *disintegrated*, as the tissue in the body can disintegrate. The power itself continues to exist, but it is misdirected. For example, the sense appetite may be conditioned by bad habits to operate too readily toward its own goal without regard for the other operations of the human person (excessive eating, or excessive use of the sex function, or readiness to anger, etc.). On the other hand, the power may be conditioned by habit and circumstances so that it does not operate as readily as it should, as when the power of will is not actuated to exercise its control over other functions.

The potentiality for operation remains in the powers of the soul of the neurotic or psychotic. But the powers of the soul are not integrated so that they accord with the total good of the whole human person.

As stated above, the will tends to possess an object presented to it by the intellect as good. "Nothing is willed that is not first known." Although this is true, it is obvious that the intellect may present to the will what is really only an *apparent* good. To the will it is, however, presented *sub specie boni*. Further, the intellect can focus upon the desirable features of an object, leaving the undesirable features out of consideration. Thus, the first step in the development of a neurosis or psychosis takes place. The person confronted by painful reality attempts to avoid suffering by focusing his attention on the more comforting aspects of various escape mechanisms (ego defenses) which the intellect presents to the will as good. The will accepts this misdirection *sub specie boni* and elicits the first act which, if frequently repeated, may result in a habit. Thus are developed the faulty habits of thinking, feeling, and willing that eventually result in neurotic disorders. Each act makes its repetition easier. As habit develops, advertence to the acts is lessened. Eventually the act may be performed automatically. *Habit may, under certain circumstances, decrease responsibility.*

The Will and So-Called Irresistible Impulse

There are specific disturbances associated with defective use of the will. The first of these is the so-called irresistible impulse. The expression "irresistible impulse" connotes a distortion of the power of the will itself. This is an inaccuracy. It is not the power of will *itself* that has been distorted as was noted above. If the patient had entertained reality judgments which were different from those he did have, he might have chosen to act in another manner. The distortion is not of the will, but of the whole person.

According to St. Thomas, there is only one irresistible object for the will — i.e., the infinitely good. That is to say, if the intellect recognized an object as being the infinite good, the will would have no other choice than to accept it. On the other hand, *if the intellect does not recognize an object as necessarily connected with infinite goodness, the will is free to accept or to reject it.* It should be noted that the infinite good irresistibly captures the consent of the will only when it is perceived *as the infinite good.* That is what takes place when the intellect of the blessed behold God face to face. But in the present life the intellect pictures God as a limited good; therefore, it does not have to love Him.

The will tends to accept any good which is less than infinite if the intellect does not recognize in the acceptance a threat to an even greater good. This is the way the intellect and will would act in an emotionally mature individual. The intellect would have a regulating and integrating role over the sensile and vegetal activities.

However, we must keep in mind that intellect and will are not the only capacities of the whole human person. He is an emotional, sensile, and vegetal being as well as intellectual. The person may choose to cultivate his sensile life at the expense of the intellectual. Thus, he might establish fixed habits whereby his emotional capacities react more readily than the intellectual, and the emotions obtain their satisfaction at the expense of the person as a whole.

The regulating and integrating rule of the intellectual powers over the lower powers is never a despotic one, even in the most perfectly integrated human personality. Its rule is rather a democratic one. That is to say, the lower powers have some autonomy of their own, and if they are not regulated, will break out and take over the person. But even here the question of responsibility is not to be ignored. Even if an individual's life is a chaos of emotions, we cannot say that he has lost his will power. What should be said is that in this particular situation the individual for one reason or another has not exercised his will power, not that his will was overrun. In certain concrete situations, an individual might be said to have had no freedom in so far as, here and now, his psychic apparatus was so conditioned by disposition and habits that these exercised their excessive influence before the individual was able to calmly deliberate. An individual with a compulsion neurosis, for example, may know what is right and yet act against his knowledge.

In determining guilt, the question will arise: To what extent did the person knowingly allow his emotions to take the ascendancy? If his emotional life is emphasized at the expense of his higher powers, it may be due to a number of factors, such as poor training by his parents. This would be a mitigating factor so far as guilt is concerned. On the other hand, an individual may have allowed his emotions to take over simply because he chose the path of least resistance. In this case, he would be far more guilty than in the other. In both cases, we should speak of an "unresisted" urge but never of an "irresistible" urge.

In brief, the will is indirectly influenced by the emotions and unconscious factors but never coerced. The will acts on the basis of conscious judgments and inclines toward the judgment which is presented to it as good.

A great deal of the confusion about psychic determinism in modern psychiatry has arisen because Freud thought that he had shown once and for all that free will is an illusion. He based this on his explanation of a number of psychic activities, such as the connection of thought associations, origin of neurotic symptoms, slips of the tongue, and acts of forgetting, among others. But anyone who understands Freud's theories and who also understands and accepts the doctrine of free will will immediately see that the instances offered in proof against free will do not pertain to the question.[10] The conditions upon which an individual makes a free decision are all *in consciousness* at the time that he makes the decision. That is to say, the premises upon which he decides to act, or not to act, are in his field of consciousness. These thoughts are influenced by other unconscious factors which are not directly available to the man making the decision. However much these conscious thoughts may be influenced by unconscious factors, it still remains true to say that the individual's decision to act is based upon those thoughts immediately available in consciousness.

This is true for both the psychotic and for his more normal confrere. For example, in the famous M'Naghton case the conscious, although delusional, thought which caused M'Naghton to kill was that the subject of his fury was his mortal enemy. That this concept was a delusion and undoubtedly arose from unconscious sources does not change the fact that his decision to kill arose from the thoughts of which he was conscious. In a recent article in a national magazine, it was asserted that "the girl who slept with the basketball player" did not know why she was doing it. I doubt very much that anyone could possess such a naïve idea. The remote unconscious factors certainly did not coerce her into so doing. To repeat, every normal human being is influenced but not coerced by his unconscious. The difference between the normal man and the psychotic is the *degree of influence* which is exerted on his actions by his unconscious. In the normal man, the power of reason *has control* over the urges arising from unconscious sources. In the psychotic, the power of reason yields its place more readily to the urges of the unconscious. Thus, reason is unseated because its control has been usurped by the lower powers. Just why reason is overwhelmed in the psychotic depends on a large number of factors, the most important being the loss of proper subjective judgment which permits the effects of childhood trauma, more immediate environmental influences, psychic threats, faulty habits, and other traumatic psychological experiences to gain access to the conscious without the usual controls. The normal and the abnormal mind do not differ qualitatively, but quantitatively. The sensitive conscience of the psychotic may lead to swift and terrifying behavior.

---

[10] Cf. Agostino Ramirez, *Unconscious Drives and Human Freedom in Freud's Psychoanalysis* (Washington, D. C.: The Catholic University of America, 1955).

It should be clearly understood in speaking of free will that no one maintains that all acts of man are free. On the contrary, there are many acts a man performs which are not free. Only those acts which follow deliberation are free acts. That is why the philosopher distinguishes between an *actus humanus* and an *actus hominis*. A human act (*actus humanus*) is a specific act resulting from a man's exercise of his human power of deliberation. An act of a man (*actus hominis*) is one that takes place without deliberation, e.g., reflex activity, digestive activity, response to stimuli and growth. Habit and bodily appetites may influence the judgment which precedes the act of the will and consequently may strongly influence its action, in which case, the will, although influenced, is not coerced. About the lack of freedom in reference to certain acts, Mercier has this to say:

> . . . all acts performed by man are not free. Only those acts are free which are the fruit of reflection. A very large percentage of acts, then, even in the most serious life, are not free because done without thought; a larger percentage are suggested simply by the imagination, controlled by passion or self-interest, or are due to routine. In the second place, it is a mistake to imagine that free acts are purely arbitrary, proceeding from a will that acts without a purpose. Truly man may be unreasonable if he like. But in point of fact, in by far the majority of cases, men are not unreasonable, but allow themselves to be actuated by a purpose. Thus, not to speak of the last intention — the seeking after supreme happiness — the instinct of self-preservation, the instinct of propagation, the natural love of parents for children, of children for parents, the striving for well-being, or for personal interest, are all so many motors to the will to which it generally responds without making a deliberate choice.[11]

Freedom of will does not mean merely arbitrariness, as if the will simply moved at random without receiving influences. On the other hand, we should not say that these influences coerce the will into a position where it can choose only one alternative. We all know how often we have had the chance to choose between two motives and we may have chosen something which at the time was less desirable than something else. For example, going to work at the office on a pleasant day instead of playing golf. Most of the arguments against freedom of the will are based on a distorted nineteenth-century concept of Newtonian physics, or upon the law of the conservation of energy. In back of the doctrine of psychic determinism is the nineteenth-century philosophy of

---

[11] Cardinal Desire Mercier, *Manual of Scholastic Philosophy* (London: K. Paul Trench, Trubner and Co., Ltd., 1916), Vol. 1, p. 275.

mechanism which Freud adopted uncritically from his contemporaries. Freud himself was not a philosopher, as he pointed out somewhat ironically in his own autobiography. Nineteenth-century mechanism has been rejected because in more recent times even in the physical universe it can no longer be held that there is absolute determinacy.

It is a mistake for a philosopher to predicate of all reality some principle which applies to only a segment of reality, just as it would be for a botanist to say that since tomatoes and lemons are both fruit, anything he says about tomatoes will apply equally to lemons.

Definition of Unresisted Urge

The following definition of unresisted urge (irresistible impulse) would include cases of scrupulosity and seems to be best: *an unresisted urge is one which, because of mental illness, so far causes the individual to lose his power of choice in regard to particular acts that in spite of the fact that he may recognize an act as wrong, he feels so impelled to act that he may be unable to adhere to what he considers right.*

Put in philosophical terms, this could be expressed as follows: an unresisted urge is one which has developed so excessively at the expense of the other psychic powers that in comparison to this urge the other powers exert negligible influence upon reason when it is called upon to make a judgment. This urge occupies the focal point of consciousness. Because it occupies this central point, it becomes the basis upon which the intellect represents an object or some course of activity as desirable to the will.

In other words, this urge has developed to such a degree that its occupancy of the whole field of consciousness for the individual precludes the entrance into consciousness of other notions which might tend to represent the urge as undesirable. Since the urge is presented to the will only as something desirable to fulfill, the individual wills to satisfy the urge. This condition occurs not as an isolated temporary mental illness, but as part of a continuing illness which both antedates and succeeds this particular act. Instances of acts of short duration are more likely to be the result of sudden passion or anger and are not properly considered under this title. It should be emphasized that the degree of resistibility is related to the severity of the illness and may vary in degree from slight to the point of complete irresistibility. This principle would apply in varying degrees to many neurotic states such as compulsive masturbation, suicidal urges, and so forth.

In summary, it may be said that the will may be affected by many factors both conscious and unconscious, such as memory, imagination, habits, emotions. Depending upon the extent to which these factors detract from freedom of choice, there will be varying degrees of responsibility.

Habits

The influence of habits on the development of both the normal and the sick personality has been mentioned frequently. A brief discussion of habits therefore seems appropriate. A *habit may be defined here as a facility in performing an action engendered by conscious repetition of the act.* Specific individual acts habitually repeated enter into the formation of the personality and character of an individual. There is, however, a reason or purpose for man's actions. A motive stands behind them and produces them. *Omne agens agit propter finem.* Each act represents the choice of one goal or object or reality and the rejection of others. At times, the choice may run counter to the urges of instinct, feelings, and emotions; at other times, it may be in accord with them. In any case, habits indicate that the process of making a choice after a certain manner has become second nature in the personality of the individual. Habits may be so much second nature that they are performed with only a minimum degree of consciousness, or even unconsciously. Habits are mere symbols or signs which reveal that a man consistently acts one way and not another.

The counselor should examine habits genetically. This means that the multiple emotions, instincts, feelings, fears, anxieties, ego-deflating experiences, and kindred situations which helped to establish the habit should be carefully analyzed and their influence on the fully developed personality be evaluated.

From psychic habits are developed man's general principles, ideals, etc., which will become manifest as his personality. These, if of the proper type, will assist him in meeting his daily conflicts intelligently, calmly, and efficiently. If the individual's habits are in accordance with reason and are based on deferred pleasure, or on the subordination of sense to reason and revelation, the principles and character will be worthy of a mature, rational being. They will lead to mental integrity and "peace of soul." Such an individual develops true basic principles, worth-while ideas, and a strong, well-integrated personality and character. He has calm of mind and peace of soul. Happiness is for him a spiritual condition. He is willing to exercise effort to preserve psychological normality, to enjoy it as one of the noblest achievements of man. If, on the contrary, the individual habitually employs unhealthy ego defenses such as withdrawal, denial, rationalization, projection, and so forth, as a means of escaping reality, these will eventually lead to mental disorders and psychic unrest. "Habit, if not resisted, soon becomes necessity."[12]

---

[12] St. Augustine.

CHAPTER XIX

THE PSYCHOLOGY OF PERSONAL RESPONSIBILITY (Continued)

Ego Defenses

The effect of habit on all aspects of the personality cannot be considered in a book of this length, but certain intellectual habits are so important in the practice of the pastoral counselor that they cannot be omitted. When an individual is confronted by an unacceptable or distasteful conflict he has two ways in which to handle it. One is by facing it realistically; the other is by attempting to avoid it through the use of some type of ego defense. Ego defenses are so named because they protect the individual from the feeling of deflation, inadequacy, or inferiority which he might experience if he faced the situation realistically. Ideally, of course, one should face conflicts squarely and solve them on a reality basis. Unfortunately, this happens infrequently because the language of reality is austere, frequently painful, and often deflating. More frequently the individual escapes from the painful conflict by the use of a variety of defense mechanisms. Neuroses and psychoses develop when the use of these defenses becomes habitual.

Definition

Ego defenses, or psychic dynamisms, are essentially protective methods of judging, reasoning, and acting, unconsciously adopted by the individual to defend himself and/or to compensate for his subjectively recognized, though not clearly perceived, distaste for or inability to face reality.

It is important to remember that *these are not consciously employed devices*. The conflict is repressed and gives rise to the various mechanisms which are unconsciously activated to bolster the individual's ego and to preserve his ego strength. The term *unconscious* will be used throughout this chapter in preference to the term *marginal consciousness*. The latter term is more correct but less commonly used and consequently less understood.[1]

Classification of Ego Defenses

For purposes of description the ego defenses are usually grouped under five headings: (A) Evasion, (B) Protection, (C) Compromise, (D) Compensation, (E) Escape. Each of these has subdivisions as follows:

A. *Evasion*

    1. Suppression
    2. Repression

B. *Protection*

    1. Rationalization
    2. Identification
        a) Identification of ourselves with the positive traits of others
        b) Identification of ourselves with the negative traits of others
        c) Identification of others with our own objectionable traits
        d) Image interchange
    3. Resistance

C. *Compromise*

    1. Substitution
    2. Sublimation
    3. Displacement
    4. Conversion
    5. Symbolization

D. *Compensation*

    1. Reaction Formation
    2. Projection
    3. Introjection

E. *Escape*

    1. Fantasy
    2. Dissociation
    3. Regression

---

[1] John R. Cavanagh and James B. McGoldrick, *Fundamental Psychiatry* (Milwaukee: The Bruce Publishing Co., 1958), pp. 89–92.

4. Denial
5. Flight
   a) Into introversion
   b) Into extroversion
6. Surrender

The pastoral counselor should be familiar with ego defenses, at least to the extent that he can recognize them in the productions of his clients. Since they occur more frequently in the abnormal personality they will not be discussed exhaustively here where we are attempting to present to the pastoral counselor a description of the "normal." The defenses are not always evidence of abnormality and may be employed by "normal" individuals. We routinely recommend, for example, that impure thoughts be *displaced* by a prayer, and many "normals" *rationalize* their behavior. The mentally ill are just like ourselves but more so.

This fact should be borne in mind — the use of ego defenses is not *per se* evidence of seriously abnormal behavior, although they will in general indicate at least an unconscious desire to escape from some aspect of reality. For more intensive study reference should be made to works on the subject.[2] For our purpose the principal mechanisms will be listed alphabetically with a definition and example of each. The pastor should become familiar with the terminology employed here and apply his knowledge of this subject in his contact with clients. The terms will be described in alphabetical order rather than in groups for ease of reference.

The Individual Ego Defenses

Compensation

No one likes to admit his shortcomings, even to himself; consequently, there is a tendency to unconsciously exaggerate one's abilities. This tendency is known as *compensation*. This must be carefully distinguished from bragging, which is a *conscious* exaggeration. Compensation occurs,

---

[2] Cf. Franz Alexander and Helen Ross (eds.), *Dynamic Psychiatry* (Chicago: University of Chicago Press, 1952); O. S. English and S. M. Finch, *Introduction to Psychiatry* (New York: W. W. Norton & Co., 1954); Frieda Fromm-Reichmann, *Principles of Intensive Psychotherapy* (Chicago: University of Chicago Press, 1950); D. Henderson and R. Gillespie, *A Text-Book of Psychiatry*, 7th ed. (New York: Oxford Medical Publications, 1951); Thomas V. Moore, *The Driving Forces of Human Nature* (New York: Grune & Stratton, 1948); J. Ernest Nicole, O.B.E., *Psychopathology* (London: Bailliere, Tindall and Cox, 1946); Joseph Nuttin, *Psychoanalysis and Personality*, translated by George Lamb (New York: Sheed & Ward, 1953); Ian Skottowe, *Clinical Psychiatry* (New York: McGraw-Hill Book Co., Inc., 1954).

for example, when an individual places excessive emphasis on his ancestors, or on his university, or on his branch of service in an effort to mask his own inadequacies or deficiencies. In the psychotic individual, compensation becomes more recognizable, as is demonstrated clearly in the schizophrenic patient who believes he is the president, a renowned leader, or even God.

Conversion

A very commonly employed defense is the conversion of emotional energy into a somatic manifestation. It is this conversion that gives the mechanism its name. There is frequently a close symbolic relationship between the conflict and the symptom. This is a primitive mechanism that follows the biblical injunction, "If your hand offends, cut it off." A hand, for example, with which a sin was committed may become paralyzed. An impulse to kill may be followed by paralysis. A painful experience may be followed by a forgetfulness or amnesia. A desire to run away in the face of danger may be followed by paralysis of the lower extremities. A fear of sinning sexually may lead to impotence, or a fear of pregnancy may lead to sterility. The manifestations of the conversion mechanism are manifold.

Daydreaming

Daydreaming, or fantasy, is a normal characteristic of the mental life. It may be defined as the act or state of dwelling amid people or scenes created by the imagination. To say that daydreaming is normal needs qualification. It is quite common in children and within broad limits may be said to be normal. Children, because of numerous restrictions, find escape into imaginative play and daydreaming, and their fantasy may even include imaginary companions and imaginary correspondents. In adults, this type of activity should not be considered normal, as in the case of a middle-aged man who insisted that his wife set a place for Mr. Roosevelt at the breakfast table each morning and then would not allow her to talk so that he could engage the President in conversation. This was ten years after Mr. Roosevelt's death.

As the child ages, fantasy should get into closer contact with reality. In the young adult, imaginations may still be somewhat grandiose, but they should be more in accord with the real potential of the individual. In the mature adult, fantasy becomes distinctly abnormal when the individual would rather daydream about doing something which he could do than actually do it. The young girl who would rather stay at home and daydream about a dance than go is definitely escaping from reality in an unhealthy way.

Denial

Denial is a commonly used mechanism in which the subject merely denies that a situation exists. He will insist, for example, that he is not sick, that his symptoms are due to organic disease, that there is nothing wrong with him. He will accept almost any explanation except that his symptoms are based on an emotional disturbance.

Reaction Formation

Reaction formation is a defense in which the patient escapes from a painful conflict by developing a trait opposite to the one he finds it painful to face. In this way, for example, an individual may express great concern for and interest in another when actually his unconscious attitude is quite the opposite. The "sugary sweet" attitude of many women barely masks the underlying hostility which they feel. A reaction formation may be the problem of the oldest daughter who has had to assume the care of aging parents and thus has missed an opportunity to marry and have a family of her own. Her excessive concern over drafts, sleep, diet, and health may actually mask an unconscious wish for the death of her parents. This is quite likely to have serious repercussions when the parent dies because of a reaction of guilt which gives rise to a depression through fear that the wish may have caused the death of the parent. The crusader may have strong unconscious feelings in favor of that against which he campaigns.

Displacement

Displacement is an ego defense in which one idea or affect is replaced by another. This term has at least two meanings. In one case, it refers to the transference of the emotion (affect) from one idea to another. This, for example, occurs in obsessions where the affect is displaced from an idea to which it was attached to another idea which would usually be indifferent to the subject. By this means the subject is spared the pain he would otherwise feel. The significant idea is then repressed. Before its displacement the emotion may be "free-floating." This means it is not attached to any specific idea. The affect may then be experienced by the subject as "anxiety," as unexplained feelings of guilt, as an unexplained feeling of euphoria, and so forth.

In the second case, the displacement results in the discharge of an emotion in other than its usual channel; for example, if hostility cannot be expressed, or there seems no other source toward which it can be directed, it may be displaced to (turned against) the individual himself, who may then experience it as a depressive reaction. If action is denied, the emotion may be expressed verbally.

Dissociation

In dissociation, a patient's ideas or emotions have reached no working agreement among themselves and become, as it were, "mixed up." Meanwhile, certain mental processes have become separated from the rest of consciousness, and these may function as a unit or as if they belonged to another person. In cases of "dual personality" this dissociated aspect of the mental life may take over and function as a separate personality by displacing the normal consciousness. This is the mechanism in conversion hysteria where it may manifest itself not only in the development of "dual" or even multiple personalities, but also in fugue states, somnambulism, automatic writing, amnesia, and so forth.

In dissociation the subject may also segregate his ideas into "logic-tight compartments" which result in the isolation of one part of the personality from others. This permits the ardent usher of the Sunday service to cheat at business all the rest of the week with the usual explanation, "Oh, that doesn't apply to me."

Extrovert

The extrovert is the "outward" type of individual. He is the doer and not the thinker; he is the one who runs away from his problems rather than take the time to think them out; he must constantly be "on the go." This tendency might be characterized as an unconscious flight into extroversion in an effort to escape from his conflict. He keeps going from one thing to another, attempting to keep busy so that "he will not have time to think."

It should be emphasized that within limits extroversion is a normal characteristic of the personality. Probably no one is completely an extrovert or an introvert. Most people possess qualities of both. The ideal would be the ambivert who possesses a balance of the desirable traits of both the introvert and the extrovert. The term has value in the appraisal of the personality, but one must be careful not to be influenced too much by casual observation of the subject. In its more pathological manifestations extroversion may be the precursor of manic behavior.

Identification

Identification is a mechanism in which the personality and actions of others who are admired are unconsciously adopted as our own. It is frequently referred to as *idealization* in the sense that the one admired is idealized and his characteristics adopted.

Wallin says that the source of the satisfaction connected with identification is largely derived from indulgence in daydreaming about the object with which the individual identifies.[3] Identification is not always a pathological mechanism. For example, we constantly urge our children, our parishioners, or our students to follow the example of erudite and holy men. We appeal to them to emulate great men of the past. In this way, it is a very desirable mechanism because a climate is set up in which a healthy growth of the individual may take place. In instances such as occur in connection with certain "comic books" and movies, an unhealthy identification may take place either with the traits displayed by the actors as they play their parts or with certain unpleasant and immoral features of the actor's private life. It is for this reason that great harm may come to an individual, especially one who is already neurotic, from books, movies, newspapers, and comics.

Image Interchange

Image interchange is a process in which qualities attributed to an individual previously admired, loved, or idealized are transferred to another. This may account, for example, for a sudden, otherwise unexplained, liking for another, or may also account for "love at first sight." What has happened in many cases of "love at first sight" is that the individual so affected has built up an idealized image of what his wife

[3] J. E. Wallin, *Personality Maladjustments and Mental Hygiene*, 2nd ed. (New York: McGraw-Hill Book Co., Inc., 1947), p. 360.

should be, which he then applies impulsively to the object of his interest. He is, indeed, fortunate if he has met the object of his dreams.[4] This interchange also works in reverse, inasmuch as it may account for sudden and apparently unexplained dislikes.

Introjection

Introjection is a mechanism whereby an individual applies elements in the environment to himself. This is the way the *superego* is supposed to be developed. The child accepts from his parents, or parental surrogates, the moral code which is later to influence his conduct. It is the closest psychoanalytic equivalent to conscience. It differs, of course, in many ways, but clinically the most important difference is that conscience is conscious, whereas, although the superego is partly conscious, it is, in large part, unconscious. But conscience and superego should not be considered mutually exclusive. It would probably be best to consider that the superego represents those aspects of conscience which have resulted from environmental influences.

Introvert

The introvert is the individual who tends to withdraw from his conflict and to think it out. He is the thinker rather than the doer. He gets his chief pleasure from within. He is a dreamer. On the surface, he is unemotional, unsociable, and inactive. He thinks much and does little. Introversion is a refuge and an escape from his conflicts. It is not necessarily an abnormal mechanism. Introverts are planners; they are the ones who make discoveries; they are the ones who think out new methods. Within certain limits, therefore, introversion is a useful mechanism. Introversion may occur in all degrees and seldom occurs in pure culture. It may be in some cases the precursor of a schizophrenic withdrawal (see *Extroversion*).

---

[4] We do not deny that young couples are capable of deep affection, but it does seem wise to think of married love as something that grows, deepens, and is gradually built into a more and more significant relationship. The most happily married couples we know seem to reflect this developmental type of marital bond. Cf. E. E. LeMasters, *Modern Courtship And Marriage* (New York: Macmillan, 1957), pp. 61–62: "Conceptualized in this way, we do not fall in love, we achieve it. This is in line with the opinion of marriage counselors that good marriages are not an accident: they are an achievement, the result of two human beings learning to live together happily and constructively."

Projection

Projection is a mechanism by which we externalize our thoughts and ascribe our own feelings to others. It is the mechanism of delusions and hallucinations. What the individual thinks of himself may be so distasteful that he cannot accept it. Instead, since it keeps crowding into consciousness, he externalizes it and then can accept it better as coming from a source outside of himself. He can then say: "*They* (the voices) say this about me." This is more acceptable than a self-accusation.

Confusion rises in this area between genuine supernatural manifestations and their distinction from delusions and hallucinations. It is not within the scope of this book to discuss this intricate subject, but the pastoral counselor should realize that a healthy skepticism concerning visions does not in any way discredit the existence of God or of holy persons or the possibility of truly supernatural visions.[5]

Rationalization

Rationalization is the unconscious finding of excuses in an effort to justify what we have already decided. It is unconscious personal deception. This differs from a common use of the term which refers to an intellectual explanation of things. The principal difference, of course, is that in its latter use the term refers to conscious "rationalization." In its use as an ego defense it is not necessarily harmful. There are very few who can face cold, grim reality without some cushioning. If a subject who was late for class blames it on the traffic, rather than his own laziness, the penalty will probably be the same. The student who fails a subject and blames the teacher rather than his own inattention, or, worse still, his own lack of intelligence, is more likely to be harmed by his rationalization.

Regression

Regression means "moving backward." It occurs (literally in certain of the psychoses and in hysteria) when the individual regresses from a mature to a less mature mental state. The schizophrenic, for example, regresses from a world of reality to a world of images and fantasy. This term should not be mistaken for "immature behavior" in which the sub-

---

[5] Cf. Mons. Alfredo Ottaviani, "On the Dangers of Credulousness," reprinted from the *Osservatore Romano* in *The Catholic Mind*, Vol. XLIX, July, 1951, No. 1063, pp. 401–406.

ject "acts as a child"; one who, in a temper reaction, for example, smashes the radio because it does not work, or tears the telephone off the wall because he keeps getting a busy signal. These individuals have probably not regressed because they were never more mature. The term *regression* should be reserved for those who had achieved a higher level of integration and then "moved backward."

Repression

In repression the individual recognizes an unpleasant complex, impulse, or conflict but does not attack it and repudiate it consciously as happens in suppression. In repression the distasteful conflict is rejected more or less consciously. The conflict which is thus repressed is not totally removed from one's psychic life; it may, and frequently does, continue to exert a dynamic, though unconscious, influence on the personality of the subject. Of all the ego defenses, repression is probably the least understood by the nonprofessional. It is difficult for him to understand how a conflict which the subject has forgotten can affect and influence his conduct. This important subject is further discussed on page 208 f.

Resistance

Resistance refers in psychoanalytic terminology to an instinctive opposition displayed toward attempts to lay bare the unconscious (see p. 91 f.).

Sublimation

Sublimation is the process of refining or purifying. It is not, strictly speaking, a mechanism of defense, but seems best described under this heading. Sublimation may be defined as the mental process of directing the aim of an unused or outdated instinctual drive to hygienic, satisfactory, and acceptable types of conduct. It differs from substitution in that in substitution we are attempting to replace one drive with another, whereas in sublimation the effort is merely to divert the unused drive into a socially acceptable channel.

Some celibate individuals have objected to the opinion that they sublimate their sexual drives into their clerical activities. This indicates a misunderstanding of the meaning of sublimation. In the first place, in most celibates the sex drive is not repressed; it is merely controlled. In any case, the energy associated with drives which are repressed is not repressed as such but as undifferentiated energy. This energy is then available for the use of the individual. Just as the electrical energy which is generated by a waterfall has no direct relationship to the results it produces, the energy of the sex drive has no direct relationship to the ultimate achievements of the individual. "Sublimation is the exchange of infantile sexual aims for interests or modes of pleasure-finding which are no longer directly sexual, although psychically related, and which are on a higher social level. The terms 'desexualized' and 'aim-inhibited' are used throughout psychoanalytic literature to describe sublimated activities. Sublimation is fundamentally an unconscious process."[6]

Substitution

Substitution refers to the technique of improving the patient's situation by offering better, more wholesome, and more constructive ideas to take the place of those that have been harmful to him. This is on the whole a healthy mechanism and is frequently usefully employed.

Suppression

Suppression is an evasion mechanism in which the individual consciously and voluntarily rejects the disturbing conflict from focal consciousness. Suppression keeps the conflict under supervision but does not solve it. Suppression, if more or less habitual, is undesirable because:

1. It does not solve the conflict.

2. It indicates the individual's basic fear of unmasking.

3. It does not produce psychic calm since the conflict is still there though in chains.

4. It gives rise to the habit of avoiding rather than solving conflicts.

5. It may require the use of alcohol or other drugs to keep it under control.

Surrender

When the struggle becomes too great for the patient, reality too painful for him to face, and no acceptable solution can be found, he may completely withdraw even his inadequate defenses and surrender. He may then retreat into a neurosis or psychosis.

Symbolization

Repressed concepts, if they return to consciousness, usually do so in a changed form which is symbolic of the underlying conflict.

---

[6] W. Healy, A. F. Bronner, and A. M. Bowers, *The Structure and Meaning of Psychoanalysis* (New York: Alfred A. Knopf, Inc., 1930), p. 248.

Such symbolism is more common in dreams than in waking consciousness. It means that the conscious symbol in some way represents an unconscious conflict. Just as a flag is symbolic of a country, or a cross may represent religion, a single idea may become symbolic of a repressed conflict which has great significance for the individual.

Symbolization according to psychoanalytic usage is an unconscious process built up on association and similarity whereby one object comes to represent or stand for (symbolize) another object, through some part, quality, or aspect which the two have in common. . . The resemblance is generally so slight or superficial that the conscious mind would overlook it.[7]

Case Report. The following case illustrates how many of these mechanisms work:

Johnny was in love with Susie. He was, thereby, acting in accordance with one of his basic *instincts* which inclines him toward *race preservation.* In fact, Johnny was very much in love with Susie, and he would spend many hours writing her letters and indulging in much fantasy about her. In his mind, he pictured her as his ideal love object. Being driven by his instincts, he enjoyed very much being with her and thereby substituted reality for his fantasies. Susie, on the other hand, although also motivated by her instincts, was not only interested in Johnny, but in others as well. In fact, Susie spread her affection to many others. Johnny continued to fantasy concerning his love ideal and built up many dreams of what would happen after his marriage. When he deemed the time appropriate, he *projected* his feelings on Susie only to receive an ego-shattering, totally unexpected scornful rejection at her hands. He became quite depressed, but attempted to repress his feeling of *rejection* by an escape into over-indulgence in alcohol. With the assistance of alcohol as an anesthetic, he was able to *repress* much of this painful experience. However, he continued to experience painful symptoms which he did not recognize as conscious responses to his inner psychic unrest which arose from his frequent exposure to objects *symbolic* of his scornful rejection by Susie. He was able to *convert* these feelings of anxiety into somatic manifestations and it was for these apparently totally unrelated symptoms that he eventually sought medical help.[8]

Summary. Intellectual habits of escape or ego defenses against conflicts and unpleasant reality are numerous. Some of the more important ego defenses have been described. Basically they all serve the same purpose, viz., to secure greater peace of soul for the disturbed individual. It should be emphasized that the occasional use of many of these mecha-

---

[7] *Ibid.,* p. 206.
[8] John R. Cavanagh, M.D., "Internist Looks at Psychosomatic Medicine," *The Bulletin,* Georgetown University Medical Center, 1950, IV, No. 2, Aug.–Sept., pp. 23–31.

nisms is not abnormal and not even undesirable. It is only their persistent use as a means of escape from reality which is pathological. A most important mechanism is *repression* because it is basic to most neurotic disorders.

The Unconscious

There is now general agreement as to the existence of unconscious psychological processes, and there is little doubt that such processes have a profound effect on the personality. These unconscious processes are especially significant for the question of moral responsibility.

While there is general agreement on the fact that there is an unconscious part of the mind, various schools of psychiatry differ among themselves when they consider a detailed explanation (see Chapter XVI). I shall attempt to outline a simple picture of the unconscious which would be generally acceptable to all schools of psychiatry. At the end of the chapter will be listed a bibliography where more details can be found.

To begin, we might ask exactly what is meant by the term *unconscious*. Obviously it means all the mental content which is not in the conscious mind. It is easy to illustrate that the mind contains contents of which it is not at the time immediately aware. If I ask you to imagine the Empire State Building, you probably can draw from your imagination a sense picture of that structure. If you had not been thinking of the Empire State Building before reading this, then the image of the Empire State Building was in your unconscious. Let me take another example: You are reading this page. While you have been reading this page, you have not carefully adverted to the whole meaningful content behind any of the words written here. To illustrate, let us take one word out of the preceding sentence: *carefully*. The word *carefully* means: *in a strictly accurate manner*. The word *accurate* means *in exact conformity to the truth*. The word *strictly* means *closely in conformity to the requirements*. Thus, the expression *strictly accurate* can mean *closely and in exact conformity to the requirements of truth*. Now, if we begin to analyze this phrase, we begin to accumulate more meaning, e.g., *closely: in union with. Exact: admitting of no deviation*. The other words of the phrase might be subject equally to further definition. Thus, we take the one word *carefully* and we recognize that behind the meaning of that word there is a whole wealth of meaning to which we do not directly advert. The meaning behind the word *carefully*, then, might be compared to an iceberg. Most of the meaning is below the conscious surface. To illustrate:

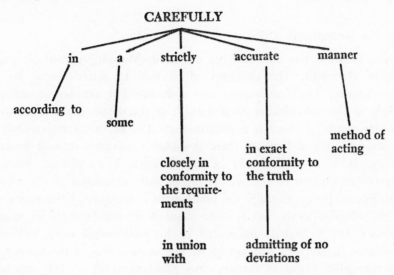

CAREFULLY

in   a   strictly   accurate   manner

according to

some

closely in
conformity to
the require-
ments

in union
with

in exact
conformity to
the truth

admitting of no
deviations

method of
acting

Now when you first came across that word *carefully*, you did not advert to all the content behind it or behind each other word. If you did, it would probably take you days to finish one page. Nevertheless, the meaning lies there in the unconscious mental contents of the reader, and these contents can be brought up if the reader stops to do so.

What I have attempted to do above is simply to illustrate that there are contents stored in the mind which have some influence on those contents at the time in the consciousness of any human person.

Much of these unconscious contents can be brought up readily, or at least without special technics. These contents are what Freud and the psychoanalytic school call the preconscious (foreconscious).

But there are other contents in the unconscious which an individual, by himself, is unable to bring up and which may be exercising harmful influences on the contents of the conscious mind. These contents of the unconscious are what psychiatrists usually mean when they speak of the unconscious.

The unconscious, as referred to immediately above, is the content of repressed mental experiences which at the time were psychic shocks, "injuries," and conflicts which the individual was unable to resolve.[9] These repressed contents of the unconscious are dynamic and may still produce conscious symptoms concerning the source of which an individual may be unaware.

Can the Unconscious Coerce?

This question has already been discussed. Motivation must in some way be conscious. The elements which lead to activity must be in consciousness. *The unconscious may influence but not coerce activity as long as the individual remains normal.* As the depth of the psychiatric disorder increases, there is a proportionate loss of moral responsibility. In the psychotic individual, there is probably complete loss of responsibility, at least in the field of his disorder. The influence of the unconscious portion of the mental life is well exemplified in the sexual field. For example, generally the homosexual is unaware of the source of his disturbed sexuality, but is quite aware of its influence on his sexual attitudes. He is strongly influenced by his homosexual drive, but not coerced to homosexual conduct by it. The same is true of the masochist and the sadist. Urges of various types affect many of us, but they are not coercive.

According to psychoanalysis, Father Tesson informs us: "You think you are acting out of generosity, religion; — in fact you are motivated by your unconscious. The unconscious motivation really causes the act. The conscious motivation is only a deception."[10]

Pseudo Virtues

Following from this same concept of unconscious influences, there is another idea which we frequently hear mentioned in psychiatric literature; this is the notion of what might be called *pseudo virtues.* This would mean that one might think he was practicing penance, whereas he

---

[9] By *repressed* we mean that the individual tried to act as if these traumata had never existed, instead of suppressing them. By suppressing them, an individual would have recognized the existence of these traumata, and, having resolved them, would have put them out of his mind. Suppression is a healthy activity. It is essential for emotional maturity. Repression, on the other hand, is unhealthy.

[10] Quoted by John C. Ford, S.J., "Depth Psychology, Morality and Alcoholism," reprinted from *Proceedings* of the Fifth Annual Meeting of The Catholic Theological Society of America, Washington, D. C., June 26–28, 1950, p. 9.

is actually deriving masochistic pleasure from his pain. Continence may really be the result, not of virtue, but of frigidity, revulsion to sex, or latent homosexuality. All of these superficial qualities, which look like virtues, may be pathological symptoms of an underlying personality disorder capable of being explained in terms of a neurotic character defect.[11]

Conclusion

It is safe to conclude that the normal individual and most neurotic individuals are responsible for their conduct and therefore culpable. In the "normal" individual the unconscious does not coerce, although it may influence. The normal man has a free will which, although influenced by numerous factors, remains free as long as he maintains good contact with reality. Responsibility decreases when contact with reality decreases. Responsibility is based on the individual's subjective concept of objective reality. If those concepts are in agreement, the individual is responsible. If they are not in accord, by reason of mental illness, he is not responsible to the extent that discord exists.

For the reader seeking a more detailed discussion of theories underlying modern schools of depth psychology, the following books are suggested:

Hall, Calvin, and Lindzey, Gardner, *Theories of Personality* (New York: John Wiley & Sons, Inc., 1957).
Mullahy, Patrick, *Oedipus, Myth or Complex* (New York: The Grove Press, 1955).
Progoff, Ira, *The Death and Rebirth of Psychology* (New York: The Julian Press, 1955).

For understanding some relation between depth psychology and moral issues see the following:

Ford, John C. (S.J.), *Depth Psychology, Morality and Alcoholism* (Weston, Mass.: The Weston College Press, 1941).
Moore, T. V. (O.S.B.), *The Driving Forces of Human Nature* (New York: Grune & Stratton, 1939).

---

[11] *Ibid.*, p. 18.

CHAPTER XX

THE SELECTION OF CANDIDATES FOR THE RELIGIOUS LIFE

When the candidate for religious life asks his opinion of his suitability for that life, the pastoral counselor needs some guidelines and these have not been very clearly delineated for him. Since this is such a frequent problem for the pastoral counselor, it was decided to include it here. The pastor must, of course, assess the individual from the religious viewpoint as well as from the standpoint of his physical and psychological adaptability to religious life. We are concerned here only with the psychological evaluation. What is written may seem more applicable to the Catholic priesthood and Sisterhood. This is my orientation and were I to attempt to write concerning all religious faiths, I would be doing so without knowledge or experience. What is said, however, would seem to be applicable to candidates for the religious life of all faiths. The pastor has an obligation to help screen his professional group so as to exclude the mentally ill.

The Problem

The prevention of mental illness in men and women in religious life is a matter of grave importance. Careful selection of candidates for such a life could result in a tremendous decrease in such illness. Many studies,[1] designed to eliminate candidates for the religious life who are poor

---

[1] William C. Bier, S.J., "Practical Requirements of a Program for the Psychological Screening of Candidates," *Review for Religious*, 13 (1954), and "Psychological Testing and the Theology of Vocation," *Review for Religious*, 12 (Nov., 1953), pp. 291–304; Edward Farrell, O.P., *The Theology of Religious Vocation* (St. Louis: Herder, 1951); A. Ple, P.P., *Unconscious Attraction to the Religious Life; II Vocation* (Westminster, Md.: Newman, 1952); Felix D. Duffey, C.S.C., *Testing the Spirit* (St. Louis: Herder, 1947); Sister M. Digna, O.S.B., "A Tentative Testing Program for Religious Life," *Review for Religious*, X (1951), pp. 75–76.

psychiatric risks, are under way, but further clarification of these tests is necessary before they can be fully accepted. There is little doubt that the seeds of neurosis and psychosis are planted and have begun to grow before the candidate enters the seminary.

Statistics on mental illness in religious are very few. Probably the most reliable figures are those published by Father Moore in 1935.[2] His figures showed that mental illness occurred as follows:

> Priests — 446 cases per 100,000
> Sisters — 485 cases per 100,000
> Brothers — 418 cases per 100,000
> General population — 595 cases per 100,000

At first glance, this ratio would appear to favor religious life as one which reduces the incidence of mental illness. If, however, we eliminate those psychoses due to syphilis, alcohol, mental deficiency, and epilepsy which are unlikely to be found in religious, the rate becomes significantly higher among those in religious life. Another interesting and significant fact elicited by Father Moore was that among religious women those in active work, e.g., teaching, there was an incidence of only 428 cases of mental illness per 100,000; whereas in the cloistered orders there were 1034 cases of mental illness per 100,000. There are no comparable figures for men, but there is no reason to believe that these would be different. There is little doubt that many mentally ill individuals seek to enter religious life. Such neurotic and prepsychotic individuals are especially attracted to cloistered life which by its nature caters to the needs of the schizoid individual. With suitable screening many individuals, who later become a serious liability, could be eliminated before entering the houses of study.

Steps Toward a Solution

1. *The recognition that neuroses may have a religious coloring.*

Religious superiors, spiritual directors, and confessors must accept the possibility of mental illness in candidates for the religious life. That such an attitude is not always present is evidenced by a patient whom I saw recently who had been accepted by five different orders and dismissed by each in turn because of mental illness. Admittedly this is

---

[2] Thomas Verner Moore, "Insanity in Priests and Religious. Part I. The Rate of Insanity in Priests and Religious," *The Ecclesiastical Review*, 95 (1936), p. 297.

an unusual case, but acceptance by one order after dismissal from another because of mental illness is not uncommon. Failure of superiors to recognize mental illness by mistaking it for sanctity is not unusual even today. Competition for candidates between different orders, as if mere numbers were important, often makes a superior reluctant to dismiss a man unless he is literally "climbing the wall."

2. *A vocation requires mental fitness for the life.*

Bouscaren defines a vocation as follows:

> A vocation to the priesthood is a call from God, which, however, is usually indicated not by an extraordinary internal inspiration, but by a right intention together with fitness for the life and work so chosen.[3]

The supernatural builds on the natural. *One should not be considered to have a true vocation as long as he is not physically or mentally fitted for such a life.* It is this requirement which places upon all a clear obligation to screen candidates for the religious life as carefully as possible. All those not suitable should be eliminated as soon as practical.[4] The sooner this can be done the better because in many orders there comes a time when the candidate can no longer be dismissed because of vows and other obligations which the order has to its subjects.

3. *The Holy Father has directed the exclusion of the mentally and emotionally unfit.*

In case there are any who hesitate to dismiss these psychiatrically unfit candidates these words of Pope Pius XI should lend support. The Holy Father said of such individuals, "there should be no human consideration or false mercy" concerning their dismissal or rejection.[5] In this same encyclical the Holy Father placed a responsibility on confessors and spiritual directors to "admonish the unsuited and unworthy . . . of their obligation to retire."[6] There could hardly be a clearer mandate than this.

4. *Certain legal problems must be considered.*

Legally and ethically, a psychiatrist or psychologist who examines a

---

[3] T. Lincoln Bouscaren, S.J., and Adam C. Ellis, S.J., *Canon Law* (Milwaukee: Bruce, 1946), p. 736.

[4] A. Ple, O.P., "Unconscious Attraction to the Religious Life," *Religious Life: II Vocation* (Westminster, Md.: Newman Press, 1952), p. 109. Quoted by William C. Bier, S.J., "Practical Requirements of a Program for the Psychological Screening of Candidates," *Review for Religious*, January, 1954, p. 13.

[5] Pope Pius XI, *Encyclical Letter on the Catholic Priesthood* (Washington, D. C.: National Catholic Welfare Conference, December 20, 1935), pp. 45–46.

[6] *Ibid.*, pp. 47–48.

religious may not reveal the results of his examination to the subject's superior without his consent which should be in writing. This has always been true, but, until quite recently, it was assumed by the subject and by the psychiatrist that the religious superior was acting *in loco parentis* and was therefore legally entitled to a report. This need for consent was brought rather forcefully to my attention recently when a member of a cloistered order brought suit against me through his parents because I gave his superior a report on his mental state. This particular aspect of the problem may be eased if the superior makes the appointment for the subject. While this does not release the examiner from the obligation of secrecy, it does indicate that the subject accepts the interest of the superior in his case by his acceptance of the appointment. This is probably the best method of handling such examinations. However, no report should be released without the subject's consent in writing. If the subject goes voluntarily to the examiner on his own, a confidential relationship is established and it is unlikely that the subject would be willing to release an adverse report.

5. *Moral aspects of some of the tests may destroy their value.*

These questions come up:

1. Does the examiner have the right or obligation to reveal to superiors highly personal matters concerning the subject?

2. Does the examiner have the right or obligation to reveal matters likely to affect the reputation of the subject?

3. Is the subject obligated to submit to a testing program?

There can be little doubt that religious superiors have the right as well as the obligation to carefully screen candidates for the religious life. It would seem to follow from this that they would have the right to refuse to accept candidates who will not perform such tests. On the other hand, certain of these tests, especially those in the form of questionnaires, ask definite questions in regard to past sinful actions. Since the subject may rightfully refuse to answer such questions, the superior cannot exclude him because of his refusal to do so. Such an impasse would invalidate many of the questionnaire type of tests. There are some who believe that the Holy Father in his April 10, 1958, address to the Rome Congress of the International Association on Applied Psychology expressed disapproval of the use of psychological tests which invade the field of conscience.

Father Vaughan feels that candidates may not be required to answer such questions:

> It should be noted that there are two modes of personality testing: the one, a projective, and the other a questionnaire type. The former does not offer any special moral problems (which have not already been treated) since it taps tendencies and patterns of behavior, but does not indicate whether the testee has committed specific sinful acts. The same does not always hold true in the case of the questionnaire. Sometimes definite questions are asked which call for admission or denial of past sinful actions. When the testee is faced with such items, he is not obligated to answer them, since no one can be forced to confess publicly past sinful acts, which are detrimental to his reputation. Hence, the employer or religious superior cannot exclude an applicant because he refuses to answer such items.[7]

6. *Religious superiors must become sensitized to the emotional problems of their subjects.*

With these considerations in mind, it is important for the religious superior to have a secure grasp of basic psychiatric concepts. He should develop a sensitivity to mental and emotional symptoms in those around him and learn to evaluate them. He should learn to accept advice from those qualified to give it on these matters. He must learn to evaluate this advice because the ultimate decision concerning the candidate must be his.

7. *Certain notions from the past must be revised.*

The most important of these is the significance of heredity in the selection of candidates for the religious life. Because of previous emphasis on this subject I would like to speak fully concerning it.

Heredity

In our present frame of reference, we are concerned chiefly with the importance of heredity as a factor in the development of character, personality traits, or mental illness.[8] By the term *traits* we mean the tendencies of an individual to grow and develop in certain ways rather

---

[7] Richard P. Vaughan, S.J., "Some Moral Implications in Psychological Screening," *ACPA Newsletter*, May, 1956, Supplemental No. 21.

[8] According to Gordon W. Allport: "Personality is the dynamic organization within the individual of those psychophysical systems that determine his unique adjustment to his environment," *Personality* (New York: Henry Holt and Co., 1937), p. 48.

than in others.[9] These traits, if biologically inherited are handed down to the offspring by the parents through the media of the chromosomes and genes, the component parts of the genetic constitution of every living organism.[10] The parental genes and chromosomes may be combined in the offspring in many different ways. There is a very slight probability that any two persons will receive exactly the same arrangement of genes, unless the parents themselves are exactly alike in their genetic constitutions. The probability of such an occurrence in the human race is very slight.[11] Biological heredity, therefore, cannot be considered the result of any force or of any influence brought to bear by the parents upon their offspring. Such heredity depends upon the individual's genetic constitution which differs from either of the parent cells.[12]

This brief outline of the genetical inheritance of physical traits does not touch upon many interesting theories of inheritance. The word theory is used very significantly in this case. The larger portion of human genetics is a matter of theory. Many of the theoretical conclusions in human genetics are very probable. These conclusions, derived from conclusions drawn from the scientific studies of other organisms, stand until they have been disproven. However, probability in a science does not help one to obtain firm convictions. Therefore, until geneticists are able to discover a satisfactory mode of experimentation upon the human genetical constitution, our data and its consequential conclusions will remain within the realm of theory.

What are we to think, then, when we are confronted by a candidate for the religious life who gives a family history of mental illness, or of alcoholism, or of psychopathy? Are we to refuse him because some have said that such conditions are biologically inherited? There is very little scientific foundation for this opinion. This is especially true if we consider that dynamic factors are important in the development of mental illness. If we accept the fact that most mental illness is acquired, then we must accept the fact that it cannot be transmitted by heredity because acquired traits are not inheritable.

---

[9] Cf. Florence Laura Goodenough, *Developmental Psychology* (New York: Appleton-Century-Crofts, 1945), p. 42.

[10] Rudolph Allers points out that "any number of individual traits do not make up character; it is not, as will be shown later, a mosaic of separate traits or elements of any kind. Character is a unity and a whole, not an aggregate," *The Psychology of Character* (New York: Sheed & Ward, 1939), p. 8.

[11] Cf. Goodenough, *op. cit.*, p. 42.

[12] Cf. *ibid.*, p. 43 ff.

The question at issue here is: Whether or not acquired characteristics may be inherited? Dr. Goodenough tells us that experiments have shown negative results. Parents, who have a special talent in a given field or who have special training for the performance of a special act, do not necessarily transmit their skill to their offspring.

> For many generations Chinese women have been accustomed to bind their feet to make them smaller, but neither the size nor the shape of the feet of their offspring has altered thereby. For many generations the tails of fox terriers were cut off, but the tails of the puppies were not diminished in size. Perhaps the best example proposed by Dr. Goodenough to illustrate her point is that children of foreign born ancestors who for many generations have spoken nothing but German, Italian, etc., have acquired through heredity no special predisposition toward the speaking of those languages rather than any other language.[13]

Textbooks of psychiatry give confused and indefinite answers to the question of heredity in mental illness. Many authors speak vaguely of a "predisposition" or "tendency" without explaining what this is or where it comes from. Because of the importance of the subject of heredity in the selection of candidates for the religious life, various contemporary authors are quoted at length so the reader can form his own estimate as to their reliability. If the questions seem too numerous, my excuse is the importance of the subject matter and the will to avoid the appearance of bias.

> Pollack and Malzberg presented a detailed study of heredity and environmental factors in the causation of mental disease. The conclusions at which they arrived are as follows: Neither dementia praecox nor manic-depressive psychosis appear in frequencies that are in accord with the requirements of simple Mendelian inheritance. Yet, though no specific law of inheritance of mental disease has been proved, the records show, they believe, that it is highly probably that there is a generalized familial basis for such disorders. This could be expressed best in the statement that the chance of developing a mental disorder is greater in some families than the corresponding chance for the general population. However, the authors state that no one appears fated to develop dementia praecox, as shown on the basis of hereditary studies, because some of the ancestors had such a disease. It requires something in addition. There must be not only the seed but the ground in which to plant the seed. Given satisfactory environmental and psychologic factors, good adjustment may be achieved. Therefore, the authors conclude that one cannot speak of hereditary and environmental factors as antithetic causes of mental disease. Both combined, often in subtle ways, create such a disorder.

---

[13] Cf. *ibid.*, pp. 61–62.

Furthermore, the authors state that both manic-depressive psychosis and dementia praecox may occur in a family in which there is no unfavorable heredity and in which mental disease has not previously appeared for at least 3 or 4 generations.[14]

An inherited predisposition to mental disorder is found in from 30 to 90 per cent of cases according to different authorities, while the average for all conditions has been estimated at from 60 to 70 per cent. But any one who is at all familiar with the collecting of statistics must know how impossible it is for them to fully represent the facts in such a matter.[15]

The whole subject of heredity, so far as it relates to insanity, is in a most unsatisfactory state, very largely because investigators have been dealing with "insanity" as if it was a simple, concrete affair instead of the infinitely complex thing it has proved to be. As I have pointed out, "insanity" is just a label for a certain form of social maladjustment that may be dependent upon innumerable factors, each one of which, in turn, may be, and probably is, highly complex.[16]

To be sure those families are rare which on careful search prove entirely free, and the cases with only a few diseased members are always the more common. Nevertheless the family predisposition is surely one of the most important determinants for the development of mental diseases.[17]

The hereditary predisposition certainly plays an important role among the causes of schizophrenia. However, we do not know in what this predisposition consists and how it manifests itself in other ways. It appears to be specific for schizophrenia.[18]

In the majority of mental illnesses it is possible to discern evidence of the presence of inherited factors, though in few, if any, are these exclusive causes of the illness.[19]

Twin studies suggest that if it were possible (though it is of dubious validity) to rate in numerical terms how much of the causation of an illness may be due to inheritance, the maximum proportion would be put at about 80 per cent. This is based on the fact that if one of a pair of

---

[14] Leopold Bellak, M.D., *Dementia Praecox* (New York: Grune & Stratton, 1948), p. 45.

[15] William A. White, M.D., *Outlines of Psychiatry* (Washington D. C.: Nervous and Mental Disease Publishing Co., 1926), p. 35.

[16] *Ibid.,* p. 34.

[17] Eugen Paul Bleuler, *Textbook of Psychiatry* (Dover Publications Inc., Macmillan Co., 1924), p. 200.

[18] Eugen Paul Bleuler, *Dementia Praecox or the Group of Schizophrenias* (New York: International Universities Press, 1950), p. 340.

[19] Ian Skottowe, M.D., *Clinical Psychiatry* (New York: McGraw-Hill Book Co., Inc., 1954), p. 52.

monozygotic twins develops certain forms of mental illness, the other will do so in approximately 80 per cent of the examples observed.[20]

This raised the question of what it is that is inherited. With rare exceptions (possibly Huntington's chorea is the only certain one, apart from some forms of mental deficiency) it is not, as it were, the whole illness, but only a proclivity or predisposition to develop the illness — but what does this mean?

A proclivity is not an abstraction, but a way of describing some peculiarity of bodily constitution, which plays an indispensable part in psychological functioning. A current hypothesis is that genetic proclivities are seen especially in the biochemistry of the body, with special reference to the speed at which various complicated processes of growth and function occur.[21]

It is easy to imagine such acquired reactions being transmitted from generation to generation as a tradition, but it remains difficult, in view of the uncertainty regarding the experimental work quoted, to think of such psychological reactions as becoming truly heritable.[22]

Up to the present time, however, our knowledge as to a hereditary predisposition to mental diseases, as in the case of many other problems concerning heredity, is incomplete and our opinions must remain subject to revision.[23]

Heredity is undoubtedly an important factor in the production of mental disease, but there is an increasing belief that it has been overemphasized.[24]

Except in rare forms of mental disease, such as Huntington's chorea, there is no conclusive evidence that hereditary transmission follows Mendelian ratios.[25]

The subject of heredity in schizophrenic reactions has been studied, but the results are not conclusive. Monozygotic twins have proven to be the most valuable source of information, but investigators have not always been careful to give adequate weight to enviromental factors. Certainly it may be said that heredity does not play as measurable a role in a schizophrenic reaction as it apparently does in a manic depressive reaction.[26]

Generally speaking, the more we study and observe, the more important become postnatal influences upon the individual in the production of mental maladjustment and the smaller becomes the amount of blame we can place upon heredity.[27]

---

[20] *Ibid.*, pp. 53–54.

[21] *Ibid.*, p. 54.

[22] David Henderson, M.D., and R. D. Gillespie, A *Textbook of Psychiatry* (New York: Oxford University Press, 1927), p. 47.

[23] Arthur P. Noyes, M.D., *Modern Clinical Psychiatry* (Philadelphia: W. B. Saunders Co., 1934), p. 71.

[24] *Ibid.*, p. 70.

[25] *Ibid.*, p. 71.

[26] O. Spurgeon English, M.D., and Stuart M. Finch, M.D., *Introduction to Psychiatry* (New York: W. W. Norton and Co., Inc., 1954), p. 344.

[27] *Ibid.*, pp. 46–47.

In the first place, I am one of those who see too many explanations by more direct nonhereditary causes in many of the defects and disorders of total behavior which we meet in our practical work.[28]

On the basis of present knowledge, all we can say is that families in which one or more members suffer, or have suffered from a functional mental disorder are somewhat more likely to produce children some of whom may develop similar conditions than those families in which no such disorders are found.[29]

In some conditions — mostly the rarer ones — heredity plays a direct and major role; in others it produces tendencies or susceptibilities, which will give way to insanity only if there is some strong, adverse environmental push.[30]

Can environmental factors or emotional stress alone produce insanity? Most authorities are not inclined to believe that except in very unusual cases, a person will not become insane unless he starts off with some inborn tendency. No more terrible, nerve-racking experiences can be imagined than those which vast numbers of soldiers and civilians underwent during World War II. Yet only a relatively small proportion became mentally diseased. Evidence indicates strongly that those who did were especially susceptible. Further, there is considerable evidence that even chronic alcoholism, syphilis or other acquired diseases, do not ordinarily result in mental derangement unless there is some predisposition; and that in very old age, while mental faculties may become weaker, actual insanity (senile dementia) tends to occur only in those persons who previously had some mental instability. Finally, there is no evidence that any one can ever "catch" insanity merely from contact with a mentally diseased person, no matter how close the relationship.[31]

This particular situation has become increasingly interesting in recent years, since the opposite view has been made the official, government sponsored doctrine of one nation (the U.S.S.R.) and has been imposed by force upon its scientists and laity.[32]

The answer is clearly and unequivocally supplied by experiments, carried out countless times in rapidly reproducing organisms, which could be followed for many generations. In no such test has an inheritable effect of the environmental ever been observed.[33]

---

[28] *The Commonsense Psychiatry of Dr. Adolph Meyer*, edited by Alfred Lief (New York: McGraw-Hill Book Co., Inc., 1948), p. 511.

[29] Winfred Overholser, M.D., and Winifred V. Richmond, *Handbook of Psychiatry* (Philadelphia: J. B. Lippincott Co., 1947), p. 16.

[30] Amram Scheinfeld, *The Human Heredity Handbook* (Philadelphia and New York: J. B. Lippincott Co., 1956), p. 128.

[31] *Ibid.*, pp. 129–130.

[32] Richard B. Goldschmidt, *Understanding Heredity* (New York: John Wiley & Sons, Inc., 1952), p. 24.

[33] *Ibid.*, p. 24.

There are several prior considerations which, even in the presence of more convincing evidence than is at present available, would raise doubt of the possibility of a physical transmission through the genes. The first of these considerations is the fact that there is a very great general acceptance of the psychogenic origin of many of these disorders. It is our own belief that all of these disorders are acquired and that, therefore, being acquired, they are not transmittable by heredity any more than the ability of the parent to play the piano could be so transmitted. The second consideration is that, since a psychosis is a psychic, unextended reality, it cannot be transmitted by physical heredity. A material reality cannot, according to the principle of sufficient reason, produce a psychic reality.[34]

Social heredity, or the effect of environment, is very important in the development of personality and mental illness. It is because of this that mental illness in the family is significant. If the candidate has been subjected to a traumatic environment and grew up in this atmosphere, it is more important than the fact that his maternal great-aunt had a schizophrenic reaction.

Until more is known of the biological inheritance of mental illness, the existence of mental illness in the family may be given little weight. Careful attention, however, should be paid to environmental influences. The circumstances under which the individual is reared are much more important than his biological family tree.

Environmental Influences

Although we need pay little attention to biological heredity, the environmental influences to which the candidate was subjected while growing up are of the greatest importance. For this reason, the longitudinal history of the candidate is of great significance. Broken homes, insecurity, living with alcoholic, criminal, or psychotic parents or siblings all leave their marks on the personality. A history of unusual ideas and disturbed behavior during the period of development may point to personality disorder or to neurosis. The seeds of neurosis may be planted in prepared soil at an early age.

Early sexual experiences are important and should be investigated. Masturbation, homosexual and heterosexual play may be significant if they persist beyond certain ages.

---

[34] John R. Cavanagh, M.D., and James B. McGoldrick, *Fundamental Psychiatry* (Milwaukee: The Bruce Publishing Co., 1958), p. 157. See also Chapter XI on "Heredity."

Inability to tolerate authority, resentment of correction, lack of sociability, scrupulosity, overreligiosity, undue suspiciousness, bed-wetting, instability, seclusiveness, sullenness, discontent, lonesomeness, depression, shyness, overboisterousness, timidity, sleeplessness, lack of initiative, lack of ambition, personal uncleanliness, stupidity, sleep-walking, suicidal tendencies are a few of the symptoms which should be sought in recording the longitudinal history.

As part of the longitudinal history a careful inquiry into motivation should be made by those responsible for selection.

Motivation

Supernatural motivation should be dominant in all cases of true vocation. Careful inquiry may reveal unusual motivations. Too frequently the supernatural motive is taken for granted and not investigated. One of my patients spent three years in the seminary before his mental illness was discovered. He used to pose in front of a mirror and make gestures in imitation of Bishop Sheen. He wanted to be a bishop, not a priest, and preach on the radio and television. Another patient in his second year of theology wanted to be a priest because he thought it would be nice to sing high Mass. This list could be extended indefinitely, especially with those who were persuaded by their parents that they had a vocation.

8. *Careful attention should be paid to studies concerning the development of acceptable procedures for conducting screening examinations.*

It is in this area that there is at present little uniformity of opinion. The problem is not the need to detect frank psychotic states. These are not frequent and are usually easily detected even by the layman. The area which must be carefully screened is that involving personality disorders, personality trait disturbances, and the psychoneuroses. These are not readily detectable and may need professional skill for their determination. The present trend is to use psychological tests for this purpose. These tests are of two types — projective, such as the Rorschach, and questionnaires. Some of the difficulties with the questionnaire type have already been discussed.[35]

It is quite likely that the pastoral counselor will not have at hand suitable reference works to which he may go for acceptable definitions of such difficult-to-define terms as personality disorders and psycho-

---

[35] See Footnote 7.

neurosis. For this reason they are reproduced here, with permission, from the official nomenclature of the American Psychiatric Association.[36]

Personality Disorders

These disorders are characterized by developmental defects or pathological trends in the personality structure, with minimal subjective anxiety, and little or no sense of distress. In most instances, the disorder is manifested by a lifelong pattern of action or behavior, rather than by mental or emotional symptoms. Occasionally, organic diseases of the brain (epidemic encephalitis, head injury, Alzheimer's disease, etc.) will produce clinical pictures resembling a personality disorder. In such instances, the condition is properly diagnosed as a Chronic Brain Syndrome (of appropriate origin) with behavioral reaction.

The Personality Disorders are divided into three main groups with one additional grouping for flexibility in diagnosis (Special Symptom Reactions). Although the groupings are largely descriptive, the division has been made partially on the basis of the dynamics of personality development. The Personality Pattern Disturbances are considered deep seated disturbances, with little room for regression. Personality Trait Disturbances and Sociopathic Personality Disturbances under stress may at times regress to a lower level of personality organization and function without development of psychosis.

1. Personality Pattern Disturbances

These are more or less cardinal personality types, which can rarely if ever be altered in their inherent structures by any form of therapy. Their functioning may be improved by prolonged therapy, but basic changes are seldom accomplished. In some, "constitutional" features are marked and obvious. The depth of the psychopathology here allows these individuals little room to maneuver under conditions of stress, except into actual psychosis.

2. Personality Trait Disturbance

This category applies to individuals who are unable to maintain their emotional equilibrium and independence under minor or major stress because of disturbance in emotional development. Some individuals fall into this group because their personality pattern disturbance is related to fixation and exaggeration of certain character and behavior patterns; others, because their behavior is a regressive reaction due to environmental or endopsychic stress.

This classification will be applied only to cases of personality disorder in which the neurotic features (such as anxiety, conversion, phobia, etc.) are relatively insignificant, and the basic personality maldevelopment is the crucial distinguishing factor. Evidence of physical immaturity may or may not be present.

3. Sociopathic Personality Disturbance

Individuals to be placed in this category are ill primarily in terms of society and of conformity with the prevailing cultural milieu, and

---

[36] *Diagnostic and Statistical Manual* (Washington, D. C.: American Psychiatric Association, 1952), pp. 34–36.

not only in terms of personal discomfort and relations with other individuals. However, sociopathic reactions are very often symptomatic of severe underlying personality disorder, neuroses, or psychosis, or occur as a result of organic brain injury or disease. Before a definitive diagnosis in this group is employed, strict attention must be paid to the possibility of the presence of a more primary personality disturbance; such underlying disturbance will be diagnosed when recognized.

Psychoneurotic Disorders: The chief characteristic of these disorders is "anxiety" which may be directly felt and expressed or which may be unconsciously and automatically controlled by the utilization of various psychological defense mechanisms (depression, conversion, displacement, etc.). In contrast to those with psychoses, patients with psychoneurotic disorders do not exhibit gross distortions or falsification of external reality (delusions, hallucinations, illusions) and they do not present gross disorganizations of the personality. Longitudinal (lifelong) studies of individuals with such disorders usually present evidence of periodic or constant maladjustment of varying degrees from early life. Special stress may bring about acute symptomatic expression of such disorders.

"Anxiety" in psychoneurotic disorders is a danger signal felt and perceived by the conscious portion of the personality. It is produced by a threat from within the personality (e.g., by supercharged repressed emotions, including such aggressive impulses as hostility and resentment), with or without stimulation from such external situations as loss of love, loss of prestige, or threat of injury.

In recording such reactions the terms "traumatic neurosis" or "traumatic reaction" will not be used; instead, the particular psychiatric reaction will be specified. Likewise, the term "mixed reaction" will not be used; instead the predominant type of reaction will be recorded, qualified by reference to other types of reactions as part of the symptomatology.

There has been a tendency in recent years to train a member of the community to conduct these tests and evaluate the results. It is obvious that such a person should be well trained because psychological tests are capricious things even in the hands of experts and would be very dangerous in the hands of the unskilled. Regardless of skill, however, I do not believe that a member of the community should conduct such tests. The tests should be interpreted by a disinterested examiner. There is too much possibility that through a variety of unconscious processes the personality of the examiner who is a member of the order would enter into his evaluation. If psychological testing of this type is to be used, it would probably be done best through the Departments of Psychology in our many universities. We are often asked if tests adapted to the special needs of the priesthood are not needed. This is neither necessary nor desirable. Ordinary psychological tests are adequate for this purpose.[37] One of the many difficulties with the psychological questionnaire type of screening is that it depends on the complete intellectual honesty of the examinee. If, for example, the question asked is, "Would you cross the street to avoid someone you didn't like?" my inclination, even if I did cross the street, would be to say "no" because I know this is the more normal answer. Are we required to incriminate ourselves?

If large numbers of individuals are to be screened and the examiners are few, psychological tests may be performed on all and those who appear to need more careful examination called in separately. No one should, however, be considered unfit on the basis of psychological testing alone. Ideally, candidates should have personal interviews with professionally qualified examiners. These individuals may be either psychiatrists or psychologists, but, as noted above, they should not be members of the same order. These examiners should preferably be of the same religious belief, and have sufficient knowledge of the vicissitudes of the religious life to be able to estimate the candidate's ability to adjust to this life. One does not, as some believe, need to be a clergyman to form such a judgment. Suitable examiners are not numerous, and the number of candidates is great. This deficiency may be solved to some extent by providing more adequate training in abnormal psychology to the members of the seminary faculty. These psychologically oriented faculty members, after a period of observation, could select certain students for more thorough examination. There should, in all cases, be careful observation during the early days and months of training in order to avoid the not infrequent tragedy of the student whose psychosis is discovered after the invitations for his ordination have been mailed. Careful screening should eliminate between 70 and 80 per cent of psychiatric risks.

Monitum From the Holy Office

On July 15, 1961, the Sacred Congregation of the Holy Office issued an official warning against the practice of psychoanalysis by clerics or religious and against its use for testing religious vocations.

The Holy Office document stated: "Since many dangerous opinions are being published and spread regarding the sins incurred by violation

---

[37] Cf. John B. Murray, C.M., *Training for the Priesthood and Personality and Interest Test Manifestations*, unpublished doctor's dissertation, Fordham University, 1957.

of the Sixth Commandment (Thou shalt not commit adultery) and regarding the imputability of human actions, the Sacred Congregation of the Holy Office established the following norms for public knowledge:

"1. Bishops, presidents of faculties of theology, rectors of seminaries and schools for Religious must require that those whose duty it is to teach moral theology and similar disciplines comply exactly with the traditional teaching of the Church (Canon 129)."

(Canon 129 provides that clerics must not neglect the study of the sacred sciences and that in their studies they must always follow the sound doctrines handed down by the Fathers of the Church and commonly accepted by the Church. They must also avoid profane novelties of expression and what is wrongly called scientific.)

The document continued:

"2. Ecclesiastical censors must use great caution in censoring and passing judgment on books and publications which deal with the sixth precept of the Decalogue.

"3. Clerics and Religious are forbidden to practice psychoanalysis according to the norms of Canon 139, paragraph two.

(Canon 139 provides that clerics must avoid affairs which, although not unbecoming in themselves, are foreign to the clerical state. Without special permission they may not practice medicine or surgery or accept certain public offices.)

The document concluded:

"4. The opinion of those who consider that a prior psychoanalytical examination is definitely necessary before receiving Holy Orders must be disapproved. Likewise disapproved are the opinions of those who hold that the so-called psychoanalytical examination and relative investigations are necessary for candidates to the priesthood and for religious profession. This applies also if it is a matter of investigating the aptitude required for the priesthood or for religious profession. Likewise, priests and men or women Religious must not go to psychoanalysts except with the permission of the Ordinary and for grave reasons."

At first glance this Monitum might appear to interfere with the very excellent programs which are being built up in the United States, as well as in other countries, for psychiatric and psychological screening of candidates for the priesthood. Closer examination and a realization that such directives of the Holy Office are intended to be interpreted strictly have allayed this anxiety. It would seem that when the monitum speaks of *psychoanalytic examination*, it means literally psychoanalytic, and not psychological or psychiatric examination. The term, "absolutely required," was also misunderstood when not kept in context. Monsignor Francis F. Reh, in a personal communication, said "that bishops and their seminary directors are not on suspect or even unsanctioned ground when they approach the psychologist's clinic for help in judging the fitness of candidates for the priesthood."

The recent warnings of the Holy See, he stated, were directed against the opinion that prior psychoanalytic direction is "absolutely required" for the reception of Holy Orders or that candidates for the priesthood or religious profession must undergo "psychoanalytic examination" properly so-called.

Within these limitations, the psychologist can be of great assistance to the seminary director in screening applicants. Monsignor Reh observed that while Canon Law and the recent letter from Rome did not call for psychological testing as a condition for admission, the "prudent employment of such assessment" could be considered in keeping with the Holy See's insistence upon careful selection. I am in complete accord with this opinion.[38]

As a routine procedure, for the present, I would suggest:

a) That all candidates have a psychological screening examination before being accepted for the seminary. The particular tests to be employed is a matter too technical for this volume and should be left to the discretion of an acceptable examiner.

b) Those showing gross abnormalities should be examined psychiatrically before being accepted.

c) Those showing lesser abnormalities may be admitted, but should be carefully observed during the early years of seminary training. For this purpose, more adequate training in psychiatric concepts must be given to the faculty.

d) These studies would, of course, be in addition to other tests of scholastic and spiritual adaptability for the priesthood.

Father William C. Bier, S.J., who has done much work in this field,

---

[38] *Personal Communication.* Monsignor Francis F. Reh commented on the *Monitum* at the Fifteenth Annual Meeting of the American Psychological Association in New York on August 31, 1961.

does not agree fully with these recommendations.[39] Father Bier would rely more on testing and feels that only a limited number of individuals need to see a psychiatrist.

9. *Regardless of the method of selection there are certain conclusions which should be immediately applicable:*

a) Doubtfully suitable candidates are likely to be problems from the beginning. Experience demonstrates that when there has been any question about the suitability of a candidate, it is more frequently confirmed than proved to be wrong.[40] These candidates should be rejected.

b) History of a previous psychotic episode should be cause for rejection. Bouscaren and Ellis[41] are more specific:

> Mental defects (defectus animi). Included under this heading are epilepsy, insanity, and diabolical possession. Once incurred, the irregularity for the reception of orders remains even though the candidate becomes entirely free from the defect which gave rise to the irregularity. If the irregularity is incurred after the reception of orders, and if it is certain that the cleric has been entirely freed from the defect which gave cause to it, ordinaries may allow their subjects to resume the exercise of the orders already received (c. 984, 3°). Many authors make an exception in the case of epilepsy with which the candidate was afflicted before the age of puberty and which, in the opinion of a reliable doctor, has entirely disappeared. This opinion may be safely followed in practice.

c) Homosexuality, when acts have been performed in the seminary, should be cause for rejection by the authorities. The obligation to refrain from sexual activity outside of marriage is the same whether the drive is homosexual or heterosexual. A student who engaged in heterosexual activity would certainly be rejected, so why not an overt homosexual? Homosexual individuals who have not performed acts in the seminary should be selected on an individual basis.

d) Individuals with severe or moderately severe personality disorders should be rejected. Sociopathic personalities of any degree should be

---

[39] Cf. William C. Bier, S.J., "Practical Requirements of a Program for the Psychological Screening of Candidates," reprinted from *Review for Religious*, January, 1954, sup. 22 ff.

[40] "Experience has taught us one thing, and that is that when there is a doubt about anyone in the novitiate, it is nearly always confirmed later; the situation does not improve. There may be exceptions, but they are few and far between." Quoted by William C. Bier, S.J., "Psychological Testing of Candidates and the Theology of Vocation," *Review for Religious*, November, 1953, p. 303. From "An Inquiry about Vocation" in *Religious Life: II Vocation* (Westminster, Md.: 1952), p. 83.

[41] See Footnote 42.

rejected. Bouscaren adds to those who should be rejected, "Trouble-makers, incorrigible youths, those who show a rebellious spirit."[42] More specifically he states:

> Absence from the Seminary: Dismissal. Whenever the students remain for any reason away from the seminary, Canon 972, par. 2, is to be observed, that is, they must be under the care of some suitable pious priest who must watch over them and train them to piety (c. 1370). Trouble-makers, incorrigible youths, those who show a rebellious spirit, and those who do not seem morally and psychologically suited to the ecclesiastical state, should be dismissed from the seminary; as should also those who make so little progress in studies that there is no hope that they will ever acquire sufficient learning; especially any should be immediately dismissed who have committed a fault against morals or against faith (c. 1371).

e) Candidates suffering from psychoneuroses should be carefully screened. Those in whom the conflict is sexual should be rejected. In the case of psychoneuroses, an individual decision must be made, but when they are severe early in training the candidate should be rejected.

f) Masturbation persisting beyond preparatory school is evidence of emotional disorder or immaturity, or both. When it persists, especially with frequency, into seminary years, the candidate should be rejected.

g) Obviously psychotic and prepsychotic candidates should be rejected.

h) Epilepsy in a candidate poses a special problem. If there is a history of only preadolescent seizures and at least five years have gone by without an attack no objection need be offered to his entering the seminary. If postadolescent seizures have occurred, a period of at least three years should be required before acceptance, and at least three years free of seizures before ordination. Epilepsy is well controlled by modern treatment and is not the type of disorder which gave rise to many of the rules against it. Most of the deterioration noted before modern therapy was due to the drugs used and not due to the disease itself. These degenerative states are seldom seen in recent years.

These I would regard as the absolute causes for rejection on psychiatric grounds. Relative indications for rejection would be too numerous to discuss in this brief presentation.

I would like to emphasize that such positive statements as those made in this section are not intended to disregard the effects of grace. Grace can produce many strange and wonderful results. Psychological screening must deal with the personality objectively. It must form an estimate

---

[42] T. Lincoln Bouscaren, S.J., and Adam Ellis, S.J., *op. cit.*, p. 742.

of the individual's ability to adapt to the priesthood on purely natural grounds.

Conclusion

More needs to be done in the matter of screening of candidates for the religious life. A start has been made. The pastoral counselor should keep abreast of the advances in this field by frequent reference to his professional journals.

APPENDIX

ROGERIAN THEORY OF PERSONALITY AND THERAPY

In presenting Rogers' *theory of personality* his own outline will be followed. He presents nineteen propositions to account for observed phenomena about behavior; some propositions are considered to be assumptions while others are thought of as testable hypotheses.

The first proposition is that *"every individual exists in a continually changing world of experience of which he is the center."*[1] This world includes all that is experienced by the individual, whether or not these experiences are consciously perceived. Rogers agrees with Angyal that consciousness consists of the symbolization of some of our experiences. Rogers feels that probably only a small portion of all possible experiences are *consciously* perceived. He states further that "many of our sensory and visceral sensations are not symbolized. It is also true, however, that a large portion of this world of experience is *available* to consciousness, and may become conscious if the need of the individual causes certain sensations to come into focus because they are associated with the satisfaction of a need."[2] He continues, "An important truth in regard to this private world of the individual is that it can only be known, in any genuine and complete sense, to the individual himself."[3]

The second proposition is *"the organism reacts to the field as it is experienced and perceived.* This perceptual field is, for the individual, *'reality.'*"[4] That is, a person reacts to things as he perceives them. His perception may or may not be in tune with things as they actually are. Each perception is considered by Rogers to be an hypothesis. These hypotheses which are tested provide much security. There are present among a person's perceptions untested hypotheses also, and these may direct behavior as much as tested hypotheses.

---

[1] Carl R. Rogers, *Client-Centered Therapy* (Boston: Houghton Mifflin Co., 1951), p. 483.
[2] *Ibid.*, p. 483.
[3] *Ibid.*, p. 483.
[4] *Ibid.*, p. 484.

The third proposition is "the organism reacts as an organized whole to its phenomenal field . . . there is increasing acceptance of the fact that one of the most basic characteristics of organic life is its tendency toward total, organized, goal-directed responses."[5] Rogers uses the concept of the individual functioning as a whole to explain the possibility of disorders.

The fourth proposition is "the organism has one basic tendency and striving — to actualize, maintain, and enhance the experiencing organism. . . . We are talking here about the tendency of the organism to maintain itself — to assimilate food, to behave defensively in the face of threat, to achieve the goal of self-maintenance even when the usual pathway to the goal is blocked. We are speaking of the tendency of the organism to move in the direction of maturation, as maturation is defined for each species. . . . It moves in the direction of greater independence or self-responsibility. Its movement . . . is in the direction of an increasing self-government, self-regulation, and autonomy, and away from heteronymous control, or control by external forces. . . . Finally, the self-actualization of the organism appears to be in the direction of socialization, broadly defined."[6] Rogers goes on to say, "The directional tendency which we are discussing will be defined most adequately by comparing the undeveloped with the developed organism, the simple organism with the complex, the organism early or low on the evolutionary scale with the organism which has developed later and is regarded as higher."[7]

In quoting Horney, Rogers says, "Horney gives a vivid description of this force as it is experienced in therapy: 'The ultimate driving force is the person's unrelenting will to come to grips with himself, a wish to grow and to leave nothing untouched that prevents growth.' "[8]

Rogers states that experience in therapy allows him to give this proposition a central place in his scheme. Elaborating on this idea, he says, "It would be grossly inaccurate to suppose that the organism operates smoothly in the direction of self-enhancement and growth. It would be perhaps more correct to say that the organism moves through struggle and pain toward enhancement and growth. The whole process may be symbolized and illustrated by the child's learning to walk. The first steps involve struggle, and usually pain. Often it is true that the immediate

[5] Ibid., pp. 486–487.
[6] Ibid., pp. 487–488.
[7] Ibid., p. 489.
[8] Ibid., p. 489.

reward involved in taking a few steps is in no way commensurate with the pain of falls and bumps. The child may, because of the pain, revert to crawling for a time. Yet, in the overwhelming majority of individuals, the forward direction of growth is more powerful than the satisfactions of remaining infantile."[9]

Rogers' *fifth proposition* is *"behavior is basically the goal-directed attempt of the organism to satisfy its needs as experienced, in the field as perceived."*[10] The need, it seems, must be experienced to be a motivating factor. It does not, however, have to be consciously experienced. It seems that by conscious experience Rogers here means symbolization. He uses the example of hunger contractions being motivating factors although not necessarily conscious, that is, not symbolized. Rogers further points out that all needs must be present to the organism to be motivating. "Behavior is not caused by something which occurred in the past. Present tensions and present needs are the only ones which the organism endeavors to reduce or satisfy. While it is true that past experience has certainly served to modify the meaning which will be perceived in present experiences, yet there is not behavior except to meet a present need."[11]

Rogers' *sixth proposition* is *"emotion accompanies and in general facilitates such goal-directed behavior, the kind of emotions being related to the seeking versus the consummatory aspects of the behavior, and the intensity of the emotion being related to the perceived significance of the behavior for the maintenance and enhancement of the organism."*[12] Rogers speaks of two kinds of emotions, "the unpleasant and/or excited feelings, and the calm and/or satisfied emotions."[13] He feels that the first of these facilitates rather than impedes goal-directed behavior except when present to an excessive degree.

Dr. Rogers distinguishes between the organism and the self, the latter being the conscious, symbolized representation of how one sees oneself. This representation may or may not be realistic and accurate. The organism is the totality of the person, conscious to an extent but for the most part unconscious, including both one's physiological and psychological make-up. Thus when he says, ". . . *the intensity of the emotion being related to the perceived significance of the behavior for the maintenance*

---

[9] *Ibid.*, p. 490.
[10] *Ibid.*, p. 491.
[11] *Ibid.*, p. 492.
[12] *Ibid.*, pp. 492–493.
[13] *Ibid.*, p. 493.

and enhancement of the organism," he includes in this proposition the notion that at times behavior will be directed toward the maintenance and enhancement of the self to the disadvantage of the organism.

Proposition seven is "*the best vantage point for understanding behavior is from the internal frame of reference of the individual himself.*"[14] This proposition is related to proposition one, that only the person himself is capable of full knowledge of his own experience. Hence, an external frame of reference is artificial. When we can adopt an internal frame of reference, we can see that "the various meaningless and strange behaviors are seen to be part of a meaningful and goal-directed activity" of the client. It is only by seeing things as the client sees them, meaningful as they are meaningful to the client, that we can predict his thinking and behavior. We can only approximate this, for to take a complete internal frame of reference is impossible. But, a number of investigators approximating the same internal frame of reference and finding agreement in their observations holds promise for the advance of scientific psychology.

Dr. Rogers feels that this phenomenological approach is further limited by the fact that much of the person's experience is not conscious to the person, and what the person is aware of must be communicated to be known by others, and we well know the inaccurate character of all communication. Rogers summarizes this point of view when he says, "It is possible to achieve, to some extent, the other person's frame of reference, because many of the perceptual objects — self, parents, teachers, employers, and so on — have counterparts in our own perceptual fields, and practically all the attitudes toward these perceptual objects — such as fear, anger, annoyance, love, jealousy, satisfaction — have been present in our own world of experience. Hence we can infer, quite directly, from the communication of the individual, or less accurately from observation of his behavior, a portion of his perceptual and experiential field. The more all his experiences are available to his consciousness, the more it is possible for him to convey a total picture of his phenomenal field. The more his communication is a free expression, unmodified by a need or desire to be defensive, the more adequate will be the communication of the field. (Thus a diary is apt to be a better communication of the perceptual field than a court utterance where the individual is on trial.) It is probably for the reasons just stated that client-centered counseling has proved to be such a valuable method for viewing behavior from the

---

14 *Ibid.*, p. 494.

person's frame of reference. The situation minimizes any need of defensiveness. . . . The person is usually motivated to some degree to communicate his own special world, and the procedures used encourage him to do so. The increasing communication gradually brings more of experience into the realm of awareness, and thus a more accurate and total picture of this individual's world of experience is conveyed. On this basis, a much more understandable picture of behavior emerges."[15]

Rogers' *eighth proposition* is "*a portion of the total perceptual field gradually becomes differentiated as the self.*"[16] Rogers pays tribute to the influence Mead, Cooley, Angyal, Lecky, and others have had upon his thinking concerning the concept of the self. With regard to the origin of the self, Rogers says, ". . . as the infant develops, a portion of the total private world becomes recognized as 'me,' 'I,' 'myself.'" The conscious self "is not necessarily coexistent with the physical organism. . . . Whether or not an object or an experience is regarded as a part of the self depends to a considerable extent upon whether or not it is perceived as within the control of the self. . . . When even such an object as a part of our body is out of control, it is experienced as being less a part of the self. The way in which, when a foot 'goes to sleep' from lack of circulation, it becomes an object to us rather than a part of self, may be a sufficient illustration."[17]

The *ninth proposition* is "*as a result of interaction with the environment, and particularly as a result of evaluational interaction with others, the structure of self is formed — an organized, fluid, but consistent conceptual pattern of perceptions of characteristics and relationships of the 'I' or the 'me,' together with values attached to these concepts.*[18]

The *tenth proposition* is "*the values attached to experiences, and the values which are a part of the self structure, in some instances are values experienced directly by the organism, and in some instances are values introjected or taken over from others, but perceived in distorted fashion, as if they had been experienced directly.*"[19] The two propositions are treated in combined fashion by Rogers. He seems to say that the child comes to differentiate himself from his environment. As he does, he

[15] *Ibid.*, pp. 495–496.
[16] *Ibid.*, p. 497.
[17] *Ibid.*, pp. 497–498.
[18] *Ibid.*, p. 498.
[19] *Ibid.*, p. 498.

learns things about himself and his environment and about the relationship between the two. He learns, "I like ice cream," "stoves are hot,"
"kittens are furry," and, most importantly, "I am loved and my parents
are affectionate to me and I like it." There are also other behaviors
which are satisfying to the child, for example, having a bowel movement
when one feels like it and where one feels like it, let us say in the bath
tub, or hitting one's baby sister. These behaviors may not be so satisfying
to the child's parents. They may say nonloving things to the child or
withdraw manifestations of affection from the child as a result of their
dissatisfaction. This, as Rogers puts it, "constitutes a deep threat to the
nascent structure of self." As a result, the child learns to distort his
perceptions. He denies that behavior, unacceptable to his parents, is
satisfying to him, and he introjects their evaluation of the behavior as
though it were his own, which it is not, and in fact is directly contrary
to his own direct valuing experience. Thus, parental values are accepted
as though they were based on one's sensory and visceral experience.
These values come to be thought of as just as "real" as those based on
one's own direct experience. Behavior is accepted on the word of others
when such behavior is not directly experienced as satisfying, and behavior
is rejected on the word of others when there is no direct experience of
such behavior as being dissatisfying. "The individual begins on a pathway
which he later describes as 'I don't really know myself.' The primary
sensory and visceral reactions are ignored, or not permitted into consciousness, except in distorted form. The values which might be built upon
them cannot be admitted to awareness. A concept of self based in part
upon a distorted symbolization has taken their place."[20]

It is from this type of thinking that Rogers draws his definition of
the self-concept or self-structure. "The self-structure is an organized configuration of perceptions of the self which are admissible to awareness.
It is composed of such elements as the perceptions of one's characteristics
and abilities; the percepts and concepts of the self in relation to others
and to the environment; the value qualities which are perceived as
associated with experiences and objects, and the goals and ideals which
are perceived as having positive or negative valence. It is, then, the
organized picture, existing in awareness either as figure or ground, of
the self and the self-in-relationship, together with the positive or negative

[20] *Ibid.*, p. 501.

values which are associated with those qualities and relationships, as they are perceived as existing in the past, present, or future."[21]

Rogers draws a blueprint for the development of a self-structure in infants which might avoid psychological difficulty in later life. When a child behaves in a way that is unacceptable to the parent, Rogers suggests that the parent develop an attitude that allows him to accept the behavior of the child as satisfying to the child, to accept the child who experiences satisfying feelings associated with unacceptable behavior, and to accept one's own feeling that such behavior is unacceptable in the family. The child is then free to act acceptably or not in the light of clearly perceived parentally invoked consequences. The most important fact here is that feelings are allowed expression, are subject to recognition, are above board, and subsequent behavior, acceptable or not, ensues based upon reality. Summarizing this viewpoint, Rogers says, "Because the budding structure of the self is not threatened by loss of love, because feelings are accepted by his parent, the child in this instance does not need to deny to awareness the satisfactions which he is experiencing, nor does he need to distort his experience of the parental reaction and regard it as his own. He retains instead a secure self which can serve to guide his behavior by freely admitting to awareness, in accurately symbolized form, all the relevant evidence of his experience in terms of its organismic satisfactions, both immediate and longer range. He is thus developing a soundly structured self in which there is neither denial nor distortion of experience."[22]

The eleventh proposition is "as experiences occur in the life of the individual, they are either (a) symbolized, perceived, and organized into some relationship to the self, (b) ignored because there is no perceived relationship to the self-structure, (c) denied symbolization or given a distorted symbolization because the experience is inconsistent with the structure of the self."[23] It seems that Rogers is saying here that some phenomena are fringe and background phenomena and have little or no relationship to my self-concept, for example, the hiss of the heater in the basement as I type this material. These phenomena are all but ignored by me. Other phenomena are symbolized, perceived, and organized into my self-structure because compatible with that structure, for example, a

---

[21] *Ibid.*, p. 501.
[22] *Ibid.*, p. 503.
[23] *Ibid.*, p. 503.

statement by my wife that she thinks I'm really getting some work done down here in the basement. Other phenomena are somewhat consciously denied or distorted, or in Freudian terms, unconsciously repressed because they are a threat to my self-concept, for example, the feeling of hate which I have for my publisher and his deadlines. This feeling is not acceptable to me because I think of myself as an even-tempered, easy-to-get-along-with person.

Basing himself on the work of Postman, Bruner, and McGinnies;[24] McGinnies;[25] and McCleary and Lazarus,[26] Rogers also notes that persons may be able to "subceive" threatening phenomena and to defend against them without consciously being aware of the threatening "subceptions" or of the defenses taken against them.

The *twelfth proposition* is "*most of the ways of behaving which are adopted by the organism are those which are consistent with the concept of self.*"[27] Rogers feels that most but not all ways of behaving in one's attempts to meet one's needs will be ways consistent with one's self-concept.

Proposition thirteen is "*behavior may, in some instances, be brought about by organic experiences and needs which have not been symbolized. Such behavior may be inconsistent with the structure of the self, but in such instances the behavior is not 'owned' by the individual.*"[28] Rogers explains such behavior by saying that strong organic cravings cry for expression but are not acceptable or admitted to awareness. These cravings do express themselves at times, as for example, when a person has had too much to drink, and cause the person to say, "I wasn't myself," or "I didn't know what I was doing." In other words, "This behavior was not owned by me, it was behavior beyond my control."

Proposition fourteen is "*psychological maladjustment exists when the organism denies to awareness significant sensory and visceral experiences, which consequently are not symbolized and organized into the gestalt of the self-structure. When this situation exists, there is a basic or potential*

[24] L. Postman, J. S. Bruner, and E. McGinnies, "Personal Values as Selective Factors in Perception," *Journal Abnorm. and Soc. Psychol.*, 1948, 43, 142–154.

[25] Elliott McGinnies, "Emotionality and Perceptual Defense," *Psychological Review*, 1949, 56, 244–451.

[26] R. A. McCleary, and R. S. Lazarus, "Autonomic Discrimination Without Awareness," *Journal Pers.*, 1949, 18, 171–179.

[27] Rogers, *op. cit.*, p. 507.

[28] *Ibid.*, p. 509.

psychological tension."[29] In explaining this proposition, Rogers says, "If we think of the structure of the self as being a symbolic elaboration of a portion of the private experiential world of the organism, we may realize that when much of this private world is denied symbolization, certain basic tensions result. We find, then, that there is a very real discrepancy between the experiencing organism as it exists, and the concept of self which exerts such a governing influence upon behavior. This self is now very inadequately representative of the experience of the organism. Conscious control becomes more difficult as the organism strives to satisfy needs which are not consciously admitted, and to react to experiences which are denied by the conscious self. Tension then exists, and if the individual becomes to any degree aware of this tension or discrepancy, he feels anxious, he feels that he is not united or integrated, that he is unsure of his direction."[30] Clinically, this condition manifests itself by the client not knowing what he is afraid of, not knowing what he wants, not being able to make any decisions, and not having any clear goal.

Rogers cites two clinically observable tension types. There is one type in which the self-concept is well formed; that is, the person has a clear, though inaccurate, concept of what he or she is. Tension arises when organic strivings contradict one's concept of self and are to a degree perceived as opposed to the self-concept. Another tension type is that in which one feels he does not have a real self, a real identity. He feels that "his only self consists of endeavoring to do what others believe he should do." In this latter case, the self is based almost entirely upon the valuations of others and only minimally on one's own sensory and visceral experience and hence provides the basis for considerable potential tension.

Proposition fifteen is *"psychological adjustment exists when the concept of the self is such that all the sensory and visceral experiences of the organism are, or may be, assimilated on a symbolic level into a consistent relationship with the concept of self."*[31] When this integration occurs, all the energies devoted to denial and distortion can be directed toward personal growth. Rogers states that research indicates that "conscious acceptance of impulses and perceptions greatly increases the possibility of conscious control."[32]

---

[29] *Ibid.*, p. 570.
[30] *Ibid.*, pp. 510–511.
[31] *Ibid.*, p. 513.
[32] *Ibid.*, p. 514.

Another noteworthy observation of Rogers is that when all one's experiences are available to consciousness, the person becomes less self-conscious, less guarded, and feels that he can freely be himself.

Proposition sixteen is "any experience which is inconsistent with the organization or structure of self may be perceived as a threat, and the more of these perceptions there are, the more rigidly the self-structure is organized to maintain itself."[33] If, for example, a mother, who thinks of herself as accepting and loving, but in fact to a notable degree rejects her child, is told that she is rejecting, she may question the evidence for such a statement, she may question the authority or training one has for making such a statement, and take other steps to keep her self-structure intact. Rogers seems to agree with Hogan in noting that "the more of sensory and visceral experience that is denied symbolization, or given a distorted symbolization, the greater the likelihood that any new experience will be perceived as threatening, since there is a larger false structure to be maintained."[34]

Proposition seventeen is, "under certain conditions involving primarily complete absence of any threat to the self-structure, experiences which are inconsistent with it may be perceived, and examined, and the structure of self revised to assimilate and include such experiences."[35]

Thus, a person's self-concept can and does change from time to time. It changes in one's ordinary development as a person through the years. We all have experiences of looking at ourselves in different ways from time to time. It also changes in therapy. According to client-centered theory, this change is attributed to counselor acceptance of the client, his thoughts, and his feelings. This allows the client, it is hypothecized, to bring into consciousness previously rejected perceptions about himself. Once in consciousness, once accepted by the therapist, they can be accepted by the client as a part of himself and incorporated into his own self-concept.

Rogers analyzes two factors that provide for the reorganization of the self-structure. First, the client is allowed to learn about himself at his own rate, each new discovery being accepted by the therapist "at a 'safe' rate . . . hitherto denied experiences are slowly and tentatively accepted."[36] Second, the therapist accepts all experiences, all attitudes, all

---

[33] *Ibid.*, p. 515.
[34] *Ibid.*, p. 517.
[35] *Ibid.*, p. 517.
[36] *Ibid.*, p. 518.

perceptions of the client, and the "introjection of the counselor attitude may be at least a temporary or partial step toward the client's experiencing of himself as acceptable."[37] Having developed an inclination toward accepting himself, the client can also assimilate experiences about himself between interviews. Our understanding, however, is incomplete. Rogers admits, "that a more refined analysis is needed of the exact conditions which are necessary to permit a reorganization of the self-concept and the assimilation of contradictory experiences."[38]

Proposition eighteen is "when the individual perceives and accepts into one consistent and integrated system all his sensory and visceral experiences, then he is necessarily more understanding of others and is more accepting of others as separate individuals."[39] This proposition is explained by saying that the person who denies sensory and visceral experiences is vulnerable to having these experiences brought to his attention by the words and behavior of another. Thus, others are seen as threats. It is only when one is able to view and accept all sensory and visceral experiences that he ceases to be vulnerable and others cease to be threats. He then no longer needs to defend against others and can relate to them as they are, separate individuals, operating in terms of their own meanings, based on their own perceptual fields.

Rogers' final proposition is, "as the individual perceives and accepts into his self-structure more of his organic experiences, he finds that he is replacing his present value system — based so largely upon introjections which have been distortedly symbolized — with a continuing organismic valuing process."[40] The client expresses the idea that he has been doing just what others thought he should do. He tries to discover what he thinks he should do. He learns to trust his own senses, his own physiological system, to provide a basis for his evaluations. "He makes a choice between two courses of action, fearfully and hesitantly, not knowing whether he has weighed their values accurately, but then he discovers that he may let the evidence of his own experience indicate whether he has chosen satisfyingly. He discovers that he does not need to know what are the correct values; through the data supplied by his own organism, he can experience what is satisfying and enhancing. He can put his confi-

---

[37] *Ibid.*, p. 518.
[38] *Ibid.*, p. 519.
[39] *Ibid.*, p. 520.
[40] *Ibid.*, p. 522.

dence in a valuing process, rather than in some rigid, introjected system of values."[41] Rogers feels that when persons analyze values in the above way, they arrive at a set of values applicable to all persons, "that the greatest values for the enhancement of the organism accrue when all experiences and all attitudes are permitted conscious symbolization, and when behavior becomes the meaningful and balanced satisfaction of all needs. . . . Since all individuals have basically the same needs . . . it is not anarchy which results, but a high degree of commonality and a genuinely socialized system of values. One of the ultimate ends, then, of an hypothesis of confidence in the individual, and in his capacity to resolve his own conflicts, is the emergence of value systems which are unique and personal for each individual, yet which are at the same time deeply socialized, possessing a high degree of similarity in their essentials."[42]

Theory of Therapy

Rogers' theory of therapy is a logical sequel to the foregoing theory of personality. He begins by considering the individual who has no thought of seeking counseling help. He sees himself as worthy and acceptable. The self-structure can be considered as an organization of hypotheses for meeting life's situations. Evidently the organization of this individual has served him well in meeting his needs. In order to serve him well, all hypotheses need not agree with objective reality. The extent to which the individual's perception of himself is not in agreement with "socially perceived reality" is a measure of his basic vulnerability. "The extent to which he dimly perceives these incongruences and discrepancies is a measure of his internal tension, and determines the amount of defensive behavior."[43] "To return to our individual, who is not yet ready for therapy: It is when his organized self-structure is no longer effective in meeting his needs in the reality situation, or when he dimly perceives discrepancies in himself, or when his behavior seems out of control and no longer consistent with himself, that he becomes 'ripe,' as it were, for therapy." Perceptions which run contrary to the established self-structure are denied or distorted.[44]

---

[41] *Ibid.*, p. 523.
[42] *Ibid.*, p. 524.
[43] *Ibid.*, pp. 191–192.
[44] *Ibid.*, p. 192.

BIBLIOGRAPHY

Alexander, Franz, and Ross, Helen (eds.), *Dynamic Psychiatry* (Chicago: Univ. of Chicago Press, 1952).

Allan, W. Scott, *Rehabilitation: A Community Challenge* (New York: Wiley, 1958).

Allers, Rudolph, M.D., "Abnormality: A Chapter in Moral Psychology. VI. Moral Responsibility of the Neurotic," *Homiletic and Pastoral Review* (1942, 42, 727–733).

—— *Character Education in Adolescence* (New York: J. F. Wagner, Inc., 1940).

—— *The Psychology of Character* (New York: Sheed & Ward, 1933).

Allport, G., *The Individual and His Religion* (New York: Macmillan, 1950).

American Association of Marriage Counselors, *Marriage Counseling* (New York: Association Press, 1958).

Anderson, George G., *Current Conditions and Trends in Relations Between Religion and Mental Health* (New York: Academy of Religion and Mental Health, 1960).

Anon., *Alcoholics Anonymous Comes of Age* (New York: Harper, 1957).

Anon., *Marriage Legislation of the Catholic Church* (Paterson, N. J.: St. Anthony's Guild, 1947).

Anon., *Mother's Little Helper* (Chicago: Franciscan Herald Press, 1960).

Aquinas, St. Thomas, *Summa of St. Thomas Aquinas* (New York: Benziger Bros., 1947).

Aring, Charles D., M.D., "Sympathy and Empathy," *Journal American Medical Association* (Vol. 167, No. 4, May 24, 1958).

Baruch, Dorothy Walter, *New Ways in Discipline* (New York: McGraw-Hill Book Co., Inc., 1949).

Berg, Charles, *The First Interview With a Psychiatrist* (London: George Allen and Unwin, Ltd., 1955).

Bernard, Harold W., *Mental Hygiene for Classroom Teachers* (New York: McGraw-Hill Book Co., Inc., 1952).

Bier, Rev. William C., S.J., "Goals in Pastoral Counseling," *Pastoral Psychology* (Feb., 1959).

—— "Psychological Aspects of Pastoral Work," in *Proceedings of the Archdiocesan Institute of Ecclesiastical Studies* (New York: St. Joseph Seminary, 1957).

—— "Religious Counseling: The Roman Catholic Church," in R. K. Hall and J. A. Lauwery's (eds.) *The Year Book of Education* (Yonkers: World Book Co., 1955).

Bier, William C., S.J., and Schneiders, A. A. (eds.), *Proceedings of the Second Institute for the Clergy on Problems in Pastoral Psychology* (New York: Fordham University, 1958).

Bingham, W. V., and Moors, B. B., *How to Interview* (New York: Harper, 1941).

Blum, M. L., and Balinsky, B., *Counseling and Psychology* (Englewood Cliffs: Prentice-Hall, 1951).

Boaatey, Trygve F., *Fundamentals of Psychoanalytic Technique* (New York: Wiley, 1954).

Bonnell, Rev. John S., *Pastoral Psychiatry* (New York: Harper, 1938).

Bordin, Edward S., *Psychological Counseling* (New York: Appleton-Century-Crofts, 1955).

Braceland, Francis J., M.D. (ed.), *Faith, Reason and Modern Psychiatry* (New York: Kenedy, 1955).

———— "A Psychiatrist Examines the Relationship Between Psychiatry and the Catholic Clergy," *Pastoral Psychology* (Feb., 1959).

Bradway, John S., "Some Domestic Relations Laws that Counselors in Marital Difficulties Need to Know," *Social Forces* (Vol. 17, October, 1938), pp. 83–89.

Brayfield, Arthur H. (ed.), *Modern Methods of Counseling* (New York: Appleton-Century-Crofts, 1955).

Brewer, John M., *History of Vocational Guidance* (New York: Harper and Brothers, 1942).

Bruckner, Rev. P. J., S.J., *How to Give Sex Instructions* (St. Louis: The Queen's Work, 1952).

Buhler, Charlotte, *Kindheit und Jugend* (Leipzig, 1931).

Bullis, H. Edmund, "An Educational Program For Development of the 'Normal' Personality," *The American Journal of Psychiatry* (Vol. 109, No. 5, Nov., 1952), pp. 375–377.

Bullis, H. Edmund, and O'Mally, Emily E., *Human Relations in the Classroom, Course I* (Wilmington: Delaware State Society for Mental Hygiene, 1947).

Burgess, Ernest W., and Cottrell, Leonard S., Jr., *Predicting Success or Failure in Marriage* (New York: Prentice-Hall, Inc., 1939).

Byrne, Rev. John T., "The Counselor and The Spiritual Director," *The Homiletic And Pastoral Review* (Vol. 59, No. 6, March, 1959).

Callis, Robert, et al., *A Casework of Counseling* (New York: Appleton-Century-Crofts, Inc., 1955).

Cammack, Rev. J. S., S.J., "Confessor and/or Psychiatrist," *Clergy Review* (1940, 18, 290–303).

The Catholic Counselor, *Readings for Catholic Counselors* (New York: The Catholic Guidance Council, 1959).

Catholic University of America, *Workshop on College Counseling and Testing, 1957* (Washington, D. C.: The Catholic University of America Press, 1958).

Cattell, Raymond B., *An Introduction to Personality Study* (London and New York: Hutchinson University Library, 1950).

Cavanagh, J. R., M.D., "Contemporary Schools of Psychiatry," *Bulletin of the Georgetown University Medical Center* (June–July, 1951, Vol. V, No. 1), pp. 91–99.

———— "The Effect of Confinement on Psychiatric Patients," *U. S. Armed Forces Medical Journal* (October, 1951, Vol. II, No. 10), pp. 1479–1482.

—————— "Emotional Problems of the School Child," *Bulletin of the Guild of Catholic Psychiatrists* (Vol. V, No. 3, April, 1958).

—————— "The Existent Woman," *Alumnae Journal of Trinity College* (Vol. 33, No. 1, Section 2, Spring, 1959).

—————— "The Father Is the Head of the Family," *Bulletin of the Georgetown University Medical Center* (Vol. XII, No. 1, September, 1958), pp. 21–27.

—————— "Frustration As A Hidden Cause of Divorce," *Sanctity and Success in Marriage* (Washington, D. C.: National Catholic Welfare Conference, 1956).

—————— *Fundamental Marriage Counseling* (Milwaukee: The Bruce Publishing Company, 1957).

—————— "Group Psychotherapy in a Naval Disciplinary Barracks," *U. S. Naval Medical Bulletin* (July–August, 1949, Vol. 49, No. 4), pp. 645–654.

—————— "Hypnosis," *Bulletin of the Georgetown University Medical Center* (Vol. 9, No. 6, July, 1956), pp. 202–204.

—————— "The Internist's Approach to Psychosomatic Medicine," *Bulletin of the Georgetown University Medical Center* (August–September, 1950, Vol. IV, No. 2), pp. 23–31.

—————— "Mental Health in the School," *Mental Health and Special Education* (Washington, D. C.: The Catholic University of America Press, 1957), pp. 215–221.

—————— "Nervous Mental Diseases," *The Ecclesiastical Review* (September–October, 1943), pp. 179–189 and 257–271.

—————— "Problem Parents," *Bulletin of the Georgetown University Medical Center* (December–January, 1950–1951, Vol. IV, No. 4), pp. 87–90.

—————— "Profile of a Probation Violator" (with Samuel Gerstein, Earl R. Peters, and Thomas J. Mathieu), *U. S. Armed Forces Medical Journal* (September, 1950, Vol. I, No. 9), pp. 1051–1064.

—————— "A Psychiatrist Looks at the Durham Decision," *The Catholic University of America Law Review* (Vol. 5, No. 1, January 1955), pp. 3–31.

—————— "A Psychiatrist Looks at Psychiatry," *Bulletin of the Georgetown University Medical Center* (Vol. 8, No. 2, November, 1954), pp. 54–64.

—————— "Psychiatry and Catholicism," *Bulletin of the Georgetown University Medical Center* (May–June, 1953).

—————— "Psychiatry, Catholic Plan," *The Sign* (November, 1950), pp. 19–20.

—————— "The Psychology of Contraception," *Marriage Magazine* (August, 1960).

—————— "Psychosomatic Aspects of Essential Hypertension," *Bulletin of the Georgetown University Medical Center* (August–September, 1949, Vol. IV, No. 2), pp. 23–31.

—————— "The Psychosomatic History," *Medical Annals of the District of Columbia* (July, 1946, Vol. XV, No. 7), pp. 325–329.

—————— "Psychotherapy by the General Practitioner," *G. P.* (July, 1954, to March, 1955).

—————— "The Responsibility of the Mentally Ill for Criminal Offenses," *The Catholic Lawyer* (Vol. 4, No. 4, Autumn, 1958).

—————— "The Teacher and Mental Health," *Mental Health and Special Education* (Washington, D. C.: Catholic University of America Press, 1957), pp. 24–62.

———— "What Is Your Psychiatric I.Q.?" *Bulletin of the Georgetown University Medical Center* (Vol. 8, No. 5, May, 1955), pp. 157–169.

Cavanagh, J. R., M.D., and McGoldrick, Rev. James B., S.J., *Fundamental Psychiatry* (Milwaukee: The Bruce Publishing Company, 1953).

Central Council for Health Education, *Six Hints to Mothers of Teenage Girls* (London: Tavistock House).

Children's Bureau, Social Security Administration, U. S. Department of Health, Education and Welfare, *The Adolescent in Your Family* (No. 347, rev. 1955).

Ciriaci, Pietro, Cardinal, "Letter on Modesty in Dress," *The Pope Speaks* (Third Quarter, 1954), pp. 289–291.

Clemens, Alphonse H. (ed.), *Marriage Education and Counseling* (Washington, D. C.: The Catholic University of America Press, 1951).

Colky, Kenneth M., *A Skeptical Psychoanalyst* (New York: Ruald Press, 1958).

Connell, Very Rev. F. J., C.Ss.R., *Outlines of Moral Theology* (Milwaukee: The Bruce Publishing Company, 1953).

———— *Some Moral Problems in Marriage Education and Counseling* (Washington, D. C.: Catholic University of America Workshop Papers, 1952).

Connors, Rev. Charles, C.Ss.P., "Teen-Agers 'Going Steady': Whose Problem?" *The Homiletic and Pastoral Review* (Vol. LVIII, No. 3, 1957), pp. 249–254.

Cottle, William C., "Which Catholics Should Counsel," *Catholic Counselor* (V. 3, Winter, 1959, 3:33, No. 2).

Cox, R. D., *Counselors and Their Work* (Philadelphia: Archives Publishing Company of Pennsylvania, 1945).

Crotty, Charles, "Marriage Counseling and Psychology," *Bulletin of the Guild of Catholic Psychiatrists* (Vol. VI, No. 4, Oct., 1959).

Cuber, John F., *Marriage Counseling Practice* (New York: Appleton-Century-Crofts, Inc., 1948).

Curran, Rev. Charles A., *Counseling in Catholic Life and Education* (New York: The Macmillan Company, 1952).

———— "The Counseling Relationship and Some Religious Factors," *Journal of Counseling Psychology* (Vol. 6, Winter 1959, No. 4, 6:4).

———— *Personality Factors in Counseling* (New York: Grune & Stratton, Inc., 1945).

Darley, John G., *The Interview in Counseling* (Washington, D. C.: U. S. Department of Labor, Government Printing Office, 1946).

Demal, W., *Pastoral Psychology in Practice* (New York: Kenedy, 1955).

Dempsey, Rev. P. J. R., O.F.M.Cap., *Freud, Psychoanalysis, Catholicism* (Chicago: Regnery, 1956).

Descartes, Rene, *The Method, Meditations, and Philosophy of Descartes*, trans. by John Veitch (New York: Tudor Publishing Co., 1901).

Deutsch, Felix, and Murphy, William F., *The Clinical Interview* (New York: Int. Univ. Press, 1955), 2 vols.

D'Evelyn, Katherine, *Meeting Children's Emotional Needs* (Englewood Cliffs: Prentice-Hall, 1957).

Drake, Lewise E., and Oetting, E. C., *An MMPI Codebook for Counselors* (Minneapolis: University of Minnesota Press, 1959).

Drolet, Howard O., A Study of the Services Facilitating Guidance Provided by the Diocesan Superintendent's Offices of Education in the United States (Washington, D. C.: Catholic University of America Press, 1959).

Dublin, Louis I., M.D., "Women Are Different," The Reader's Digest (Dec., 1950) Your Life (Dec., 1950) (New York: Kings Way Press, Inc.).

Eaton, Joseph W., Ph.D., "The Assessment of Mental Health," The American Journal of Psychiatry (Vol. 108, No. 2, August, 1951), pp. 81–90.

Eisenstein, V., Neurotic Interaction in Marriage (New York: Basic Books, 1956).

English, O. S., M.D., and Finch, S. M., M.D., Introduction to Psychiatry (New York: Norton, 1954).

Erickson, E. H., Childhood and Society (New York: Norton, 1950).

Evaluation in Mental Health (Washington, D. C.: U. S. Government Printing Office, 1955).

Ferm, V., A Dictionary of Pastoral Psychology (New York: Philosophical Library, 1955).

Fleege, U., Self-Revelation of the Adolescent Boy (Milwaukee: The Bruce Publishing Company, 1945).

——— Personal Problems of the Modern Adolescent (Washington, D. C.: The Catholic University of America, 1945).

Flood, Rev. Peter, O.S.B. (ed.), New Problems in Medical Ethics (Westminster, Md.: Newman Press, 1955), 3 vols.

Ford, C. S., and Beach, F. A., Patterns of Sexual Behavior (New York: Harper, 1951).

Ford, J. C., S.J., Depth Psychology, Morality and Alcoholism (Weston, Mass.: Weston College Press, 1951).

——— Man Takes a Drink (New York: Kenedy, 1955).

Ford, Rev. J. C., S.J., and Kelly, Rev. G., S.J., Contemporary Moral Theology, Vol. I (Westminster, Md.: Newman, 1958).

Fostering Mental Health in Our Schools, Yearbook, Association for Supervision and Curriculum Development (Washington, D. C.: National Education Association, 1950).

Frankl, V., M.D., The Doctor and the Soul (New York: Knopf, 1955).

Freud, S., "Three Contributions to the Theory of Sex," in The Basic Writings of Sigmund Freud (New York: Modern Library, 1938).

Froehlich, Clifford P., and Hoyt, Kenneth, Guidance Testing and Other Student Appraisal Procedures for Teachers and Counselors (Chicago: Science Research Associates, 1959).

Fromm, Erick, M.D., Escape From Freedom (New York: Farrar & Rinehart, 1941).

Fromm-Reichmann, Frieda, M.D., Principles of Intensive Psychotherapy (Chicago: University of Chicago Press, 1950).

Garrett, Annette, Interviewing, Its Principles and Methods (New York: Family Welfare Association of America, 1942).

Gayle, R. Finley, Jr., M.D., "Conflict and Cooperation Between Psychiatry and Religion," reprint from Pastoral Psychology (Nov., 1956).

Gemelli, Rev. A., O.F.M., *Psychoanalysis Today* (New York: Kenedy, 1955).

Gill, Merton, M.D., Newman, Richard, M.D., Redlich, Frederich C., M.D., *The Initial Interview in Psychiatric Practice* (New York: International Universities Press, Inc., 1954).

Gleason, Rev. Robert W., S.J., "Homosexuality: Moral Aspects of the Problem," *The Homiletic and Pastoral Review* (Vol. LVIII, No. 3, 1957), pp. 272–278.

Goldbrunner, J., *Cure of Mind and Cure of Soul* (New York: Pantheon Books, 1958).

Greenleaf, Walter J., *Guide to Occupational Choice and Training* (Washington, D. C.: Government Printing Office, 1947).

Group for the Advancement of Psychiatry (Committee on Public Education), *The Psychiatrist in Mental Health Education: Suggestions on Collaboration with Teachers* (Report No. 35) (New York: Publications Office, 1790 Broadway, November, 1956).

———— (Committee on Preventive Psychiatry) *Promotion of Mental Health in The Primary and Secondary Schools: An Evaluation of Four Projects* (Report No. 18) (Topeka, Kans.: 3617 W. 6th Ave., Jan., 1951).

———— (Committee on Psychiatry and Law), *Criminal Responsibility and Psychiatric Expert Testimony* (Report No. 26) (Topeka, Kans.: May, 1954).

Gruenberg, Sidonie (ed.) (in co-operation with the Child Study Association of America), *Our Children Today* (New York: Viking, 1955).

Guilford, J. P., *Fields of Psychology* (New York: Van Nostrand Co., Inc., 1950).

Hadfield, J. A., M.D., *Mental Health and the Psychoneuroses* (London: George Allen and Unwin, 1952).

Hadley, John M., *Clinical and Counseling Psychology* (New York: Knopf, 1958).

Hagmaier, Rev. George, C.S.P., and Gleason, Rev. Robert W., S.J., *Counseling the Catholic: Modern Techniques and Emotional Conflicts* (New York: Sheed & Ward, 1959).

Hahn, Milton E., and Maclean, Malcolm S., *Counseling Psychology*, 2nd ed. (New York: McGraw-Hill Book Co., Inc., 1955).

———— *General Clinical Counseling* (New York: McGraw-Hill Book Co., Inc., 1950).

Haley, Rev. Joseph E., C.S.C., *Accent on Purity* (Notre Dame: Fides Publishers, 1960).

Hall, C. S., and Lindzey, G., *Theories of Personality* (New York: Wiley, 1957).

Hardee, Melvene D., *The Faculty in College Counseling* (with two chapters by Orrin B. Powell) (New York: McGraw-Hill Book Co., Inc., 1959).

Harsh, C. M., and Schrickel, H. G., 2nd ed., *Personality: Development and Assessment* (New York: Ronald, 1959).

Harvey, Rev. John F., O.S.F.S., "Counseling is a Complex Art," *Catholic Educator* (27:367–70; 513–16; April, 1957).

Healy, W., Bronner, A. F., and Bowers, A. M., *The Structure and Meaning of Psychoanalysis* (New York: Alfred A. Knopf, Inc., 1930).

Henderson, D., M.D., and Gillespie, R., M.D., 7th ed., A Text-Book of Psychiatry (New York: Oxford Medical Publications, 1951).

Hiltner, Rev. Seward, Pastoral Counseling (New York: Abingdon Press, 1949).

—— The Christian Shepherd; Some Aspects of Pastoral Care (New York: Abingdon Press, 1959).

Hoch, P., M.D., and Polatin, P., M.D., "Pseudoneurotic Forms of Schizophrenia," Psych. Quarterly (23:248, 1949).

Hollander, I. Fred, Rabbi, Hoffman, Hans, Astley, Royden, C., M.D., and Bier, Rev. William, C.S.J., Some Considerations of Early Attempts in Cooperation Between Religion and Psychiatry, Symposium No. 5, Group for the Advancement of Psychiatry (March, 1958).

Horney, Karen, M.D., Neurosis and Human Growth (New York: Norton, 1950).

Hostie, Rev. R., S.J., Religion and the Psychology of Jung (New York: Sheed & Ward, 1957).

Hunter, Edith, The Questioning Child and Religion (Boston: The Starr King Press, 1956).

Jacobi, Yolande, The Psychology of C. G. Jung, rev. ed. (New Haven: Yale University Press, 1951).

Jager, Harry A., "The Guidance Program Broadens Its Base," Occupations (Vol. 27; 469–473; April, 1949).

Jesus-Marie, Rev. B. de (ed.), Conflict and Light: Studies in Psychological Disturbances and Readjustment (New York: Sheed & Ward, 1952).

Joseph, H., and Zern, G., The Emotional Problems of Children: A Guide for Parents (New York: Crown, 1954).

Josselyn, Irene M., The Adolescent and His World (New York: Family Service Association of America, 1952).

Jung, C. G., M.D., Psychology of Dementia Praecox, Authorized trans. with an introduction by A. A. Brill (New York and Washington: Nervous and Mental Disease Publishing Co., 1936).

Kelly, Rev. G., S.J., The Good Confessor (New York: Sentinel Press, 1951).

—— Guidance For Religious (Westminster, Md.: Newman Press, 1956).

—— Modern Youth and Chastity (St. Louis: Queen's Work, 1952).

Kelly, Rev. George A., The Catholic Marriage Manual (New York: Random House, 1958).

Kelly, Rev. William A., "Training the Catholic Counselor," The Catholic Counselor (Vol. 1, Winter Number, 1957, No. 2).

Kirsch, Rev. Felix M., O.F.M.Cap., Training in Chastity (Huntington, Ind.: Sunday Visitor Press, 1952).

Knoebber, Sister M. Mildred, The Self-Revelation of the Adolescent Girl (Milwaukee: The Bruce Publishing Company, 1937).

Kotinsky, Ruth, and Witmer, Helen L. (eds.), Community Programs for Mental Health (Cambridge, Mass.: Harvard University Press, 1955).

Kowitz, Gerald T., and Kowitz, Norma G., The Elementary Classroom (New York: McGraw-Hill Book Co., Inc., 1959).

Kuhlen, Raymond G., The Psychology of Adolescent Development (New York: Harper and Brothers, 1952).

Layton, Wilbur L., *Counseling Use of the Strong Vocational Interest Blank* (Minneapolis: University of Minnesota Press, 1958).

Leach, Max, *Christianity and Mental Health* (Dubuque, Iowa: Wm. C. Brown, 1957).

Leem, Edward, *What Is Education?* (New York: Sheed & Ward, 1944).

Lemkau, Paul V., M.D., "Prevention of Psychiatric Illnesses," *J.A.M.A.* (October 27, 1956), pp. 854–857.

Leonard, Mrs. Neuton P., *Happy Journey*, 4th printing (Washington, D. C.: National Education Association, 1933).

Linn, L., and Schwarz, L. W., *Psychiatry and Religious Experience* (New York: Random House, 1958).

Lobb, Lois G., M.D., "The Mental and Emotional Needs of Children," *The Catholic Charities Review* (Sept., 1950).

Lydon, Rev. P. J., D.D., *Catholic Teaching on Marriage and Divorce* (New York: The Catholic Information Society, n.d.).

McDaniel, Henry B., *Readings in Guidance* (New York: Holt, 1959).

McGinnies, Elliott, "Emotionality and Perceptual Defense," *Psychological Review* (1949, 56, 244–451).

McKinney, Fred, *Counseling for Personal Adjustment in Schools and Colleges* (Boston: Houghton Mifflin, 1958).

McLaughlin, Rev. Gerard L., S.J., *A Counselor's Guide to the Social Services of Massachusetts* (Boston: Daughters of St. Paul, 1959).

Mailloux, Rev. Noel, O.P., "Modern Psychology and Moral Values," *Pastoral Psychology* (1954, 5, 11–16).

—— *The Proceedings of the Institute for the Clergy on Problems in Pastoral Psychology* (New York: Fordham University Press, 1956).

Malm, Marguerite, and Jamison, Olis G., *Adolescence* (New York: McGraw-Hill Book Co., Inc., 1952).

Mandel, Sherman, "The Differentiation of Emotional Responses in Infants," *Journal Comp. Psych.* (7:265, 335, 1927).

Maxson, Howard F., "Dimensions of Counseling," *Medical Arts and Sciences* (Vol. XIV, No. 1, 1st Quarter, 1960).

May, Rollo, *Existence* (New York: Basic Books, Inc., 1958).

Menninger, Karl A., M.D., *Theory of Psychoanalytic Technique* (New York: Basic Books, 1958).

Mercier, Cardinal Desire, *The Duties of Married Life* (London: Catholic Truth Society, 1908).

—— *Manual of Scholastic Philosophy* (London: K. Paul Trench, Trubner and Co., Ltd., 1916), 2 vols.

Miller, D. F., *Blueprint for Raising Children* (Missouri: Liguorian Press, n.d.).

Misiak, H., and Staudt, Virginia, *Catholics in Psychology* (New York: McGraw-Hill Book Co., Inc., 1954).

Moore, Rev. T. V., M.D., *Nature and Treatment of Mental Disorders* (New York: Grune & Stratton, Inc., 1943).

—— *Personal Mental Hygiene* (New York: Grune & Stratton, Inc., 1944).

—— *The Driving Forces of Human Nature* (New York: Grune & Stratton, Inc., 1948).

Mudd, Emily H., M.D., *Man and Wife* (New York: W. W. Norton and Co., 1959).
——— *The Practice of Marriage Counseling* (New York: Association Press, 1951).
Mullahy, Patrick, M.D., *Oedipus, Myth and Complex* (New York: Hermitage Press, 1948).
Myers, George E., *Principles and Techniques of Vocational Guidance* (New York: McGraw-Hill Book Co., Inc., 1941).

National Catholic Welfare Conference (Family Life Bureau), *Marriage Counseling* (Washington, D. C.: National Catholic Welfare Conference, 1950).
National Conference of Catholic Charities, *Religion and Mental Health* (Washington, D. C.: National Conference of Catholic Charities, 1950).
National Marriage Guidance Council, *Syllabus for the Training of Marriage Counselors* (London, W. C. 1, 1949).
Nicole, J. Ernest, O.B.E., *Psychopathology* (London: Bailliere, Tindall, and Cox, 1946).
Nuttin, Rev. Joseph, S.J., *Psychoanalysis and Personality*, trans. by George Lamb (New York: Sheed & Ward, 1953).

O'Brien, Rev. John A., Ph.D., *Why Marriages Fail* (Notre Dame: Ave Maria Press, 1959).
——— *Catholic Marriage: How Achieve It?* (Huntington, Ind.: Our Sunday Visitor Press, 1952).
Odenwald, Robert P., M.D., "The Priest as Counselor," *Conference Bulletin*, Archdiocese of New York (Vol. 33, No. 2, 1956).
O'Doherty, Rev. Eamonn, "Religion and Psychiatry," *The Catholic Medical Quarterly* (Vol. III [XXI], No. 3, April, 1950).
——— "Religion and Mental Health," *Catholic Mind* (1957, Sept.–Oct., 413–421).
Osborne, E., *Understanding Your Parents* (New York: Association Press, 1956).

Parks, John, M.D., "Womanhood After Fifty," *Medical Arts and Sciences* (Second Quarter, 1959).
Patrice, Sister Jean, C.S.J., *Your Family Circle* (Milwaukee: The Bruce Publishing Company, 1952).
Patterson, C. H., *Counseling the Emotionally Disturbed* (New York: Harper, 1958).
——— *Counseling and Psychotherapy: Theory and Practice* (New York: Harper, 1959).
Pepinsky, Harold B., and Pepinsky, Pauline N., *Counseling Theory and Practice* (New York: The Ronald Press, 1954).
Pius XI, *Christian Marriage* (*Casti Connubii*) (New York: The America Press, 1936).
——— "Encyclical Letter on Christian Marriage," *The Ecclesias. Review* (Vol. 84, 1931).
——— *On the Christian Education of Youth* (New York: Paulist Press, n.d.).

Pius XII, "Allocution to Catholic Mothers," *Acta Apostolicae Sedis* (Vol. 33, Nov. 26, 1941), pp. 450–458.
——— *Counsel to Teaching Sisters* (Washington, D. C.: National Catholic Welfare Conference Publications Office, 1943).
——— *Humani Generis* (New York: Paulist Press, 1953).
——— *Moral Questions Affecting Married Life* (New York: Paulist Press, n.d.).
——— "The Moral Limits of Medical Research and Treatment," *Catholic Mind* (1953, 51, 305–313).
——— "Psychotherapy and Religion," *Catholic Mind* (1953, 51, 428–435).
Plé, Rev. A., O.P., "St. Thomas and the Psychology of Freud," *Cross Currents* (1954, 4, No. 4, 332).
Poage, Rev. Godfrey, C.P., and Treacy, John P., *Parents' Role in Vocations* (Milwaukee: The Bruce Publishing Company, 1959).
Porter, E. H., *An Introduction to Therapeutic Counseling* (Boston: Houghton Mifflin, 1950).
Postman, C., Bruner, J. S., and McGinnies, E., "Personal Values as Selective Factors in Perception," *Journal Abnorm. and Soc. Psychol.* (1948, 43, 142–154).
Preston, George H., *The Substance of Mental Health* (New York: Farrar & Rinehart, 1943).

Ramirez, Agostino, *Unconscious Drives and Human Freedom in Freud's Psychoanalysis* (Washington, D. C.: The Catholic University of America, 1955).
Rees, S. R., M.D., "Mental Health and Health Education," *World Mental Health* (8:4, pp. 174–179, November, 1956).
Reid, Dorothy, and Snyder, William, "Experiment in 'Recognition of Feeling' in Non-directive Psychotherapy," *Journal of Clinical Psychology* (Vol. III, No. 2, April, 1947), pp. 128–135.
Rennie, Thomas A. D., and Woodward, Luther E., *Mental Health in Modern Society* (New York: Commonwealth Fund, 1948).
Ringel, E., and Van Lun, W., *The Priest and the Unconscious* (Westminster, Md.: Newman Press, 1954).
Robinson, F. P., *Principles and Procedures in Student Counseling* (New York: Harper and Brothers, 1950).
Rogers, Carl R., "A Theory of Therapy, Personality and Interpersonal Relationships, as Developed in the Client-centered Framework," pp. 184–256, in Sigmund Koch, *Psychology: A Study of a Science* (New York: McGraw-Hill Book Co., Inc., 1959).
——— *A Concept of the Fully Functioning Person* unpublished manuscript (mimeo.) (Univ. Chicago Counseling Center, 1953).
——— *A Counseling Viewpoint* (New York: Commission on Religion and Health, Federal Churches of Christ in America, 1945).
——— *Clinical Treatment of the Problem Child* (Boston: Houghton Mifflin, 1939).
——— *Counseling and Psychotherapy* (Boston: Houghton Mifflin, 1942).
——— *Dealing With Social Tensions* (New York: Hinds, Hayden and Eldredge, 1948).

———— "Persons or Science: A Philosophical Question," *Am. Psychologist* (1955, 10, 267–278); also published in *Cross Currents* (Summer, 1953, 3, 289–306).

———— "Some Observations on the Organization of Personality," *Amer. Psychologist* (1947, 2, 358–368).

———— The *Implications of Client-Centered Therapy for Family Life*, paper given to Chicago Chapter of Int. Soc. Gen. Semantics, April, 1953.

———— *This Is Me: The Development of My Professional Thinking and My Personal Philosophy*, paper given at Brandeis University, Nov., 1955.

Rogers, Carl R., and Dymonds, R. F. (eds.), *Psychotherapy and Personality Change* (Chicago: Univ. of Chicago Press, 1954).

Rogers, Carl R., and Wallen, J. L., *Counseling With Returned Servicemen* (New York: McGraw-Hill Book Co., Inc., 1946).

Rogers, Natalie, "Changes in Self-Concept in the Case of Mrs. Ett," *Personal Counselor* (1947, 2, 278–291).

———— "Measuring Psychological Tension in Non-Directive Counseling," *Personal Counselor* (1948, 2, 237–264).

Rosenthal, Maurice J., and Sullivan, Mary E., *Psychiatric Consultation in a Public Child Welfare Agency* (Washington, D. C.: United States Department of Health, Education and Welfare, Social Security Administration, Children's Bureau, 1959).

Royce, Rev. James E., S.J., *Personality and Mental Health* (Milwaukee: The Bruce Publishing Company, 1955).

Ryan, John, M.D., *Medical Aspects of Marriage* (London: Burns, Oates and Washbourne, Ltd., 1951).

Sackett, Rev. Frederick D., O.M.I., "The Spiritual Director in an Ecclesiastical Seminary," *Universitas Catholica Ottaviensis Dissertationes in Facultatibus Ecclesiasticis Conscriptae. Series Canonica Tomus 13* (University of Ottawa Press, 1945).

Schmiedeler, Rev. Edgar, O.S.B., *Your Child's World* (New York: Paulist Press, 1951).

Schneiders, Alexander A., *Personal Adjustment and Mental Health* (New York: Rinehart, 1955).

———— "Personality Needs, Religion and Psychotherapy," *MD International Symposia* (Psychiatry and Religion) (1955, 44–46).

———— The *Psychology of Adolescence* (Milwaukee: The Bruce Publishing Company, 1960).

Sechrest, Carolyn A., *New Dimensions in Counseling Students; A Case Approach* (New York: Bureau of Publications, Teachers College, Columbia University, 1958).

Segal, Stanley J., "The Role of the Counselor's Religious Values in Counseling," *Journal of Counseling Psychology* (Winter, 1959, Vol. 6, No. 4).

Servo, P. H., *What Is Mental Illness?*, U. S. Dept. of Health, Education and Welfare, No. 505, 1957.

Sheen, Most Rev. Fulton S., *The Woman*, 4th ed. (Huntington, Ind.: Our Sunday Visitor Press, 1952).

Sheerin, J., "Confession and Psychiatry," *Homiletic and Pastoral Review* (1950, 1, 215–219).

Shostrom, Everett, L., and Brammer, Lawrence M., *The Dynamics of the Counseling Process* (New York: McGraw-Hill Book Co., Inc., 1952).

Siekmann, T. C., "The Important Years to Implant Solid Traits of Character," *Catholic Education* (October, 1953).

Skidmore, Rex A., Garrett, Hulda Van Steeter, Skidmore, C. Jay, *Marriage Consulting* (New York: Harper and Brothers, 1956).

Skottowe, Ian, *Clinical Psychiatry* (New York: McGraw-Hill Book Co., Inc., 1954).

Stafford, Rev. John W., C.S.V., "The Equipment of the Marriage Counselor," *Marriage Counseling* (Washington 5, D. C.: Family Life Bureau, National Catholic Welfare Conference, n.d.).

———— "What Is a Catholic Counselor?" *The Catholic Counselor* (Vol. 1, Winter Number, 1957, No. 2).

Steenberghen, Fernand Von, *Psychology, Morality and Education* (Springfield, Ill.: Templegate, 1958), translation by Ruth Mary Bethell.

Stanford, Rev. Edward V., O.S.A., *Preparing for Marriage* (Washington, D. C.: Archbishop Carroll High School, 1957).

Stevenson, George S., M.D., *Mental Health Planning For Social Action* (New York: McGraw-Hill Book Co., Inc., 1956).

Stoops, Emery, and Wahlquist, G. L., *Principles and Practices in Guidance* (New York: McGraw-Hill Book Co., Inc., 1958).

Strange, Ruth, *Counseling Techniques in College and Secondary School* (New York: Harper, 1949).

Sullivan, Rev. William P., *Divorce and Remarriage* (Brooklyn, N. Y.: International Catholic Truth Society, n.d.).

Symposium, *Working Relationships Between Pastor and Psychiatrist* (published by the Institute For Mental Health, St. John's University, Collegeville, Minn.).

Syracuse University, *New Frontiers in Guidance-personnel Work. Lectures given at a workshop at Syracuse University in July, 1958, jointly sponsored by the Syracuse University Division of Summer Sessions and National Association of Women, Deans and Counselors* (Syracuse, N. Y.: Syracuse University Press, 1959).

Terruwe, A. A. A., *Psychopathic Personality and Neurosis*, translated by Conrad W. Boors and Jordan Aumann, O.P. (New York: P. J. Kenedy, 1958).

Thilges, Rev. John, S.V.D., *Speaking of Purity* (Techny, Ill.: Mission Press, 1949).

Thomas, Rev. John L., S.J., *Beginning Your Marriage* (Chicago: The Cana Conference, 1955).

Thorne, Frederick C., *Principles of Personality Counseling: An Eclectic Viewpoint* (Brandon, Vt.: Journal of Clinical Psychology, 1950).

Thorpe, Louis P., *The Psychology of Mental Health* (New York: The Ronald Press Co., 1950).

Tolbert, E. L., *Introduction to Counseling* (New York: McGraw-Hill Book Co., Inc., 1959).

Topp, Robert F., "Preadolescent Behavior Patterns Suggestive of Emotional Malfunctioning," *Elementary School Journal* (February, 1952), pp. 340–343.

Tyler, Leona E., *The Work of the Counselor* (New York: Appleton-Century-Crofts, Inc., 1953).

U. S. Dept. of Health, Education and Welfare, *Evaluation in Mental Health* (Washington, D. C.: Supt. of Documents, 1955).

Van Greunsven, Rev. Norbert, J.J., "A Priest Looks at Marriage Counseling," *Bulletin of the Guild of Catholic Psychiatrists* (Vol. 4, No. 4), Oct., 1959.

VanderVeldt, Rev. James H., O.F.M., and Odenwald, Robert P., M.D., *Psychiatry and Catholicism*, 2nd ed. (New York: McGraw-Hill Book Co., Inc., 1957).

Vaughan, Rev. R. P., S.J., "Religious and Psychotherapy," *Review for Religious* (1958, 73–81).

Vincent, Clarke E., *Readings in Marriage Counseling* (New York: Thomas Y. Crowell Co., 1957).

Wallis, John H., and Booker, H. S., *Marriage Counseling* (Hordon, Routledge & Icegon, Poul, 1958).

Warters, Jane, *Techniques of Counseling* (New York: McGraw-Hill Book Co., Inc., 1954).

Watson, J. B., *Psychology From the Standpoint of a Behaviorist*, 3rd ed. rev. (Philadelphia and London: J. B. Lippincott Co., 1924).

Werth, Rev. Alvin, O.F.M.Cap. and Mihanovich, Clement S., *Papal Pronouncements on Marriage and the Family* (Milwaukee: The Bruce Publishing Company, 1955).

White, Rev. Victor, O.P., *God and the Unconscious* (London: Harvill, 1952).

Williamson, E. G., *Counseling Adolescents* (New York: McGraw-Hill Book Co., Inc., 1950).

Wise, Carroll A., *Pastoral Counseling* (New York: Harper, 1951).

——— "Client-Centered Counseling and the Pastor," *The Journal of Pastoral Care* (Vol. VII, Fall, 1953, No. 3).

Woodworth, R. S., *Contemporary Schools of Psychology* (New York: The Ronald Press Co., 1931).

Wrenn, C. Gilbert, *Guidance in Education Institutions*, 37th Yearbook of the National Society for Study of Education, 1938.

Zilboorg, Gregory, M.D., *A History of Medical Psychology* (New York: Norton, 1941).

——— *Freud and Religion* (Westminster, Md.: Newman Press, 1958).

INDEX